The Essential Guide to Secondary Teaching

Other titles in the series

Cousins: *The Essential Guide to Shaping Children's Behaviour in the Early Years*

Dix: *The Essential Guide to Classroom Assessment*

Dix: *The Essential Guide to Taking Care of Behaviour*

Dix: *The Essential Guide to Taking Care of Behaviour for Learning Support and Teaching Assistants*

Senior: *The Essential Guide to Teaching 14–19 Diplomas*

Thompson: *The Essential Guide to Understanding Special Educational Needs*

Trant: *The Essential Guide to Successful School Trips*

Walker: *The Essential Guide to Lesson Planning*

Woods: *The Essential Guide to Using ICT Creatively in the Primary Classroom*

The Essential Guide to Secondary Teaching

Susan Davies

Longman
is an imprint of

Harlow, England • London • New York • Boston • San Francisco • Toronto • Sydney • Singapore • Hong Kong
Tokyo • Seoul • Taipei • New Delhi • Cape Town • Madrid • Mexico City • Amsterdam • Munich • Paris • Milan

PEARSON EDUCATION LIMITED

Edinburgh Gate
Harlow CM20 2JE
Tel: +44 (0)1279 623623
Fax: +44 (0)1279 431059
Website: www.pearsoned.co.uk

First published in Great Britain in 2010

ISBN: 978-1-4082-2452-6

British Library Cataloguing-in-Publication Data
A catalogue record for this book is available from the British Library

Library of Congress Cataloging-in-Publication Data
Davies, Susan, 1957-
  The essential guide to secondary teaching / Susan Davies.
    p. cm.
  Includes index.
  ISBN 978-1-4082-2452-6 (pbk.)
  1. Education, Secondary--Great Britain. 2. Teachers--Training of. I. Title.
  LA635.D33 2010
  373.1100941--dc22
                          2010010955

10 9 8 7 6 5 4 3 2 1
14 13 12 11 10

Typeset in 10/12pt Frutiger Light by 3
Printed by Ashford Colour Press Ltd, Gosport

Contents

About the author vii
Author's acknowledgements viii
Publisher's acknowledgements ix

Part 1   School organisation 1

Chapter 1 The school as an organisation 3
Chapter 2 Organising pupils for learning 11

Part 2   Teaching and learning 25

Chapter 3 The National Curriculum 27
Chapter 4 Boys and girls are different! 39
Chapter 5 Poverty, ethnicity and pupil attainment 53
Chapter 6 Readability, reading ages and writing frames 73
Chapter 7 Personalised learning – every child matters 89
Chapter 8 Learning to teach and teaching to learn – planning lessons 107
Chapter 9 Storing data and organising lesson plans 129
Chapter 10 Using classroom supports to maximise pupils' learning 139

Part 3   Behaviour management 151

Chapter 11 Behaviour – let's start at the very beginning 153
Chapter 12 Behaviour management – teachers rule, OK! 167
Chapter 13 Promoting inclusion in our schools 191

Part 4 Assessment for learning 205

Chapter 14 Assessment for learning – marking for success 207
Chapter 15 Pupil data – what is it and how is it gathered? 229
Chapter 16 How schools use data to improve achievement 241
Chapter 17 Reporting to parents – best practice 255

Part 5 The pastoral programme and the curriculum 271

Chapter 18 The role of the form tutor and pastoral team 273
Chapter 19 The PSHE curriculum in our schools 285
Chapter 20 Pupil induction and transition from Key Stage to Key Stage 299
Chapter 21 Attendance, child protection and anti-bullying strategies 309

Part 6 School improvement and continuing professional development 321

Chapter 22 School inspections – what makes a good school? 323
Chapter 23 Applying for a job, preparing a lesson and the interview 337
Chapter 24 Continuing professional development 347

Conclusion 352

Index 353

About the author

Susan Davies is headteacher of an 11–18 secondary school in Bridgend, South Wales. During over 30 years in teaching she has worked in a number of schools based both in rural and urban areas. She was formerly a deputy headteacher in a large inner city school where she was in charge of teaching and learning and curriculum planning. For more than a decade she was actively involved in mentoring, training and supporting both student teachers on placements and NQTs embarking on their first teaching role. She was the winner of the 2001 Teachers' Award, 'Leadership in a Secondary School'. For six years she has been a judge for the Teachers' Awards Welsh Panel. Susan Davies is a well-known educational consultant and a trained school inspector. This is her sixth educational book.

Author's acknowledgements

In my case writing books is a team effort so this book is dedicated to my very own home team: to Gareth, my best friend, who bought me my first computer 20 years ago and continues to encourage me – keeping my feet on the ground even if at times my head is in the clouds! To Hannah, Rachael and Alys who continue to make even rainy days sunny. To Anne Griffiths, a great teacher, who shares a passion for looking at the stars! And with grateful thanks to Catherine Yates and Katy Robinson, Pearson Education, for their hard work and support.

Finally, thanks to the teachers who made a difference in my life and maybe did not realise it at the time. In particular, Mrs James at Nottage Primary School, Porthcawl, for teaching me to read when all around had given up; and Mr Wyn Derrick, Mr Euros Rees, Mr A. C. Rees, Mrs Susan Rees and Mrs Marion Williams, all at Amman Valley Comprehensive School.

Publisher's acknowledgements

We are grateful to the following for permission to reproduce copyright material:

Figures and Tables

Crown copyright material is reproduced with the permission of the Controller of HMSO and the Queen's Printer for Scotland; Text on pp.17–18 from Harlen, W. and Malcolm, H. (1997), Setting and streaming: a research review, SCRE; Extracts in Chapter 5 from Blanden, J. et al, 'Family income and educational attainment: a review of approaches and evidence for Britain', *Oxford Review of Economic Policy*, Summer 2004, 20:2 by permission of Oxford University Press; Extracts on pp. 75–6 adapted from Keith Johnson's TimeTabler website, www.timetabler. com; extracts from *A Proper Bike* and *The Holiday* by Rod Hunt, illustrated by Alex Brychta (Oxford Reading Tree, 2004), text copyright © Rod Hunt 2004, illustrations copyright © Alex Brychta 2004, reprinted by permission of the publishers, Oxford University Press; 'Identifying types of writing' on p.84, Reprinted by permission of HarperCollins Publishers Ltd © (2001) J. Strong and 'Using a writing frame' on p.85, Reprinted by permission of HarperCollins Publishers Ltd © (1997) J. Strong; TASC wheel figure on p.98 © Belle Wallace 2000, Used with permission, Education South East/ TASC International, www.tascwheel.com; 'What is your primary learning style?' p.112 used with permission from Accelerated Learning Systems Ltd; Extracts in Chapter 14 from *Inside the Black Box: Raising Standards through Classroom Assessment* © Black and Wiliam, 1998. Reproduced by permission of GL Assessment and *Working Inside the Black Box: Assessment for Learning in the*

Classroom, by Black, Harrison, Lee, Marshall and Wiliam. Copyright © 2004 Dylan Wiliam. Reproduced by permission of GL Assessment Ltd; 'Baseline assessment' extract in Chapter 15 with permission from The Association for Achievement and Improvement through Assessment; job advert in Chapter 23 used with permission from The City of Leicester College.

Picture credits

p.59 from John Birdsall/Press Association Images; p.108 from John Birdsall/Press Association Images; p.149 from John Birdsall/Press Association Images; p.155 from Brian Mitchell/Photofusion Picture Library; p.161 from John Birdsall/Press Association Images; p.177 from John Walmsley Education Photos, Educationphotos. co.uk/walmsley; p.211 from Jacky Chapman/Photofusion Picture Library; p.242 from Ian Shaw/Alamy; p.278 from Christa Stadtler/Photofusion Picture Library; p.316 from John Birdsall/Press Association Images.

Every effort has been made by the publisher to obtain permission from the appropriate source to reproduce material which appears in this book. In some instances we may have been unable to trace the owners of copyright material and would appreciate any information that would enable us to do so.

Part

1

School organisation

newly qualified teachers (NQTs). However, you will eventually find yourself alone in front of a class.

You will have to:

- follow the SOW set by your HOD
- plan lessons that are part of the programme of study
- follow a recognised syllabus for those pupils taking external examinations
- be responsible for the pastoral welfare of a class either as the class teacher or form tutor
- be aware of the vision for the school's future as outlined in the SDP
- follow whole school procedures and policies on marking, bullying, etc. that you will need to familiarise yourself with and adhere to
- use the staff handbook to obtain information about the day-to-day running of your school and its policies and procedures, such as those mentioned above
- familiarise yourself with the school prospectus (all schools must have one and the information it contains is determined by statutory guidelines).

You will also have to work with a variety of colleagues. You may have pupils who need support and will be following specific programmes of study determined by the special educational needs (SEN) department or a behaviour support team of educational psychologists (EPs). These pupils will have:

- learning support assistants (LSAs) or
- pastoral support assistants (PSAs) or
- Ethnic Minorities Language Advisory Service (EMLAS) support assistants.

You will be expected to work with these support people and take into account when planning lessons any:

- individual learning programmes (ILPs) or
- educational behaviour plans (EBPs).

Who will help me in my school?

The mentor

The mentor supports and helps you with any school-based problems. They can act as a go-between for you and your HOD or line manager. However, most teachers are very approachable and you can normally discuss specific issues with them directly.

What does a member of the senior management team do?

A member of the senior management team:

- is appointed by the governing body of the school
- has specific whole school responsibilities
- may be responsible for a subject area and be formally linked to it
- makes decisions about the staffing and financial running of the school
- plays a part in writing the school development plan (SDP) – this plan is reviewed annually but most schools now have a plan that covers three years so that longer term, more strategic planning can take place
- monitors, evaluates and reviews the progress of initiatives, departments or year groups
- chairs meetings of academic and pastoral leaders
- meets with the team on a regular basis, normally weekly.

What are the functions of middle managers?

To be an effective organisation the school needs to have key personnel with specific responsibilities. Middle managers play an important part in day-to-day running, ensuring that teaching and learning is effective. They check that the SOWs are being followed and that pupils are making progress in line with their age and ability, against targets, and in comparison to similar pupils from similar schools. They are experts in their subject, ensuring that any changes in the programme of study at any Key Stage are interpreted and included in their SOW (see Chapter 16 on data handling).

In a secondary school the pastoral coordinator (PC) or Head of Year ensures that pupils in that year group are making the necessary progress. However, instead of looking vertically at attainment in a subject through Years 7–13, as an HOD would do, a PC is interested in a specific year group's performance in all subject areas to check that attendance, attitude and behaviour are likely to ensure successful outcomes for their year.

What is expected of me and how do I fit into a school?

Mentors are appointed in secondary schools to give new teachers support, whether they are students, i.e. those undergoing initial teacher training (ITT), or

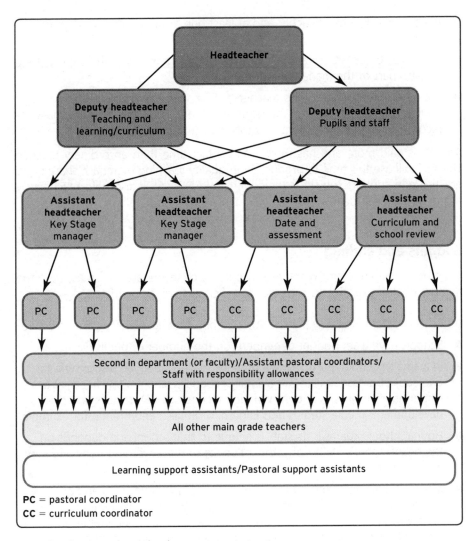

Example of a secondary school management structure

The senior management team

The headteacher, deputy headteachers and assistant headteachers form the senior leadership group (SLG) or senior management group (SMG) of a secondary school.

- there is usually a headteacher and at least one but normally two deputy headteachers
- there may be assistant headteachers, who are a rank below the deputy (they are also part of the management team)
- there may be advanced skills teachers (ASTs), who may be paid on a similar scale to members of the leadership team. ASTs have been formally recognised as being excellent classroom practitioners.

An AST is paid more and has more non-contact time than an ordinary teacher. The AST will use this time to produce high-quality teaching materials, share good practice and support subject leaders with the SOW. ASTs also help teachers by acting as a critical friend.

Budgets and staffing

If a school – regardless of whether it is primary or secondary – is small, then the number of staff available to carry out specific tasks will be restricted.

- Schools differ in the way they deploy staff but most are hierarchical in structure.
- Schools have a set budget dependent on the number of pupils.
- In a smaller school, particularly a primary, teachers may be responsible for two subject areas. Similarly, in a small secondary school a teacher may be responsible for physics and information technology (IT), textiles and child development, media studies and English, or English and drama, for example.
- How a school organises its staff is unique to that school and depends on the headteacher's philosophy, the influence of the governing body and very often the budget!
- Many schools are changing the way they organise themselves and at secondary level this has meant a flattening of the management structure. Where this has occurred the deputy headteachers have been replaced by assistant headteachers, thus removing a layer of the organisation. The headteacher may have as many as seven assistant headteachers, with one normally designated senior to deputise and make decisions in the headteacher's absence.

The management of a typical secondary school is shown in the figure overleaf.

other aspects of their work. **This chapter is intended to help you identify who you may need to approach for help and to give you an overview of how a school may be structured.**

Secondary schools vary in size dramatically and this affects how an individual school is structured. Secondary schools normally have a headteacher and at least one deputy headteacher, larger schools may have more than one. Secondary schools also employ assistant headteachers who are also members of the senior leadership group (SLG).

In addition, there are other teachers who make up the middle management team. They may have an allowance for taking responsibility for a subject area or areas throughout the school, and this may have been agreed when they were first appointed. These teachers write the scheme of work (SOW), which is a programme of study followed by all teachers of a subject, and ensure that the National Curriculum guidelines for the programme of study in a subject are being followed. The SOW takes account of all statutory needs and ensures that what is taught is the same for all pupils, i.e. is consistent. Finally, they are also responsible for monitoring, evaluating and reviewing (MER) work in that subject throughout the school (see box).

Monitoring, evaluating and reviewing (MER)

The best way to know what is going on in any classroom is to look at the pupils' books or to sit at the back of a number of lessons. Trainee and new teachers do a lot of this. When planning any new initiative it is important to think about how you will monitor, evaluate and review its success. Writing down clear success criteria for the outcome of any project *before* you begin is a good place to start. We will look at this in more detail in Chapter 22. See also Chapters 14, 15 and 16.

How secondary schools are organised

Secondary schools have subject leaders called:

● head of department (HOD) or
● curriculum coordinator (CC) or
● head of faculty (HOF), where a faculty system operates.

Size affects the organisational structure – the smallest secondary schools are usually as big as the largest primary schools. In secondary schools:

The school as an organisation

What this chapter will explore:

- How secondary schools are organised
- The senior management team
- What is expected of me and how do I fit into a school?
- Who will help me in my school?

This chapter is intended to give an overview of how a typical school is organised and the people you are likely to work alongside. Many of the concepts first mentioned here will be explored in more depth in later chapters in the book. Though secondary schools do vary organisationally they are for the most part hierarchical. Knowing the role of individual staff within the establishment is important. New teachers will need support not just with classroom teaching of their subject but also with

The finance manager/bursar

In a small school this may be the headteacher, but in a large school there will be someone with that specific job description or role. See them for issues to do with salary and finance.

The caretaker

See the caretaker or a departmental technician for all issues to do with your classroom, for example if you need new bulbs, electric plugs, extension cables or special equipment. Science, IT and technology departments in secondary schools have technical support staff.

The health and safety officer (HSO)

Every school has an HSO and any issues to do with your room or the school environment in general that come under health and safety need to be recorded and submitted to them. The HSO will ensure that remedial action is taken quickly to prevent accident and injury.

Child protection officer (CPO)

Every school has to appoint a CPO. The CPO works with organisations such as:

- social services
- the Young Offenders Team (YOT).

The CPO also works with looked-after children, children who are in some form of care other than with their natural parents.

The CPO will be in charge of all multi-agency liaison that goes on, and in most schools a deputy headteacher takes on this role.

You must report to the CPO any concerns you have about the safety of children. Any disclosure that is made to you suggesting that a child is at risk or that a crime has been committed must be immediately notified to the CPO verbally and later in writing, so that accurate records can be kept. The CPO will then make a decision about how to proceed.

The HOD or subject mentor

In a secondary school there is someone who will:

- provide leadership for the department and initial teacher trainee or NQT

- advise on issues to do with classroom practice
- advise you about lesson planning
- give you guidance about your teaching
- suggest strategies for managing children's behaviour
- observe your lessons
- check that your class books are marked regularly and accurately
- be a critical friend.

The headteacher and deputy headteachers

Do not be afraid to approach these people for help and guidance on whole school policies that you may not fully understand. They can also help you to understand the important role that you play within the school as a front-line classroom teacher.

Other teachers and staff

Every teacher in the school was once in the position you are now in – new to the school and the job. These people can help you with discipline issues or in getting to know the school and its staff better. Every school is unique and getting to know its idiosyncratic running style is useful. Your colleagues are an invaluable source of knowledge on all sorts of issues.

Why not try this?

- If you are already in a school compile a list of those people who make up the senior managers of the school.
- What responsibilities does your mentor have in addition to being a mentor?
- Who is in charge of health and safety and child protection? Find out from these people what their duties entail.
- What other information do you wish to know about responsibilities and roles?

ongoing. So, some suggestions for further reading are provided at the end of the chapter.

You can adjust your teaching to take account of the way departments or classes are organised.

What is banding?

Banding is the placing of pupils within a class into ability groupings. Although it is more common in primary schools it is also used in secondary schools, where it describes a slightly different teaching arrangement – a large year group is sometimes divided into two or more groupings. Pupils can be of equal ability or differentiated on criteria similar to streaming (see below).

Banding can ease timetabling problems. Look at this structure where you need ten teachers to teach a specific subject at the same time:

10D	10E	10W	10I	10DX	10S	10A	10N	10T	10X

In a secondary school this could happen when you are teaching the core subjects of English, maths and science. It would mean that all the teachers of English would be teaching at the same time, something a department might not want. Maybe not all the teachers want to teach the General Certificate of Secondary Education (GCSE) or maybe the department has some non-specialists who are not able to offer GCSE but are competent lower school English teachers.

Therefore, to offer the best academic experience the school may want to split the year group into two equal bands and timetable one half for English at the same time as the others have maths, for example. This would alleviate any staffing problems and ensure that the best-suited teachers are used for any particular group. In this structure you can now use staff more flexibly as you are not committed to using the whole of a department to teach a year group. From the timetable's point of view it is also easier. Let us assume that while the DEWIX band has English, the SANTX band has maths:

10S	10A	10N	10T	10X

10D	10E	10W	10I	10DX

However, there are five subject teachers of English and five of maths who are not yet scheduled for any classes at that time, so the school could use these 'free' teachers elsewhere. Therefore, some of a maths or English department may be

teaching lower school classes while GCSE is being taught. Likewise, they may be used to teach sixth form classes while GCSE is ongoing.

When you split the cohort the two halves may be of equal ability, but some schools have banded pupils in such a way that one half of the band contains the top 30 pupils in a year group. This means that resources can be put in place to support these very able students and that subject leaders can ensure that the work that is set is challenging enough for these pupils. However, if all your brightest pupils are in one half of the year group, then it can present problems. The obvious disadvantage to this is that it skews the ability range of the two halves, in that one contains all your most able pupils, whilst the other half does not have any significant high flyers. Some schools like this express group system and others think that the disadvantage of one half of the year group being devoid of the top pupils is detrimental, feeling that a good spread of very able pupils can significantly pull up the standards of other students. However, it is worth remembering that banding pupils means that you can still teach in mixed ability groups or sets within that band, depending on the philosophy of the school as a whole and the subject teams.

What is streaming?

This is when pupils remain in ability-based classes for all subjects. This does not take account of the fact that a pupil may be good in one subject but struggles in another.

What is setting?

Pupils are grouped according to ability for individual subjects. This means that a pupil can be in the top set for maths but in a lower set for English, or vice versa. In many schools the core subjects of English, maths and science are setted subjects but many others are taught in mixed ability groups.

What is a mixed ability group?

This is a class of pupils that are not selected in any way by ability, reading age, etc. It represents a cross-section of pupils of different abilities and if the school has pupils from a wide socio-economic base it will also reflect that mix.

What research has been done and what findings are relevant to new teachers?

Much research has been done on the effects of pupil groupings on learning outcomes but the results are not at all conclusive:

- Some evidence suggests that setting and streaming can negatively affect results attained by those pupils.
- Some evidence suggests that grouping by ability improves results.
- Some evidence is inconclusive, suggesting that grouping by ability has a negligible effect.

This ambiguity occurs because this is not an easy area to research, given that there are difficulties in setting up an experiment that compares like with like. These are some of the difficulties that researchers have encountered:

- Teachers are not uniform in their approach to teaching and the teaching methods they employ. This may be even more marked now as some schools use interactive whiteboard and information technology to a much higher degree than others.
- Mixed ability classes may vary in the range of ability reflected in the group.
- Setted groups may actually have a large spread of ability within them, almost equivalent to that of some mixed ability groups.
- Class sizes may vary.
- The degree of differentiation that occurs may differ widely.
- The curriculum content may be different.

(You can read more about this research via the link on the book's website, at www.pearsoned.co.uk/essentialguides.)

In order to get over some of the difficulties that have arisen in this area of research, Harlen suggests that we should apply the concept of 'best evidence synthesis'.

> *'In best evidence synthesis, criteria are identified for good quality research yielding the best evidence in a particular field. Research studies are then compared against the criteria and those that best match the criteria list are regarded as the most reliable.'*

(Harlen, in Slavin, 1986)

Harlen suggests that research based solely on measurements and comparison of achievements of pupils in both ability and mixed ability groups is inadequate. In order to get a full picture, researchers need to seek the views of the

learners themselves about what they think of the way they are organised for learning. This kind of study is discussed later in the chapter. (Visit the website at www.pearsoned.co.uk/essentialguides for a link to this research.)

How do we organise our pupils for learning? How might my subject area be organised, and why?

In the UK there is a long tradition of grouping by ability in secondary schools. There is also evidence that in-class grouping by ability is widespread in primary schools. Streaming and setting in primary schools is only possible in large schools and therefore is not as prevalent as it is in secondary schools.

The 1970s and 1980s was a period when mixed ability teaching was more popular. This was due to the general public's concern for 'educational equality', but the pendulum swung back in the 1990s to favour ability groupings for the following reasons:

● The Educational Reform Act of 1988 required schools to adopt the National Curriculum. Many teachers felt that this programme of study made it difficult to teach in mixed ability groups.

● Schools had to be seen to be academically successful in order to attract pupils and compete in the 'league tables', and middle-class parents like setting, feeling that their children are better catered for in these ability groupings.

● The government's White Paper *Excellence in Schools* (DfEE, 1997, p 38) revealed the Labour government's commitment to setting: 'Unless a school can demonstrate that it is getting better than expected results through a different approach, we do make the presumption that setting should be the norm in secondary schools.'

Reid et al. (1981) found that the nature of the subject could affect how pupils were organised for learning. If a subject required pupils to work through a body of knowledge in a logical sequence, the problems of teaching in mixed ability groups were thought to be insurmountable. In contrast, subjects that could be taught in a thematic or modular manner lent themselves more readily to a mixed ability approach. A further factor was the role of the teacher in the classroom context. If the teacher was central to the lesson and was the major resource, fewer opportunities existed for mixed ability teaching. It was suggested that for this reason modern linguists were less likely to be enthusiastic about mixed ability groupings. Setting is also prevalent in maths, science and English – the core subjects.

Case study

One research study in detail

What new teachers need to know about the effects of setting and streaming

The research study carried out by Boaler (1997) is particularly interesting as it looks at both attainment and the attitude of the learners to the way they are organised for learning. The research included case studies of two year groups containing over 100 pupils in two schools. The study focused on the teaching of maths where in one school it was taught in sets and in another in mixed ability groups. The pupils were matched according to:

- ability
- ethnicity
- sex
- socio-economic status.

The pupils were observed in lessons and interviewed and assessed regularly. This research was different in that it took into account not only how well the children were doing but also their own perceptions of the positive and negative learning experiences that they were undergoing.

The results were as follows:

- In the mixed ability school the pupils attained higher GCSE grades and significantly more A–G passes. This is despite the fact that pupils were of the same ability in both schools at the start of their schooling, measured using national and standardised tests.
- In the school that used setting, the biggest determining factor upon achievement at GCSE was social class. This was a more important determinant than the ability measure taken on entry to the school. In the mixed ability school there was no link between social class and achievement.
- The effects of setting disadvantaged a significant proportion of top set pupils. A number of pupils were negatively affected by pace and the pressure put upon them because they were in a top set, and there were expectations formed within these groups of how well these pupils should do. This was shown to disadvantage girls more than boys. These girls had previously been successful in mixed ability groups at Key Stage 3.

→

- In interviews (see below) the pupils stated that working at the pace of the class was not always conducive to success. It negatively affected their understanding as they were either forced to work too fast, which led to a lack of understanding and anxiety, or they were forced to work too slowly and this led to disaffection and underachievement. In mixed ability classes where pupils worked at their own pace they reported a greater level of understanding.

- In the school that used setting, social class influenced setting, which resulted in disproportionate numbers of working-class pupils being allocated to low sets.

- Pupils who are entered for maths GCSE can enter one of two tiers of examination (this is currently under review). It was found that those pupils who were entered for examinations where they could not access the higher grades became demotivated or disillusioned. They believed that they could have done better if they had been allowed to.

What the pupils say and why new teachers should listen

'Lessons are difficult and if you can't answer he says, "You won't be in set 1 next year – you are in set 1 you shouldn't be finding this difficult."'

(School R boy, set 1)

'He explains work like we're maths teachers – really complex, I don't understand it.'

(School R boy, set 1)

'It's just our group who keeps changing teachers. Why? 'Cause they don't think they have to bother with us, I know that sounds really mean, but they don't think they have to bother with us, 'cause we're group 5 so if they have a teacher who knows nothing about maths, they'll give them to us, say a PE teacher.'

(School R girl, set 5)

'You have to come in, sit down, there's stuff on the board and he says copy it. It's too easy, it's far too easy.'

(School A boy, set 6)

→

'I can get high if I'm pushed as hard as I can to get up there, but it's not easy when you just do the same things over and over again. How can you move up? There is nothing you can do, he has no idea how we're doing, he hasn't taken our book in once.'

(School R girl, set 5)

'We have different books – high books, medium books, low books, so everyone has the right amount of work – no-one's doing nothing too hard or too easy. If you think it's too hard or too easy you just tell Miss and she gives you the right level.'

(School W boy, set 3)

'I prefer groups when we're all mixed up like in form groups. 'Cause we're all mixed up, a variety of clever and dumb. So the dumb learn from the clever and then sometimes the clever can't do it, so they'll learn from people who aren't as good, 'cause sometimes they're good at some things but not others.'

(School W boy, set 3)

'It was last week, we were doing bar charts and pie charts and all that and I think I was the third person in the class who got it properly – we had to make it into a graph, it was good.'

(School C girl, mixed ability)

Visit the book's website at www.pearsoned.co.uk/essentialguides for more on this research.

Source: Harlen and Malcolm (1997)

What are the problems associated with streaming and mixed ability teaching? What should new teachers be aware of?

Gregory (1984) identified the following problems with streaming and mixed ability teaching:

- Lower teaching expectation is followed by poor pupil progress (Winn and Wilson, 1983, citing Tuckman and Bierman, 1971).

- Teacher behaviour and school organisation respond differentially to different ability groups. Upper ability groups receive more teacher time, more praise, less direction and criticism. In contrast, teachers of low ability groups stressed basic skills, facts and drill, and used unimaginative teaching approaches. Lower ability groups had fewer science materials, poorer library facilities and less competent teachers.

- Mixed ability teaching involved more work for the teacher as the burden of preparation is daunting (Wilcox, 1961; Davies, 1975; Kelly, 1975).

- Many teachers were not trained to teach mixed ability groups (Collier, 1982).

- Bright pupils in mixed ability classes are not being stretched academically (HMI, 1978; Wragg, 1984); in fact these researchers experienced great difficulty in finding any mixed ability teaching and reported that less able children were not being catered for.

- Even teachers considered to be effective in handling mixed ability classes often resorted to whole class teaching and made no provision for the least able. They often had discipline problems. They streamed the class into ability groups and gave no evidence of any kind of selective approach to pupils of differing abilities (Kerry, 1982a, 1982b).

Gregory concluded that on the whole the problem with setting or streaming was lowered teacher expectation for the lower ability groups. With mixed ability teaching the problem seemed to lie in the fact that there was no evidence to suggest that such groupings enhanced social interactions. The need for large amounts of supplementary materials did not seem to have been met. Many teachers, despite the mixed nature of the group, seemed to resort to a whole class approach to teaching that was wholly inappropriate.

What are the problems associated with setting pupils for learning? What new teachers need to know!

The following have been identified:

- Pupils in a set are often treated as a homogenous group when the ability range in a set can be every bit as wide as that found in a mixed ability class.

- Setted lessons are often observed to have pupils tackling identical work at an identical pace and the pace is determined by a small number of students.

- Teachers of pupils in a low set have low expectations of the group and tend to set work that is too easy.

- It seems that placing pupils in a set creates definite expectations that override any need to see pupils as individuals with individual learning requirements.

- Teachers of pupils in a top group set a pace that is too fast for many in the group and the pressure to succeed makes many anxious.

- Pupils who are entered for examinations where they can access only a low grade are disillusioned.

- Teachers of low sets are often non-specialists, whereas research has suggested that the low sets often benefit from the most specialised teachers. Low sets are more likely to have more teachers in the course of their studies than top sets.

- Pupils in low sets should be able to move into a higher set if they work hard. This cannot happen if the content base of work they are provided with is too easy or is not detailed enough. The gap widens between the sets and makes movement upwards very difficult. Research has shown that movement from set to set is not as widespread as it should be.

- In setted lessons teaching tends to be more restricted in style with teachers relying on chalkboard teaching and textbook work, with a narrower range of attainment being catered for.

- Setting does not always accomplish what it is supposed to do – to match the work set to the needs of the pupil.

'There is no evidence that any particular way of organising classes or teaching groups in itself improves learning. The main determinant of effective learning is teaching which is responsive to the key needs of learners.'

(Boyd and Simpson, 2000)

Key ideas summary

This chapter shows a new teacher how schools organise pupils for learning. The research would seem to be inconclusive, suggesting that no one system of banding, setting or streaming can be said to produce better results. However, the pupils themselves suggest that what works best for them is when the teacher is indeed responsive to their individual needs, whatever they may be. The most effective progress occurs when teachers work with pupils to set individual targets. These are based on knowledge of prior learning (see Chapter 15 on data) and an awareness of preferred learning styles (see Chapter 8). In addition, the teacher uses →

'assessment for learning' techniques to show the pupil how to progress in a detailed step-by-step manner.

Good teachers realise that within any class, whether it is banded, streamed or set, there will be a range of pupils with different strengths and weaknesses. There will also be pupils who learn in different ways depending on the individual preferred learning style of the pupil. The best teachers will ensure that their lesson is differentiated so that pupils who are finding the topic easy will be able to develop and enrich their learning and not be held back. Those who find the topic or area of work more challenging will be supported so that they will in time get to a competent level of under-standing. This range of ability is always present in any class taught in a school. (There is more on lesson planning in Chapter 8.)

Pupils also highlight how schools treat different groups of pupils within the school. Pupils from low sets suggest that they are given poorer teachers who are not subject specialists or are perceived to be weaker teachers. When setting works well, pupils will see that hard work or aptitude will allow them to move to a higher group. Pupils clearly identified times when this could not happen. This was because they were possibly not taught the skills needed to progress upwards and were therefore disenfranchised by the methods used to organise pupils for learning. Pupils are human and can perceive and feel annoyed by actions that clearly discriminate against them and prevent their progression.

Why not try this?

Consider the following questions:

- When you were in school how were your classes grouped for learning? Which subjects were taught in sets and which subjects were taught in mixed abil-ity groups?
- Did you experience the same feelings about this as the pupils who were surveyed?
- Ask how pupils are grouped in your school now.
- Do different subjects group pupils in different ways? If so, find out why this may be the case.

Going further

Boaler, J. (1997) 'When even the winners are losers: Evaluating the experiences of top set students', *Journal of Curriculum Studies*, 29(2), 165–82.

Boaler, J., Wiliam, D. and Brown, M. (2001) 'Students' experiences of ability grouping – Disaffection, polarisation and the construction of failure', available at www.nottingham.ac.uk/csme/meas/papers/boaler.htm.

Boyd, B. and Simpson, M. (2000) 'Developing a framework for effective learning and teaching in S1/S2 in ANGUS Secondary Schools', Arbroath: Angus Council Education Department.

Collier, F. (1982) 'A retreat from mixed ability teaching', in Sands, M. and Kerry, T. (eds), *Mixed Ability Teaching*, London: Croom Helm.

Davies, R.P. (1975) *Mixed Ability Grouping Possibilities and Experiences in Secondary Schools*, London: Temple Smith.

DfEE (1997) *Excellence in Schools*, White Paper, London: HMSO.

Gregory, R.P. (1984) 'Streaming, setting and mixed ability grouping in primary and secondary: some research findings', *Educational Studies*, 10(3), 209–26.

Harlen, W. and Malcolm, H. (1997) *Setting and Streaming: A Research Review*, Edinburgh: SCRE, available at www.scre.ac.uk.

HMI (1978) 'Mixed ability work in comprehensive schools', Matters for Discussion Series 6, London: HMSO.

Kelly, A.V. (1975) *Case Studies in Mixed Ability Teaching*, London: Harper and Row.

Kerry, T. (1982a) 'Mixed ability teaching in the humanities', in Sands, M. and Kerry, T. (eds), *Mixed Ability Teaching*, London: Croom Helm, pp 61–70.

Kerry, T. (1982b) 'The demands made on pupils' thinking in mixed ability classes', in Sands, M. and Kerry, T. (eds), *Mixed Ability Teaching*, London: Croom Helm, pp 82–104.

Reid, M., Clunies-Ross, L., Goacher, B. and Vile, C. (1981) 'Mixed ability teaching: Problems and possibilities', accessed through a summary by Upton, D., *Educational Research*, 24(1), Slough: NFER Nelson.

Slavin, R.E. (1986) 'Best evidence synthesis: An alternative to meta-analytic and traditional reviews', *Educational Researcher*, November, 5–11.

→

Tuckman, B.W. and Bierman, M. (1971) *Beyond Pygmalion, Galatea in the Schools*, New York: ERIC.

Wilcox, J. (1961) 'A search for multiple effects of grouping upon growth and behaviour of junior high school pupils', Unpublished dissertation, Cornell University, New York.

Winn, W. and Wilson, A.P. (1983) 'The affect and effect of ability groupings', *Contemporary Education*, 54, 119–125.

Wragg, E.C. (ed.) (1984) *Classroom Teaching Skills: The Research Findings of the Teacher Education Project*, London: Routledge.

Chapter

2

Organising pupils for learning

What this chapter will explore:

- What is banding, streaming, setting and mixed ability teaching?
- What research has been done and what are the findings?
- How do we organise our pupils for learning?
- What are the problems associated with streaming and mixed ability teaching?
- What are the problems associated with setting pupils for learning?

This chapter provides new teachers with an overview of how schools might organise their pupils for learning. It also examines some of the major research that has highlighted the advantages and disadvantages of some of these pupil groupings. This is a huge research area and it is impossible to do it justice in one chapter, particularly when research is

Part 2

Teaching and learning

The National Curriculum

What this chapter will explore:

- Who decides what is taught in our schools?
- What is a scheme of work?
- What is a departmental handbook and what is a staff handbook?
- What are the golden rules when planning a curriculum?

In this chapter you will find information about why schools teach the subject range, content and skills that they do. This is not something arbitrary – the programmes of study and the schemes of work are based on directives from the curriculum authority for each of the four nations. Read on to find out how what we teach is determined and how consultations in our four nations work.

country that makes up the UK there is a curriculum authority that determines we teach in our schools and how it is to be assessed:

- In England it is the Qualifications and Curriculum Authority (QCA).
- In Northern Ireland it is the Council for the Curriculum, Examinations and Assessment (CCEA).
- In Scotland it is the Scottish Executive Education Department (SEED).
- In Wales it is the Department for Children, Education, Lifelong Learning and Skills (DCELLS)

All of these authorities have websites and it is worth visiting these to download any materials that you need. The book's website has links to these, at www.pearsoned.co.uk/essentialguides.

Who decides what is taught in our schools?

The consulting committees that have provided us with a curriculum are made up of representatives of the curriculum authority, but they always contain teachers or headteachers as well. In addition, representatives of teaching unions or professional bodies may be present. These committees provide schools with a framework from which to work. For example, in the box below is an extract taken from the Scottish curriculum framework. It outlines the new broad areas of learning that schools will need to cover.

The four capacities

The purpose of Curriculum for Excellence is encapsulated in the four capacities – to enable each child or young person to be a successful learner, a confident individual, a responsible citizen and an effective contributor.

The experiences and outcomes in the range of curriculum areas build in the attributes and capabilities which support the development of the four capacities. This means that, taken together across curriculum areas, the experiences and outcomes contribute to the attributes and capabilities leading to the four capacities.

The expanded statements of the four capacities can also form a very useful focus for planning choices and next steps in learning. The attributes and capabilities can be used by establishments as a guide to assess whether the curriculum for any individual child or young person sufficiently reflects the purposes of the curriculum.

Taken as a whole, the experiences and outcomes embody the attributes and capabilities of the four capacities. →

Successful learners
with:
- enthusiasm and motivation for learning
- determination to reach high standards of achievement
- openness to new thinking and ideas

and able to:
- use literacy, communication and numeracy skills
- use technology for learning
- think creatively and independently
- learn independently and as part of a group
- make reasoned evaluations
- link and apply different kinds of learning in new situations.

Confident individuals
with:
- self-respect
- a sense of physical, mental and emotional well-being
- secure values and beliefs
- ambition

and able to:
- relate to others and manage themselves
- pursue a healthy and active lifestyle
- be self-aware
- develop and communicate their own beliefs and view of the world
- live as independently as they can
- assess risk and make informed decisions
- achieve success in different areas of activity.

To enable all young people to become:

Responsible citizens
with:
- respect for others
- commitment to participate responsibly in political, economic, social and cultural life

and able to:
- develop knowledge and understanding of the world and Scotland's place in it
- understand different beliefs and cultures
- make informed choices and decisions
- evaluate environmental, scientific and technological issues
- develop informed, ethical views of complex issues.

Effective contributors
with:
- an enterprising attitude
- resilience
- self-reliance

and able to:
- communicate in different ways and in different settings
- work in partnership and in teams
- take the initiative and lead
- apply critical thinking in new contexts
- create and develop
- solve problems.

The four capacities

Source: www.ltscotland.org.uk/curriculumforexcellence/curriculumoverview/aims/fourcapacities.asp

This framework outlines how pupils should be assessed and how schools should report this to parents. When a school is inspected, the inspection team ensures that the curriculum framework that is laid down as a statutory requirement is being taught and assessed appropriately and that nothing is omitted.

Although an individual authority's curriculum reflects commonality with the rest of the UK, it will be unique in that it is influenced by national need. For example, in the Welsh curriculum bilingualism is mentioned – this may or may not be perceived as a need by the other three nations. Over the past 20 years there

have been significant changes to the curricula in schools and this is a continuing process. The most recent review of the curriculum in England (www.qca.org.uk) states that the curriculum should enable all young people to become:

- successful learners who enjoy learning, make progress and achieve
- confident individuals who are able to live safe, healthy and fulfilling lives
- responsible citizens who make a positive contribution to society.

At the beginning of any framework there is a general statement of intent as to what the general curriculum will contain. Curriculum authorities do not just launch a new curriculum. First, there is a prolonged period of consultation and then a framework document will be circulated. At the same time pilot projects will take place and finally the new curriculum will be phased into the whole country. It is true that all authorities are currently reviewing their provision and that is why it is important for all teachers, whether new to the profession or established, to read the relevant documentation. Primary teachers need to be aware of the whole document because they teach a range of subjects or cover the whole of the foundation phase. However, secondary staff are normally subject teachers of one or at most two subjects. Therefore, the subject-specific information that relates to their subject will need to be read in the form of a programme of study for that subject. However, all subject schemes of work will need to take account of cross-curricular themes, dimensions that could be delivered within that subject area, enterprise, health and well-being, sustainability, global awareness, cultural diversity, relationships, self, etc.

Why not try this?

Go to the curriculum authority that serves the school that you are in (see Going further, p 37). Find the relevant information either for the age range you are teaching or for your subject. Compare this to the scheme of work that you are following in your classroom.

What is a scheme of work?

The scheme of work (SOW) is the programme of study that teachers in a school will follow and is usually prepared by the subject leader or the team leader. At Key Stages 3 and 4 it is normally subject based. The SOW should be a working document and teachers should refer to it on a regular basis. All teachers are monitored by their line managers and part of this process ensures that the SOW is

being followed. The SOW should indicate a timescale for the learning outcomes. This means that you should be able to plan what learning will take place every week, month, half-term and so on.

Some schemes of work are now placed on departmental or school websites to allow parents and other staff to see what is going on across the school. It also means that you can give potential new staff a copy of the SOW – a much more dynamic way of showcasing the work of a department or school. (Examples of SOWs can be found at www.pearsoned.co.uk/essentialguides.)

New teachers may find themselves in charge of an area of learning and may have to write an SOW shortly after completing training. The table below shows what an SOW could contain.

Topic/ tasks	Aims and learning objectives	National Curriculum attainment targets and teaching methods	Skills	Resource Different-iated (D) Standard (S)	HW/ CW	Time	Assessment	Cost

What should a scheme of work contain?

- The class/year or Key Stage it is prepared for.
- The topic to be covered.
- The timescale allowed for that particular subject/topic (this can be in terms of lessons or weeks).
- The resources available or that may be required (this may refer to worksheets, videos, software, overhead projectors, practical equipment).
- The cost of delivering that element of the course in time and within budget.
- The assessment procedures that will be used to determine how well pupils have learnt and how this is to be differentiated for all learners. (See Chapters 8 and 14 for information about differentiation that is useful in this context.)

Why not try this?

Look at the SOW for the main subject that you are teaching. How many different methods are used to assess how well a pupil is doing? (See Chapter 14 for more on assessment and marking.)

> ## How can you assess what has been learnt?
>
> Here are some ideas that may apply to your subject:
>
> - question and answer in written form/essay/practical task/oral/assessment test
> - any other means that will tell you how well your pupils have understood what you have taught.
>
> Assessment should be linked to the marking policy of the learning area/ subject area of the school.

Key skills are developed within areas of work. All subjects should contribute to the provision of key skills within the school. For example, it is important that any lesson plan clearly and fully indicates the key skills being developed alongside the subject being taught. In addition, it is important that pupils learn how to assess their strengths and weaknesses, i.e. learn how to self-evaluate.

TOP TIP!

Key skills are now a vitally important part of the work done in secondary schools. All subjects are expected to include all these key skills at certain appropriate points in the SOW. Look at your main subject SOW again and try to see where the key skills would be delivered. Are they highlighted in any way?

Key skills now form an important part of all classroom learning. Traditionally, hard skills are communication, application of number and IT; soft skills are problem solving, working with others and improving own learning – these are now referred to under the one term, 'key skills'. Many schools also teach thinking skills, and teachers may need to indicate on a scheme of work exactly where these are taught within the subject curriculum.

Cross-curricular links

It is expected that pupils have an understanding of environmental issues, careers guidance, study skills, economic and industrial awareness, health education, and in Wales the Curriculum Cymreig. Some of this learning occurs in discrete lessons, possibly as a part of the Personal, Social and Health Education (PSE/PSHE) programme, but it could occur in a subject lesson, for example:

- a lesson of English where students are learning how to answer essay questions (study skills)
- a geography lesson where pupils are studying population migration (economic and industrial awareness).

See Chapter 19 for more on PSE/PSHE.

What is a departmental handbook and what is a staff handbook?

A handbook, like the SOW, is a working document and will be regularly updated. It ensures that there is consistency in operational procedures within the department and any policy documents.

Here is a list of areas that you may expect to find in a departmental handbook:

- departmental aim with a brief outline
- factual information – this will include details about staff, resources, pupil organisation, support staff and their roles
- staff arrangements for meetings, induction arrangements and training and monitoring procedures
- a calendar of important events in the school year, key assessment, coursework, reporting deadlines
- policies on presentation of work, marking, differentiation, homework, numeracy, IT, literacy
- cross-curricular dimensions like economic and industrial awareness that might form a feature of the curriculum in your country
- ethos and environment for pupils – departmental displays, discipline procedures, equal opportunities, child protection, health and safety (note that health and safety and child protection organisation will be in line with a whole school policy and must be adhered to carefully)
- improvement planning for that subject or area of learning that should include clear success criteria and a monitoring, evaluating and reviewing strategy
- a review of the success of prior developments
- staff development
- key issues such as how pupil progress is tracked and the strategies used for improvement
- syllabus information and contact addresses
- schemes of work

- preparation for parents' evenings, pupil reviews – what records you want available
- departmental guidelines on reporting to parents and the use of assessment for learning in everyday marking
- how quality assurance is provided within the department
- how the school contributes to extra-curricular aspects
- how the department or area contributes to the moral, social and corporate life of the school (later in your working life when applying to go through threshold you will need to show how you have contributed to the life of the whole school)
- links with other schools, other agencies and the community.

This may seem an extensive list but in fact many of these areas can be covered in a short paragraph and where necessary there will be appendices. A school or departmental handbook gives a very important insight into how the school or area of learning is run.

TOP TIP!

If you are going to a school for an interview you could ask to see its handbook while you are there. It is also the case that as a new teacher you may find yourself in charge of a learning area or subject area, so it would be good practice to produce your own handbook.

Many schools now produce a staff handbook, which is a reference document that explains how a school runs. It gives a list of staff with responsibilities; information about the day-to-day running of the school; lesson times; important information about school procedures, like how to organise a school trip; important forms that can be photocopied as and when required; and the school calendar. In most staff handbooks you will find whole school policies on child protection, bullying, assessment, homework, etc.

TOP TIP!

Some handbooks will also contain information about job descriptions. They are a really useful reference tool, especially for new teachers, so make sure that you get one, and when on initial teacher training ask to see if your current school has one you could look at.

What are the golden rules when planning a curriculum?

Remember that the term curriculum refers to all the learning experiences put in place by a school to achieve determined and specified educational objectives.

● The curriculum should contain the statutory requirements set out by your curriculum authority both academically through subject teaching and through the personal and social education offered.

● It should reflect the unique nature of your school within the community. For example, if you live in an industrial area you may see engineering on the curriculum; if you live in an area of outstanding natural beauty or where tourism plays a major factor this too could influence what is included in the school curriculum.

● The curriculum should allow students to have breadth and balance to their learning. By 'breadth' we mean that pupils should have the opportunity to engage in the *nine areas of learning* (see box below). By the term 'balance' we mean that they should all be given appropriate attention in relation to one another. Time should be evenly distributed between all areas of learning.

● It should be relevant to the pupils you are teaching and reflect their present and future needs in a rapidly changing world. This can be seen in the way that IT is being used more in schools. In addition, pupils are getting more adept at using IT at a younger age. This affects the way that IT is incorporated into schemes of work in all subjects and at all levels, reflecting the future needs of these pupils.

● The curriculum should be differentiated and should allow children of all abilities and learning needs to achieve their potential.

The nine areas of learning

● Aesthetic and creative

● Human and social

● Linguistic and literary

● Mathematical

● Moral

● Physical

● Scientific

● Spiritual

● Technological.

For more information, see *Curriculum from 5 to 16* (HMI, 1985).

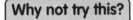

> Try to identify in your school areas of the curriculum that have been affected by the strengths of members of staff, or by its location, or by the nature of the pupil intake.

The hidden curriculum

Finally, the X factor within a school and the curriculum is something called the 'hidden' curriculum. It is best described as everything that happens once you walk through the door into school; not necessarily what happens in the classroom but in the corridors and social areas of the school. This hidden curriculum is what affects the ethos of the school. If a school values its staff and pupils, and teaches respect and moral responsibility overtly in its everyday dealings with one another and the community, then the hidden curriculum will be a positive one. The hidden curriculum is basically to do with the way messages are conveyed to pupils through their experience with the school. It is what they learn through overt and covert 'messaging' – what is seen to be acceptable behaviour and everyday practice.

Why not try this?

- Have a look at the website for your curriculum authority for information about your own subject specialism as it applies in the secondary sector.
- Have a look at an SOW for another subject area in your school. Compare it to your own subject SOW. Are they both written in a standard format? Some schools insist that all SOWs follow a standard format and others do not.
- Do both SOWs contain similar information?
- Do you prefer one to another, and if so, why?

Going further

HMI (1985) *Curriculum from 5 to 16: Curriculum Matters 2*, London: HMSO.

Learning and Teaching Scotland (1999) *A Curriculum Framework for Children 3 to 5*, available at www.ltscotland.org.uk. Originally published by Scottish Consultative Council on the Curriculum.

Learning and Teaching Scotland, www.ltscotland.org.uk/curriculumforexcellence/curriculumreview – the four capacities

www.nicurriculum.org.uk – The Council for the Curriculum, Examinations and Assessment (Northern Ireland)

www.qca.org.uk – The Qualifications and Curriculum Authority (England)

www.qca.org.uk/key-stages-3and-4/aims – National Curriculum: Curriculum purpose, values and aims

www.scotland.gov.uk – The Scottish Executive Education Department

http://wales.gov.uk/topics/educationalskills – Department for Children, Education, Lifelong Learning and Skills (Wales)

Boys and girls are different!

What this chapter will explore:

- What do we know about boys and girls?
- Why are boys and girls different?
- How are boys and girls doing academically?
- Proven strategies to enhance progress in the learning environment

This chapter suggests ways in which good teaching can help narrow the gap in attainment between boys and girls. It is now recognised that boys and girls have different learning preferences and different strengths and weaknesses. To narrow the attainment gap it is important to identify the differences in learning styles and skills as well as suggesting strategies that will definitely benefit both sexes, thus enabling boys to achieve more in line with girls.

What do we know about boys and girls?

Gender is only the fifth most important factor that will influence educational achievement. A child's socio-economic background, ethnicity and the prior learning that they bring to school will have more to do with their success than their sex. So why focus so publicly on this area of concern? In truth, because we know that the strategies that are available will make a difference and are easier to identify and consistently implement within a school. Chapter 5 considers strategies that have brought about improvement in performance in children from ethnic minority groups or from underprivileged backgrounds. For information on how linguistic and ethnic backgrounds can affect learning, see Chapters 6 and 13.

The following is a generalisation – there will always be girls and boys who will be different. However, for the most part the following differences between the sexes are true.

The average boy

The average boy has some or all of the following characteristics:

- Solves mathematical problems non-verbally.
- Is better at mental rotation and does not need to turn the map upside down to follow the route!
- Likes data, systems and facts.
- Is more likely to read non-fiction than fiction.
- Is a risk taker and a doer.
- Is highly influenced by his peers.
- Requires more space.
- Learns by doing and by experience, so is an experiential learner.
- Is more likely to be left-handed.
- Has a larger right brain hemisphere (for mathematics and spatial skills) in contrast to the left (for language).
- Talks and plays more with inanimate objects.
- Is less able to follow linear processes and pay attention to detail on the way.
- Has a shorter concentration span and is easily bored.
- Is more likely to be disruptive.
- Is more likely to need help with his reading.

- Is three times more likely than the average girl to be dyslexic.
- Is more likely to need special educational support.
- Is more likely to be excluded permanently.
- Is less able to think reflectively but more willing to think speculatively.
- Has weaker planning and organisational skills.
- Likes subjects such as maths, physics, technology, IT, business studies and physical education.

The average girl

The average girl has some or all of the following characteristics:

- Plans out tasks.
- Is more organised.
- Spends more time on homework and coursework.
- Is a reflective thinker.
- Balances her schoolwork with her life outside school.
- Likes relationships and people.
- Dislikes taking risks and is overly cautious.
- Is less influenced by peer pressure.
- Has better listening and oral skills and is more likely to talk while solving mathematical problems.
- Is a natural student.
- Has a larger left brain hemisphere.
- Is less likely to be dyslexic or myopic.
- Learns by adopting a step-by-step approach.
- Suffers fools in the classroom and tolerates poor delivery more readily.
- Underestimates her ability and often lacks confidence.
- Is slow to anger.
- Is more likely to smoke.
- Is less likely to take up teacher time or receive praise in the classroom.
- Likes English, modern languages, drama, dance, textiles, religious studies, PSE, humanities, art, music, biology, chemistry.

Why are boys and girls different?

Current brain research asserts that many of the differences between boys and girls are pre-ordained. What happens to the foetus in its early weeks in the uterus is crucial. At six or seven weeks of age, a surge of testosterone begins changing the embryos that have inherited the male chromosome into boys. This change in the sex hormone levels affects the way that male and female brains develop.

- A boy's brain is larger than a girl's. However, the girl's brain is more dense and the *corpus callosum* is larger. (The *corpus callosum* is the bundle of nerves that connects the right- and left-hand sides of the brain.)

- The girl's brain develops before the boy's and this gives her certain advantages over him.

- In both boys and girls the left side of the brain controls thinking and develops later than the right – this is the part that deals with spatial relationships. In boys this time delay in the development of the right and left sides of the brain is even more pronounced.

- When the right side of the brain is ready to start sending connecting nerves to the left, the cells are not yet in existence in the boy's brain. This causes the connecting fibres to go back and form connections within the right side of the brain. This makes the right side of a boy's brain well connected and partly explains why he may be good at maths and tasks that require spatial abilities.

- The larger *corpus callosum* allows both sides of the brain to talk to each other more efficiently. This could explain why it is commonly thought that women are better able to multi-task.

- Boys' brains have less serotonin than girls'. Serotonin is a chemical that soothes emotions, is supposed to aid in forming judgements and lessens the likelihood of an impulsive response. Serotonin, or the lack of it, makes boys more likely to be impulsive and fidgety.

- The female brain is as active at rest as the activated male brain.

- Research on reading has shown that when a girl is reading more of her brain is lit up during the activity than is the case with a boy's brain. This suggests that she is bringing more 'brain power' to the experience.

- Growing evidence suggests that boys and girls are greatly affected by the hormone surges in the womb while they are foetuses.

How are boys and girls doing academically?

Background statistics

Even at an early age girls are outperforming boys in English:

- At age 7, 85% of girls gained a level 2+ while only 72% of boys achieved this.
- Some 30% of girls attained a level 3 and only 20% of boys, and by the end of primary schooling girls are on average half a level ahead of boys in English.
- National statistics show that this gap continues and widens until GCSE, where the gap in performance in English is one of the highest.

However, in a study conducted in 1996, Sammons et al. showed that background factors such as being the youngest in the family or being poor were more influential and continued throughout schooling. For instance:

- boys born in September had a 30% chance of gaining a level 3 while for girls that figure was 50%
- boys and girls born in August had a 10% or 17% likelihood, respectively, of gaining a level 3 in the Key Stage 1 tests
- boys on average tend to be 11 months behind in oracy, 12 months behind in literacy and 6 months behind in numeracy on entry to secondary school.

It is important to bear in mind that in the days of the 11+ examination, pass rates were lowered for boys to ensure that an equal number of boys and girls were able to go to a grammar school. A generation earlier than this, items were dropped from the Stanford-Binet IQ test when women outperformed men on the test. Now girls outperform boys in GCSE:

- Of 5.6 million entries, 63.4% of girls attained five A–C grades while the figure for boys was 53%.
- Research (Mansell, 2003) has recently shown that at age 14, Key Stage 3 boys outperformed girls in maths and science, with girls well ahead in English.
- By the age of 16, girls achieved higher results in all three subjects and had a bigger overall lead than at Key Stage 3.

The GCSE system, with its reliance on sustained work throughout the course and the production of coursework, suits girls:

- Even when the coursework requirement went down from 100% to 40%, girls still outperformed boys by 17%.

● In IT, traditionally thought of as a male subject, girls have outperformed boys with 8.7% more achieving a C grade or above.

It has been suggested that vocational courses may suit boys better as they provide a skills-based approach to learning; yet even here vocational results for 2002 at intermediate level show that girls were ahead of boys. For the first time the trend has also been extended to universities:

In 2005/06, 58% of all higher education qualifications were awarded to women.

In 2005/06, more women than men gained National Vocational Qualifications and Scottish National Qualifications (56% vs 44%).

Latest data also suggest that for the first time more women are gaining university places than men.

'Good equal opportunities in the classroom is about getting the girls into doing and the boys into thinking.'

(Hannan, 2000)

Ensuring equal opportunities

It is important that we recognise the differences that exist between the boys and girls we teach. It is also vitally important that as good teachers we ensure that every child is afforded an equal opportunity to succeed. However, we must remember that the gender gap is only one factor affecting a child's academic achievement. In order to bring about real improvement it will be necessary to find strategies to help those who come to school ill-prepared due to their linguistic, socio-economic or ethnic background. These factors present a far greater challenge and call for a determined vision and whole school strategy to enable these children to overcome their disadvantage. However badly middle-class boys are doing they are still achieving more than working-class girls. Of the 40,000 16 year olds who leave school every year with no qualifications, a third are female and the majority are still from depressed socio-economic backgrounds. The table on the next page supports the view that gender is only the fifth most important determinant of a child's academic ability, coming far below prior attainment in school and social background.

GCSE attainment in England and Wales[1]: by parents' socio-economic classification (2002)

	5 or more GCSE grades A*–C	1–4 GCSE grades A*–C2	5 or more GCSE grades D–G	1–4 GCSE grades D–G	None reported	All
Higher professional	77	13	6	–	3	100
Lower professional	64	21	11	2	2	100
Intermediate	52	25	17	2	4	100
Lower supervisory	35	30	27	4	4	100
Routine	32	32	25	5	6	100
Other	32	29	26	4	9	100

All figures are percentages.
[1] For pupils in Year 11. Includes equivalent GNVQ qualifications achieved in Year 11.
[2] Consists of those with 1–4 GCSE grades A*–C and any number of other grades.

Source: DfES (2002)

If males and females are really from two different planets, is it possible to get both sexes down to earth and achieving equally? As a result of concern over the achievement of boys, the Department for Education and Skills commissioned research by Homerton College, Cambridge (DfES, 2000) to look at the small minority of schools that have managed to help boys *without* disadvantaging girls.

Initial research findings show that some schools have altered teaching methods and have broken lessons down into smaller units. Others have allowed five-minute breathers for boys. In yet others, single-sex lessons have worked and seem to have resulted in some improvement in examination results. A wider range of teaching styles has brought an all-round improvement in a Wolverhampton secondary school. However, the next phase is to identify what methods could be applied generally to bring about all-round success. Therein lies the problem – what appears to work in one school may make no difference, or indeed retard progress, in another. Success, however, does seem to depend not on mentoring or single-sex classrooms but on a culture of high expectations and good relationships between pupils and staff.

More about this research can be found at www.pearsoned.co.uk/essentialguides.

What do we mean by high expectations and good relationships?

- Be explicit about what you aim to achieve in the long term with the class you are teaching. How would you feel if you attended a course where no one told you the expected outcomes and how to achieve them? Boys and girls like to have a structure in which to work.

- Break the long-term goal down into short-term targets and have a strategy, so that at the start of every lesson you are clear about the intended learning outcome and how this fits into the 'big picture'. Boys like to work to short-term goals and be rewarded by success.

- Be honest and say that every pupil is different, and as the term progresses you will set individual targets for improvement. (These will be based on assessments of written, oral, practical work, etc.) Again this will work for boys and girls.

- Celebrate success and share this with the class – reward hard work. A lesson where pupils are allowed to listen to headsets as they work and occasionally have a small snack or drink goes down well. (Although check that this is in line with school policy!)

- Clear aims and objectives need to be shared. Examples of good work completed by previous groups or sharing good work from within the group gives pupils a goal to aim for.

Proven strategies to enhance progress in the learning environment

Research has shown that there are a number of strategies that can be used to narrow the gap in attainment. Look at the Top Tips! boxes which follow for some ideas to try with your classes.

Remember, because the strategies will work for both boys and girls the gap in performance will still exist; but you will have gone some way towards narrowing it.

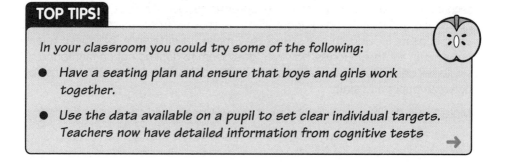

TOP TIPS!

In your classroom you could try some of the following:

- *Have a seating plan and ensure that boys and girls work together.*

- *Use the data available on a pupil to set clear individual targets. Teachers now have detailed information from cognitive tests*

(CATs) and standard assessment tests (SATs), etc. about a pupil's potential. They also have reading and spelling ages.

- Assessment for learning strategies are highly successful (see Chapter 14).

- Ensure that the lesson has a clear structure and that all tasks are time related. Boys need to be set challenging tasks.

- Try to make pupils compete against themselves rather than each other. Boys would rather 'opt out' than fail. Try the approach of 'In this lesson you need to focus on your ...'.

- Remind everyone that they are in competition with other schools – this makes the contest important but avoids competitiveness within the class itself.

- Mentor individual pupils within your class by monitoring them closely and telling them that you are watching their progress: this could be over a week or a half term. Do not try to go for a longer period as pupils need short-term goals and successes to build up confidence. Set a target and suggest a reward. Some pupils actually like a phone call home to tell parents they are doing well. For some it is a welcome change from the other type of call!

- Use questioning techniques that encourage boys to develop reflective skills where they need to speculate and hypothesise within a time regime.

- Encourage mixed pairs to discuss answers collaboratively as this improves the oracy of boys but also encourages girls to develop risk-taking strategies.

- Have clear behaviour rules. Avoid rudeness, disrespect, sarcasm and unfairness, all of which ruin the atmosphere of a classroom. Use your eyes and facial movements to control a class and not your voice, except when absolutely essential.

- Use writing frames – these are plans that pupils can follow in order to complete a piece of work. Many contain key words and paragraph openings that help pupils. These 'scaffold' a pupil's writing. Examples of writing frames can be found in Chapter 6.

Geoff Hannan (2000) suggests a 'Going for 5' strategy. This can be used in any subject and involves asking the pupils to write down five things they have learnt about, for example, erosion, the circulatory system or Romeo.

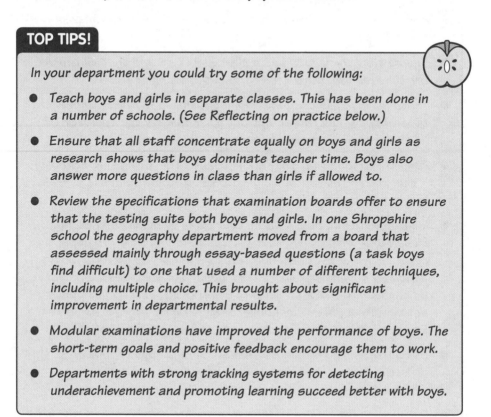

TOP TIPS!

In your department you could try some of the following:

- *Teach boys and girls in separate classes. This has been done in a number of schools. (See Reflecting on practice below.)*

- *Ensure that all staff concentrate equally on boys and girls as research shows that boys dominate teacher time. Boys also answer more questions in class than girls if allowed to.*

- *Review the specifications that examination boards offer to ensure that the testing suits both boys and girls. In one Shropshire school the geography department moved from a board that assessed mainly through essay-based questions (a task boys find difficult) to one that used a number of different techniques, including multiple choice. This brought about significant improvement in departmental results.*

- *Modular examinations have improved the performance of boys. The short-term goals and positive feedback encourage them to work.*

- *Departments with strong tracking systems for detecting underachievement and promoting learning succeed better with boys.*

Reflecting on practice

The single-sex classroom experience

In one school this strategy was used in an English department with a Year 8 cohort. Two equally matched classes of only boys or girls were taught by a teacher of the same sex as the class. The average examination mark was noted for both classes prior to the experiment, and the aim was to see a rise in both classes' performance in the next round of examinations. The results were interesting: the boys' performance actually worsened while the girls' improved.

Questionnaires were used to find out what the boys and girls thought of the arrangement and whether they wished to stay in their present class without the opposite sex. The responses were unanimous. →

The girls' response

The girls preferred to be taught away from the boys. Reasons cited included:

- being able to hold discussions in a mature fashion and have their say
- being able to have more teacher time
- preferring the literature they chose to study as it interested them and was 'girly' in subject matter
- preferring a girls-only class in general.

The boys' response

The boys hated the whole experience of being taught in an all-male group. The teacher of the boys' group also begged to be allowed to teach girls again; the experience of having an all-male class had not been a pleasant one for him either!

The outcome

Due to the fact that this strategy was intended to narrow the gender gap and not widen it, a decision was made to revert to mixed class teaching. This was by no means a strictly 'controlled' experiment, but it does echo an article in the *Accelerated Learning* newsletter (2002) suggesting that although we know there are differences between boys and girls 'it is a bold leap to say that they are so different we should teach them in different ways', and in this case in different classrooms!

TOP TIPS!

At a whole school level you could try the following:

- Adopt a consistent approach to seating plans for boys' and girls' learning.
- Put in place mentoring schemes for those pupils who are not going to achieve without intervention. Traditionally schools put together a list of pupils who would not achieve five A*–C grades without a tutor who could negotiate strategies with them for success. This scheme does not have to be applied solely to pupils in Year 11. In fact many staff would say that this is too late and early identification of pupils at risk is better practice. It is

→

possible to identify children at age 8 who would benefit from help and as time progresses this age could be reduced even further.

- Use mentoring schemes to provide equal opportunities and be accessible for any pupil who needs them. Mentors can be teachers, pastoral or senior staff, or professionals from outside the school who agree to meet with their mentee on a regular basis.

- Use rewards to celebrate all kinds of achievement.

- Ensure that an ethos of learning is cultivated within the school and targets are shared with the pupils. For example, your target could be 'this year we want to get x percentage of five A*–C grades'; or 'this year we want all pupils to improve their reading age by x months'. This sets a clear agenda for learning success. It is also important to share the performance of boys and girls in the school and gender differences.

- Hold boys-only assemblies to discuss the factors that will prevent boys from achieving and put in place clear strategies to see they are minimised.

- Have strong pastoral teams that set clear targets for the pupils and have clear expectations about behaviour and learning outcomes.

- Encourage pupils to take responsibility for their own learning and contribute to their own success.

- Have a consistent policy about feeding back information to pupils on their attainment and how they can improve.

Curriculum areas all play a significant part by putting in place schemes of work that present pupils with a challenge, particularly from one year to the next or from one Key Stage to the next.

Key ideas summary

Research shows us that there is a difference in the way that boys and girls learn and that teachers need to be aware of the strategies that can be used to narrow the gap between boys' and girls' attainment.

Why not try this?

Taking Geoff Hannan's advice on board, consider the following:

● Rank five things that you could use in your classroom that you think might improve boys' attainment.

● Think about the department you are in at present. What strategies, if any, are being used to narrow the gender gap? What is proving to be effective?

● Which of the strategies mentioned in this chapter might work in your department?

● Write down any strategies that your school is using. Which is the most effective? Are there any listed above that you think could be effective?

Going further

Accelerated Learning newsletter (2002) April, available at www.alite.co.uk.

Bradberry, M. (2002) 'Boys and girls', *ParentLife*, October, available at www.lifeway.com.

Curtis, P. (2003) 'Miliband pledges to tackle boys' failure in schools', *Guardian*, 11 July.

DfES (2000) 'Raising boys' achievement', a report by Homerton College, Cambridge, London: DfES, available at www.standards.dfes.gov.uk.

DfES, (2002) 'Youth cohort study', London: DfES, available at www. statistics.gov.uk/STATBASE.

Gurian, M., Henley, P. and Trueman, T. (2001) *Boys and Girls Learn Differently: Action Guide for Teachers*, San Francisco, CA: Jossey-Bass.

Hannan, G. (2000) *Raising Boys' Achievement*, Oxford: Heinemann.

Mansell, W. (2003) 'Gender gap widens in teenage years', *Times Educational Supplement*, 7 February.

Sammons, P. et al. (1996) 'The impact of background factors on pupil attainment and progress in Scottish schools', ISEP, Policy Paper No. 1, SEED.

→

The Scottish Office (1999) 'Raising standards: setting targets', in *Primary School Support Pack: Gender Issues in Raising Achievement*, Edinburgh: SOED.

Ward, H. (2004) 'Reading proves harder for boys', *Times Educational Supplement,* 21 May.

Poverty, ethnicity and pupil attainment

What this chapter will explore:

- The effect of poverty on attainment
- Ethnicity and educational attainment
- Best practice to reduce the attainment gap

In the previous chapter gender was identified as one of the causes of poor attainment in schools. Whilst not the most significant, the fact is that gender differences in attainment can be markedly reduced by intervention strategies that a school or a teacher has control over. The same is not strictly true of attainment gaps that are caused by poverty, ethnicity and social background. Research has suggested that cohesive government socio-economic and education policies are needed for strategies to be successful to combat these causes. However, there are strategies that

schools and teachers can use that will help all pupils, particularly those whose educational outcome could be affected by their parent's income or ethnicity. The chapter starts with a list of possible strategies.

Examples of strategies to help pupils

- Introduce breakfast and after-school clubs to ensure that pupils have a healthy start to the day and a quiet place to complete homework. Where possible, access to IT facilities and the internet are useful.
- Ensure that, where possible, support is provided for those who may be at risk due to social circumstances. Use teaching assistants and language support assistants fully in your classroom, targeting specific pupils for help where possible.
- Ensure that where setting occurs it is not further disadvantaging those who are socially disadvantaged.
- Ensure that there is movement between sets and that pupils feel that if they work hard they can progress.
- Ensure that as teachers you know your pupils, differentiate work appropriately and make certain that good quality teaching and learning takes place in your classroom.
- Ensure that you track the progress of pupils in your classroom who may be disadvantaged due to their background.

The effect of poverty on attainment

'By the age of six, clever children from poor homes have already fallen behind less able pupils from wealthy backgrounds in the classroom.'

(Bennet, 2005)

The Rowntree report, published in December 1999, points to continuing and possibly worsening inequalities in education. It reported that two million children lived in homes where there was no one in paid employment. The report also reveals a significant difference in pupil performance in primary schools where there were over 35% of pupils in receipt of free meals. Research shows that pupils in secondary schools that have a high percentage of pupils on free school meals are less likely to have a high percentage of pupils gaining five A*–C grades at GCSE (see table opposite).

'Poverty is the best predictor of inspection grades, according to an analysis of more than two years of figures from Ofsted. Teaching, management and school ethos are consistently judged to be better in secondary schools with wealthier pupils ... based on figures that show that only 4% of schools where more than a third of pupils received free school meals were given the top grade for quality of education.'

(Analysis by Karl Turner, deputy headteacher of Byng Kenrick Central School, Birmingham, cited in Cassidy, 1999)

Proportion of pupils achieving expected level by IDACI decile of pupil residence (England, 2007)

| | Key Stage 1 | | | | Key Stage 2 | | |
| | % achieving level 2 or above | | | | % achieving level 4 or above | | |
IDACI decile	Reading	Writing	Mathematics	Science	English	Mathematics	Science
England							
0–10% most deprived	73	68	83	80	68	66	79
10–20%	77	72	85	83	71	68	81
20–30%	79	75	87	85	74	71	83
30–40%	82	79	89	88	77	73	86
40–50%	85	81	91	90	80	77	88
50–60%	87	84	92	92	83	79	90
60–70%	89	86	93	93	85	81	91
70-80%	90	88	94	94	87	83	92
80–90%	91	89	95	95	89	85	94
90–100% least deprived	93	91	96	96	91	88	95
Percentage point gap between most and least deprived	20	23	13	16	23	22	16
Odds ratio between least and most deprived	4.9	4.8	4.9	6.0	4.8	3.8	5.1

→

| | Key Stage 3 | | | Key Stage 4 | | |
| | % achieving level 5 or above | | | % of pupils at the end of Key Stage 4 achieving | | |
IDACI decile	English	Mathematics	Science	5+ A*–C	5+ A*–C incl. English and mathematics	Any passes
England						
0–10% most deprived	57	60	54	42.3	25.3	95.0
10–20%	62	64	59	45.2	29.9	96.1
20–30%	66	69	65	49.1	34.2	96.8
30–40%	71	73	70	53.9	39.2	97.5
40–50%	75	77	74	58.8	44.7	98.1
50–60%	78	80	78	63.0	49.5	98.4
60–70%	81	82	81	67.1	53.8	98.7
70-80%	84	85	83	70.3	57.8	99.0
80–90%	86	87	85	73.7	61.9	99.1
90–100% least deprived	89	89	89	78.6	68.4	99.3
Percentage point gap between most and least deprived	32	29	35	36.3	43.1	4.3
Odds ratio between least and most deprived	6.1	5.4	6.9	5.0	6.4	7.5

Source: SFR38/2007 National Curriculum Assessment, GCSE and Equivalent Attainment and Post-16 Attainment by Pupil Characteristics, in England 2006/07

Jesson and Gray's Nottinghamshire study of 1991 (www.literacytrust.org.uk) revealed that half of pupils receiving free school meals had low GCSE scores as opposed to one-sixth of pupils who did not qualify for free school meals. The table above shows educational outcomes for pupils in areas of high to low social deprivation and the relationship between outcome and deprivation is stark. England has the highest population of the four nations making up the UK. It would be unusual if this pattern were not typical.

Did you know?

● Social mobility has fallen since 1960 and now one in four children live in poverty compared with one in eight in 1979 (Jesson and Gray, 1991).

- Despite all efforts, who your parents are affects educational outcomes (Jesson and Gray, 1991).

- The Department for Children, Families and Schools (DCFS) is to spend £5 million over three years on extending reading recovery programmes (www.dcfs.gov.uk).

- Social class and poverty are the most significant factors affecting achievement (Jesson and Gray, 1991).

'Government analysis of the so-called education "class" gap in primary schools reveals that while all pupils are doing better in 2004 than in 1998, those from higher income families made more progress than those on free school meals.'

(Ruth Kelly, quoted in Ward, 2005)

School readiness

School readiness is a term that refers to a child's ability to go to school ready to learn, having already gained social, mental and physical skills that will prepare them for class learning beforehand. Many programmes are already running in the UK to help prepare children for school. These programmes are intended to identify and support those children already at risk of failing before they get to school because their homes have in some way failed to prepare them sufficiently for school success. Early years education for three and four year olds, increased childcare places, library schemes, SureStart Initiatives and advertising by the Basic Skills Agency about the importance of reading, literacy and numeracy hours in primary schools, the New Deals and the New Opportunities Fund (latterly The Big Lottery Fund) have all contributed to an improvement in school readiness for many children. Evaluations in the USA and here suggest that this type of early intervention has had positive outcomes. Some of the strategies used in primary schools have informed current secondary intervention schemes for pupils who are not 'school ready'.

In the 1970s a debate raged about the level of language that pupils needed to enable them to learn effectively. Bernstein (1971) suggested that children who came from a middle-class background where language was highly developed and used for socialisation purposes were more likely to develop an elaborate code of language. This elaborate code was akin to the language that a child would be exposed to in a classroom. It was not that the words used were more complex or the vocabulary more flowery, just that children who used this code were able to describe fully experiences that did not rely on the experience being shared. Conversely and generally, the child from a working-class background would have a restricted code of language that would arise from the fact that language was used functionally – and would be characterised by greater use of dialect and

possibly be less likely to be grammatically accurate – but this restricted code relied on a shared experience. Everybody uses this restricted code sometimes. Bernstein argued that what separated some children from others was that all children could use the restricted code but not all children could use the elaborate code. It was felt that this restricted code was less likely to prepare the child for the language that they would be exposed to in a classroom, with a middle-class teacher speaking an elaborate code in front of them, and it was the children with both codes who were most likely to flourish linguistically and be able to tackle effectively the linguistic tasks that may be set for them.

It is likely of course that a child's readiness to attend school and learn is not dependent on one factor such as linguistic competency, though this is of course important. It is more the case that a whole range of competencies including the linguistic needs to be in place. The home environment also has to promote school readiness through the availability of books, time spent reading with children, visiting libraries and possibly encouraging children to spend less time in front of a television where it is used as a way of avoiding talking and as a surrogate parent.

Does income affect educational outcomes?

Although random assignment experiments are rare in the UK, the Educational Maintenance Allowance (EMA) was piloted in 15 local authorities in the UK from 1999 onwards. It offered pupils from low-income families a weekly financial payment of up to £40 per week for two years, provided they stayed on in full-time education. Attendance was monitored and the allowance withdrawn for non- or poor attendance. Bonuses were also offered as an incentive for pupils to complete the course. Ashworth et al. (2001) report evidence of the impact of the programme. Comparisons were made to pupils in 11 areas where EMAs were not being paid. Evaluations suggest that enrolment increased by 6% in pilot areas. There were no increases in drop-out rates and the stay-on rates into the second year improved. The EMA was introduced nationally at the start of 2004–05.

In the UK, Gregg and Blanden (2004) show how not only is there a link between educational outcomes and poverty but also that the link strengthened between children born in the 1950s and those born 20 years later. They also considered whether income was the cause of poor educational attainment or whether other causes such as background, latent intelligence or educational attainment level of parents were also contributory. Their results indicated that income had a causal relationship with educational attainment.

Gregg and Blanden point to recent evidence that the relationship between family income and children's educational outcomes has actually increased over successive cohorts.

'The intergenerational transmission of income has increased for children born in 1970 (British Cohort Survey) compared with those born in 1958 (National Child Development Survey).'

(Gregg and Blanden, 2004)

The impact of poverty on educational attainment

Gregg and Blanden posed the following question:

'Is it money itself that makes a difference to educational attainment and life opportunities?'

(Gregg and Blanden, 2004)

The hypothesis being posed is that if educational achievement is determined by innate ability, parental education, parenting skills and lifestyle (i.e. other factors not linked to income) then income *per se* should not affect educational outcomes. However, the issue is not clear cut given that other factors can be influenced by socio-economic circumstances, for instance the ability to pay for:

● good quality childcare

● books and educational materials to support learning

● access to a quiet work space

- separate bedrooms
- extra-curricular and social activities that aid the development of the mental, physical and social child
- life chances
- the neighbourhood you live in
- the quality of housing (many children live in substandard housing)
- the quality of school your child goes to.

Gregg and Blanden suggest that if these are important then the increasing inequality in family income between the rich and the poor will inevitably mean that poor children will continue to do less well. They estimated how income and educational attainment were related in three time periods using data from:

- the National Child Development Study (NCDS): children born in the first week of March 1958
- the British Cohort Survey (BCS): takes all children born in the same week in April and follows them at intervals until, to date, age 30
- the British Household Panel Survey (BHPS): a household survey that started in 1991 with 10,000 households. These are sampled on an annual basis and the most recent data are from 2001.

The disadvantage of the BHPS was its small effective sample size as, unlike the other studies, there are fewer children of a particular age in each wave.

Gregg and Blanden looked at the percentage of people from each cohort studied who gained:

- a degree
- A levels or equivalent
- GCSE or Certificate of Secondary Education (CSE – no longer in use) at grade 1, O levels, or equivalent
- below this level.

This measure of attainment is gathered at age 33 for the NCDS sample, at age 30 for the BCS sample and at age 22 or 23 in the BHPS sample. Gregg and Blanden acknowledge that in the last sample this could potentially bias the income effects upwards if poorer young people take longer to gain a higher-level qualification.

Gregg and Blanden also added in controls for family background, sex of child, family size, parental age, race and parental education. Even with the controls in place the relationship between income and attainment remained strong. The raw relationship between family income and education over time had strengthened between the NCDS sample and the BCS sample. Gregg and Blanden did find evidence in the BHPS sample that the likelihood of gaining low-level qualifications

had improved but the chance of going on to gain a degree had lessened with each successive sample studied. In addition, they found that parental education did have some effect on child outcomes and the implied income relationships were reduced by a fifth to a quarter.

Gregg and Blanden summarised their work as follows:

- there was a relationship between family income and educational attainment
- the link between income and attainment had strengthened over time
- there was a causal impact between income and educational outcomes.

Evidence of changes over time in the causal relationship between income and attainment proved to be inconclusive. This is due to the impossibility of estimating this link in a consistent way across the models.

Gregg and Blanden suggest that a one-third reduction in family income from the mean of £140 per week is significant, reducing the chances of obtaining a degree by around 4 percentage points. They then posed the question: Was this a large shock compared with the 4 percentage points difference it made? Using their models they attempted to compare the probability of someone in the 90th percentile of the income distribution with someone in the 10th percentile gaining a degree. They reported that:

'Results from the BHPS which control for the post-education income give a larger estimate of the income effect. This combined with greater income inequality, means that the predicted gap is larger, with the probability of degree attainment at the 10th percentile 0.21 and 0.42 at the 90th. These results demonstrate that when combined with substantial income inequality the impact of income has important implications for educational inequality.'

(Gregg and Blanden, 2004, p262)

Gregg and Blanden concluded that if £7000 was significant then redistribution of wealth through taxes and benefits was not likely to bring the income that the poor received up sufficiently close to the mean. However, if initiatives to improve early years learning and extra resources to schools were targeted to those who most need them these could indeed be beneficial. They were optimistic about efforts that had been made post-1997 to address these issues and indicated that educational investments like the EMA and pre-school programmes could be successful in creating a more equal society where the educational gap in attainment between the rich and the poor is reduced.

Recent evidence suggests that between 2003 and 2007 there has been an improvement of 11.1 percentage points in the average attainment of free school meal (FSM) pupils at GCSE (5+ A–C). This compares favourably to the improvement of 7.6 percentage points for non-FSM pupils. Put simply, the gap

in the performance of pupils on free school meals versus those who are not is reducing. However, the average attainment of FSM pupils still remains low (Deprivation and Education, March 2009).

In 2003 just over a quarter reached the threshold. In 2007 just over a third did.

The following tables show how family background and income can impact on educational achievement and outcomes.

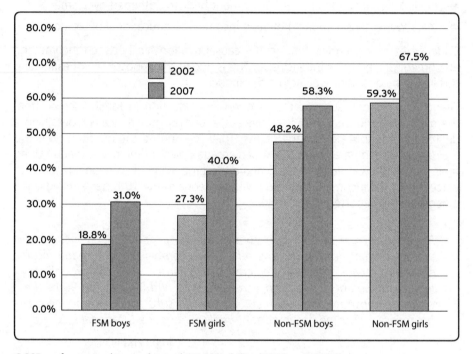

GCSE performance by gender and FSM eligibility (2002 and 2007)

Source: SFR38/2007 *National Curriculum Assessment, GCSE and Equivalent Attainment and Post-16 Attainment by Pupil Characteristics, in England 2006/07* and SFR04/2004 *National Curriculum Assessment and GCSE/GNVQ Attainment by Pupil Characteristics, in England, 2002* (final)

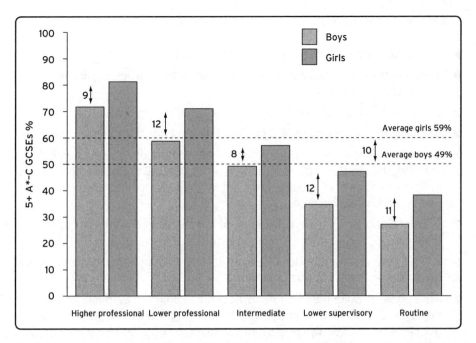

Percentage of pupils gaining 5+ A*–C GCSEs by gender and occupational class (2004)
Source: Youth Cohort Study, reproduced from DfES (2007)

Ethnicity and poverty

As has been suggested, during the last part of the twentieth century the average British family became 40% better off in real terms. At the same time the numbers of children in poverty rose. This has affected several types of economically vulnerable family groups. If the lowest 30% of income distribution were taken to represent the poorest families then the following percentage of family groupings would be included (Marsh and Perry, 2003, p1):

- 86% of all workless families.
- 79% of all single lone-parent families.
- 73% of all large families.
- 68% of all young mothers.
- 66% of all formerly partnered mothers.
- 65% of ethnic minority families.

In addition, the following have been found to be true:

● Ethnic groups are not spread evenly demographically.

● Some communities marry younger and have larger families, particularly Bangladeshi and Pakistani.

● Ethnic groups are more likely to have more children than whites.

● Black Caribbeans are more likely than whites to have one child.

● The extent of child poverty among some ethnic minority groups, particularly Bangladeshi and Pakistani, is high. Seven out of ten Bangladeshi children live in households with an income 60% below the national median compared to one in three white children.

● 41% of Caribbean children and 36% of Indian children live in similar income brackets.

● White pupils achieved better GCSE results overall than Bangladeshi/Pakistani/ Black African/Black Caribbean pupils.

● An analysis of white pupils on free school meals who achieved a level 5 in Key Stage 3 national tests at age 14 found that only one-third went on to get five A*–C GCSEs. By contrast, of the Chinese pupils on free school meals 73% gained five A*–C grades or more and for Indian pupils it was 66%. Black Caribbean pupils also did better than poor white counterparts, at 46%. The findings were mirrored at GCSE for those who achieved level 4 or 6 at Key Stage 3, just above or below the expected level 5 (Mansell, 2003).

The following graph shows the GCSE attainment of non-FSM and FSM pupils by ethnic group.

What are the causes of poverty among ethnic minority groups?

The causes of poverty are varied and include the following:

● Higher rates of unemployment, which could be as a result of not speaking the language and having to take lower paid manual jobs despite qualifications that would normally provide people with a higher income.

● Higher rate of couples neither of whom works.

● Low levels of qualifications/literacy that might naturally result in the securing of lower paid jobs.

● Low pay for certain ethnic groups despite the fact that both partners are employed.

● Lone parenthood rates that are overly high compared to other groups despite the fact that the lone parent may be employed.

All these factors contribute to families ending up in the lowest quintile.

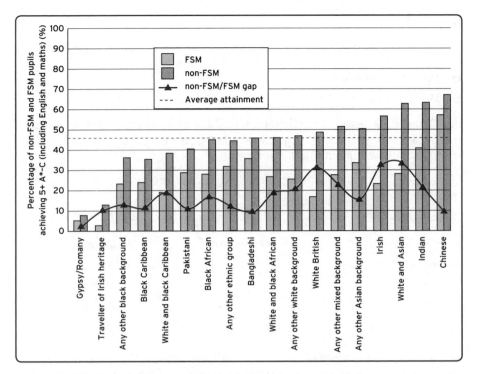

GCSE attainment of non-FSM and FSM pupils by ethnic group (2007)

Source: SFR38/2007 National Curriculum Assessment, GCSE and Equivalent Attainment and Post-16 Attainment by Pupil Characteristics, in England 2006/07

The impact of poverty and ethnicity on educational outcomes

Recent data supports the view that despite poverty other ethnic groups on the whole achieve better than their white poor counterparts. When it comes to attaining GCSEs, 52% of white pupils attained five A*–C grades but so did over 60% of Indian children. The suggestion is that although many Asian children grow up in impoverished conditions family expectations remain high and while Pakistani and Bangladeshi children may not achieve level 2 qualifications (i.e. the equivalent of A*–C grades by age 16) they are more likely to stay on in school post-16.

In 2003 the Aiming High Strategy was launched to raise achievement of ethnic minority pupils. In England a range of targeted programmes have been launched.

Key facts

The proportion of black and ethnic minority pupils has increased since 2004:

- 18–21% in primary
- 15–17% in secondary.

By 2010 it is expected they will represent 20% of all pupils. However, most of the pupils who make up this group go to schools in conurbations like London, Manchester, Birmingham, Cardiff and so on.

Exam results for many ethnic minority (EM) groups are improving, as shown in the table below:

Ethnic group	Results 2003	Results 2006
Black Caribbean	33%	44%
Bangladeshi	46%	56%
Pakistani	42%	51%

However, schools engaging in the Aiming High initiatives show a higher than average rate of progress, for example the proportion of pupils achieving level 5 in the 52 schools involved in the Minority Ethnic Achievement Programme (MEAP) at Key Stage 3 has been greater than the national average. Improvements of 7% were recorded compared to 4–6% nationally.

However, it is still the case that the exclusion rates for black pupils remain disproportionate. A new pilot programme in response to 'Getting it, getting it right', the black pupils exclusion report, is planned to try to remedy this (DfES, 2006).

Including gender in the breakdown of deprivation and ethnicity effects shows that there are some differences by gender within ethnic groups, but on average no significant gender effect can be seen.

Important points

One of the most recent research studies (Deprivation and Education, March 2009) on outcomes for ethnic minority pupils states that FSM white British boys achieve amongst the lowest GCSE results. The gap between their attainment and white British boys not on FSM is 27%. This is the same gap seen between white British girls on FSM and their non-FSM counterparts.

For every ethnic minority group apart from Gypsy/Roma results are improving.

Deprivation as measured by FSM is strongly associated with poorer performance on average at every Key Stage.

Looking at progress between Key Stages it can be seen that for every prior attainment point in every subject, FSM pupils on average make less progress than non-FSM pupils. High-attaining FSM pupils are more likely to fall back, whilst low-attaining FSM pupils are less likely to improve than non-FSM.

There is no direct relationship between attainment by ethnic group and the size of the FSM; there are examples of both high- and low-performing ethnic groups with a small FSM gap.

Findings from PISA, who carry out the world's largest education surveys, show that deprivation has a negative impact on attainment across all OECD countries.

In education authorities where the Ethnic Minorities Achievement Grant (EMAG) is distributed these authorities have begun to gather and analyse a huge amount of information about the attainment of ethnic minority groups.

> *'Emphasising the difference in attainment between groups can be part of a necessary analysis of inequalities in educational outcomes. However, care should be taken that such an approach does not lead to a hierarchy of ethnic minorities based on assumptions of ability.'*
>
> (Gillborn and Safia Mirza, 2000)

Every main ethnic group had achieved significantly well to top an attainment league table in at least one local authority (LA) out of the 118 that responded with evidence. This suggests that all pupils irrespective of race and background can achieve academically. Our role should be to identify why one ethnic group can achieve in one LA and underachieve in another. Research evidence also shows that all ethnic groups are seeing a year-on-year rise in attainment. However, it is also true that for some groups the gap is widening, i.e. other groups are improving at a faster rate, and so the attainment gap is widening faster than they are improving. This is certainly true of Black Caribbean, Pakistani and Bangladeshi pupils, who continue to improve but not as quickly as their white counterparts or some other ethnic groups, particularly Indian and Chinese children.

Case study

One local authority's findings

Local authorities gaining EMAG are not all consistent in the way they collect data. However, it is possible using the results available to see worrying trends in the potential versus the attainment of at least one ethnic group. →

The LA collecting the data serves one of the biggest minority populations in Britain and has been alerted to this worrying trend. In this LA, at Key Stage 1, black pupils were the highest achieving cohort in the authority with scores 20% above that of other children in the authority. By the end of Key Stage 2 they were beneath the authority average and by age 16 were 21 points below the average within the authority.

The gathering of data and the tracking of progress and identification of such underachievement are vital if schools and the LA want to improve the attainment of pupils in this ethnic group in the future. Strategic plans for the authority, the school development plans and funding will all need to be deployed effectively to bring about change. Research applicable to all schools with minority ethnic groups suggests that to counteract this underachievement in particular we need to examine how we treat these pupils, and ensure that our discipline systems are fair and consistent and that expectations for all pupils are high.

Best practice to reduce the attainment gap

Gender underachievement is easier for schools to combat than underachievement caused by poverty or ethnicity, which rely on national strategies. Many strategies that are working to reduce attainment gaps are reliant on government funding and initiatives, and rely on a national vision and drive to counteract disadvantage and deprivation. The use of early reading schemes, SureStart programmes, EMAs, pre-school programmes, library schemes and New Deals all help to reduce disadvantage. Resources should be targeted at those most at risk and children with poorly educated mothers could need extra support. To do this schools will have to work with and through the community to bring about improvement. Where significant improvements have been made in attainment for those at risk of failure, this has been done through family learning classes and reading schemes that take place outside the school day. It is also important that LAs strategically deploy staff and funds to support schools that have a high percentage of pupils who qualify for free school meals. Higher staffing ratios, greater support for pupils through increased use of learning support assistants and, where appropriate, support from English as an Additional Language (EAL) teachers and behaviour support teams are vital.

It is important that schools avoid becoming schools for one ethnic minority or another – schools should be representative of society both in the economic and ethnic mix of pupils who go there. Research has also suggested that poor white children are actually underachieving significantly, as are boys and certain ethnic minority groups.

With this in mind we should specifically track and monitor the following:

- performance of boys versus girls
- performance of children who are eligible for free school meals versus children who are not
- performance of ethnic minority children versus other ethnic groups in the school. Research has shown that it is possible that some ethnic groups will strive in some schools and not in others and identifying trends is vital.

Comparing all of these children's potential against final achievement and ensuring they are on track to achieve that target is essential to ensure a successful outcome for all children irrespective of background. It is also necessary for LAs to take a lead on this and work with schools to ensure that all schools set targets to ensure that these groups do attain. At the same time the targets that schools are setting should be rigorous so that over time Black Caribbean and Bangladeshi children actually manage to close the widening attainment gap. It is worth remembering that the social class attainment gap at Key Stage 4 as measured by the percentage point difference is three times wider than the gender gap.

Schools that are making a difference

Blair and Bourne (1998) researched primary and secondary schools in a number of LAs who seemed to be making a difference to the ethnic children in their areas. They visited 11 primary and 18 secondary schools; all schools had over 10% of their students from Bangladeshi, Black Caribbean or Pakistani communities. The schools were:

- all attaining at or above the national average for A–C grades obtained, or at or above the national average for Key Stage 1 and 2 results, or
- though not yet at national levels, making significant movements towards the national average, or
- outperforming similar schools with similar free school meals, EAL students and levels of attendance.

Blair and Bourne found that where schools were making a difference there were common identifiable features that could be contributory to these results. They also suggested that these initiatives are transferable between schools with different intakes and in different contexts.

Initiatives to follow and adopt

The following list of possible initiatives is based on Blair and Bourne (1998):

- The headteacher provides a strong lead on inclusion and equal opportunities.

- Pupils and their parents are listened to by the school and the school makes an effort to learn from experiences with families.
- There are strong and careful links made with the communities.
- There are clear procedures for dealing with racist incidents and racist bullying and these are carefully investigated and dealt with judiciously.
- Work progresses on strategies to prevent exclusions.
- There are high expectations of the teachers and students and clear systems for targeting, tracking and monitoring individual students.
- Monitoring by ethnicity is embedded and ensures that the schools know whether all pupils are achieving in line with expectations.
- The schools all value the diverse mix of pupils in their midst and make an effort to promote their culture, language and ethnicity.
- The schools that are successful also value the white children and ensure that there are equal opportunities for all.
- Schools have strong behaviour policies that are consistently applied.
- Schools encourage children to set their own targets or assess their own progress.
- Schools encourage a range of after-school and lunchtime clubs intended to support those who might be least motivated.
- Mentors are used to encourage children in the schools.
- Schools use all the help available from the LA to support their vision and make it a reality.
- Schools have induction and intensive language and literacy programmes for beginners in English.
- Schools offer a broad range of modern languages including languages spoken in the local community at secondary school level.

Why not try this?

Looking at the above list of initiatives:

- List the initiatives that a teacher in a classroom could apply.
- Which would need to be whole school?
- Which need to be LA and which rely on national strategy?

Going further

Ashworth, A. et al. (2001) 'Education maintenance allowance, the first year: A quantitative evaluation', DfES Research report 352, Norwich: HMSO.

Bennet, R. (2005) 'Labour failed poorest children', *The Times*, 25 February.

Bernstein, B. (1971) *Class, Codes and Control*, Vol. 1, London: Routledge and Keegan Paul.

Blair, M. and Bourne, J. (1998) *Making the Difference: Teaching and Learning Strategies in Successful Multi-Ethnic Schools*, London: The Open University.

Cassidy, S. (1999) 'Wealth wins top marks', *Times Educational Supplement*, 21 May.

Deprivation and Education (2009) *The Evidence on Pupils in England, Foundation Stage to Key Stage 4*, Schools Analysis and Research Division, London: DCSF.

DfES (2006) 'Getting it, getting it right', London: DfES.

Gillborn, D. and Safia Mirza, H. (2000) *Educational Inequality Mapping Race, Class and Gender: A Synthesis of Research Evidence*, London: HMSO.

Gregg, P. and Blanden, J. (2004) 'Family income and educational attainment: A review of approaches and evidence for Britain', *Oxford Review of Economic Policy*, 20(2), 245–63.

Jesson, D. and Gray, J. (1991) *The Link Between Poverty and Exam Results: 1991 Pupil Performance in Context*, Nottingham: Nottingham Education Committee.

Joseph Rowntree Foundation (1999) 'Rowntree report on child poverty', December.

Kober, C. (ed.) (2003) *Black and Ethnic Minority Children and Poverty: Exploring the Issues*, London: End Child Poverty.

LSE (2005) 'Policies towards poverty, inequality and exclusion since 1997', a study of findings by members and associates at the London School of Economics, available at www.jrf.org.uk.

Mansell, W. (2003) 'Deprived white pupils bottom of teenage pile', *Guardian*, 4 July.

➜

Marsh, A. and Perry, J. (2003) in Kober, C. (ed.) *Black and Ethnic Minority Children and Poverty: Exploring the Issues*, London: End Child Poverty.

Ward, L. (2005) 'Catch-up lessons to help bridge class gap in school', *Guardian*, 27 July.

www.dcsf.gov.uk

www.literacytrust.org.uk

Readability, reading ages and writing frames

What this chapter will explore:

- What is readability?
- How do we assess reading age?
- What are text types and writing frames?

It is important that all teachers, irrespective of their subject specialism, understand about readability and reading ages, as, over time, every teacher will present their classes with a variety of materials and resources. Some will come from textbooks, examination or test papers and some you will make yourself. In this chapter we explore the importance of matching materials to the individual pupil and the positive effect that this can have on their learning experience.

'If a teacher is to plan individual instruction to meet specific needs, the first task is to assess the attainment level of every child and provide each with reading material of the right level of ability.'

(DES, 1975)

All teachers need to understand what a specific reading age means in terms of the children and the individuals being taught within the classroom. A pupil's reading age will significantly affect their ability to engage in your subject whatever it might be. Remember it is the responsibility of all teachers to help pupils overcome obstacles that prevent their learning, whatever that obstacle might be.

This chapter also looks at text types and writing frames. Teachers need to be able to categorise the different writing that pupils are expected to undertake in the classroom. In the primary school much work is done to ensure that pupils understand different text types. This is developed further in secondary school where pupils build on their ability to write in the style of journalists, report writers, advertisers and so on. Writing frames have traditionally been used to 'scaffold' pupils' own writing and have proved to be very useful tools for learning.

What is readability?

Readability refers to all the factors that affect a pupil's success in reading and understanding a text and include:

● the motivation and interest of the pupil

● the way the material is presented, the font size, the legibility, use of illustrations, layout, visual impact and clarity

● the complexity of the words used in relation to the reading ages and the experience the reader brings to the text, i.e. its conceptual level.

How can you interest and motivate pupils to read?

It is true that pupils have little chance of avoiding using the materials presented to them. However, there are ways that we can encourage pupils to read and encourage compliance. We can use praise, merits and rewards and ultimately their own success in the subject to promote greater interest. In addition, we can make sure that the materials we provide have been chosen carefully, that the reading material is matched to the reader and that where possible the material is visually attractive and produced on good quality paper.

How can you ensure resource material is appropriate?

Research has shown that pupils find it more difficult to read non-fiction than fiction and therefore it is helpful if the reading age of a non-fiction text is slightly lower than the average of a class. If your class is aged 12, the reading age will probably vary between 8 and 16 years with the average being clustered around the 12 mark. (How to gauge the reading level of a text is discussed later in the chapter.) Remember though that the reading level of a text is a break-off point for a reader of that reading age. The break-off point means that pupils who have a reading age of 10 are at their outer limit of reading capability and reading comprehension when they read an extract that requires a reading age of 10. This is because most readability formulae are based on a correct answer score in a comprehension test. If a book has a reading level of 10, an average 10 year old would score only 50% on a test of comprehension on that text. If our class only scored 50% on a comprehension test would we then assume they had fully understood the text? Probably not!

Why not try this?

What is wrong with the passage below?

Gingnahc Smoor.

Over the last few years there has been a gniworg tserestni in srevoekam of all kinds not just snedrag, but slaudividni and homes. This has meant that the noisivelet skrowten have jumped on the bandwagon and have provided a elohw egnar of new semmargorp designed to cater for our curiosity. A whole new breed of seitirbelec has been born who are on these semmargorp, we want to know everything about them. These seitirbelec have become dlohesuoh seman and their lives fascinate us. One of the most suomaf is from the ginnedrag dlrow, eilrahc kcommid is a well known erugif and her face is familiar to us all. I am now an Xtreme expert on all sorts of srevoekam and I am not the only one, this is true of sdierf, sevitaler and sruobhgien. What will the next mad ezarc be I wonder!

Finding it hard to read and understand? Then reverse the letters for the unfamiliar words so that the heading becomes *Changing Rooms*, and so on.

See if you agree with these criticisms:

● The font is too small at 10pt and research suggests that 12pt suits fluent readers. The less fluent the reader the more likely it is that a larger font is more appropriate. At the secondary level though, older pupils do not want to be labelled as 'slow' and this often happens when 'big' print is used. Teachers need to be sensitive to this issue. Comic Sans is one of the most

→

legible fonts for use on worksheets and for pupils of all ages, and is the one favoured by a lot of 'literacy across the curriculum' schemes. However, you may want to vary the font throughout your worksheet. Research also suggests that using a variety of fonts throughout the text aids learning as it breaks the material up into 'visual' units.

- The line length is too long: 10–12 words is the suggested optimum length.
- The words used are unfamiliar to a reader and hinder understanding.
- The spacing between the lines is too narrow.
- There is a lack of visual illustrations, which might help understanding.
- The sentence structure is quite complex and the number of words that are polysyllabic raise the reading level considerably. For instance:
  - This short sentence needs a reading age of less than 9 years.
  - This longer sentence, which contains an adjectival clause and polysyllabic words, has a reading age of more than 16 years.

(Based on 'Readability' by Keith Johnson, www.timetabler.com)

Below are some questions about the passage. You will be able to answer them – yet you may not have understood much of what you have been reading.

1. What has happened over the last few years?
2. What has jumped on the bandwagon?
3. What has been born?
4. What is this person an Xtreme expert in?

This can happen in your classroom. You have presented your class with new terminology that they may not understand. You include a task like this with all your unfamiliar words. You ask questions, as has been done above, and the pupils answer them correctly. The exercise merely proves that they can locate an answer, *not* that they understand it.

Why not try this?

The readability game: version 1

One of the most important factors affecting readability is the language that is used. Key words should be clearly explained to the class and where possible definitions of these words should be displayed around the room.

→

One technique for doing this that has been successful is to give the pupils a passage containing a number of words they should know but may not. In pairs, ask them to underline any words they are not sure of. Then ask them to get into groups of four. In the group of four look at the underlined words. If anyone in the group can explain any of the underlined words then they do so. The group of four now identify a new group of words made up of any they still don't know and get rid of any that they have had explained to them. The group now is doubled and becomes eight. The process is repeated. Finally, the teacher goes through any words that are still unknown and checks that the ones the pupils do know have been properly understood.

Health warning. Do this only in a class where you have good control!

The second version can be used as an alternative to the above for a change or with a class who are more difficult to control.

Why not try this?

The readability game: version 2

Make a set of cards for each pupil — one red, one amber, one green.

Read the passage aloud, pausing over new or unfamiliar words. Ask the class to hold up a card to show their level of understanding of the word.

Green — I know this word and can use it correctly and understand what it means in this subject.

Amber — I think I know what this word means.

Red — I haven't got a clue.

The cards allow the teacher to see at a glance the number of pupils in the class who understand the key words used. It also keeps a firm hand on what is going on in the classroom and ensures that all pupils are involved in the lesson. No time for messing about! Choose someone with a green card in their hand to explain what the word means. Go through the passage in this way until all the words have been explained. Sometimes you may wish to choose someone with an amber card to explain what they think the word means.

To check that the information has been retained, this exercise can be attempted at the beginning of a future lesson as a quick lesson starter.

See Chapter 8 for other examples of lesson starters.

TOP TIPS!

When making your own worksheets:

● *Ensure that they are legible. The font size should be at least 12pt and you should be sensitive to the font you are using. Comic Sans is easy to read whilst others are not so easy for some pupils, especially if they are written in small point size. Remember that pupils in secondary schools do not want to be stigmatised by having worksheets that look like they were prepared for much younger pupils.*

● *Ensure that the paper quality is good. This seems a minor point but the paper quality affects legibility and the motivation of the pupils reading it.*

● *Ensure that headlines are used to mark off sections of the text and change fonts to provide visual blocks of work that can be easier to recall.*

● *Ensure that illustration is used where possible. However, the illustrations need to be relevant to the subject and placed appropriately in the text.*

● *Ensure that the readability level of the text allows pupils to fully engage with the material. Ensure that key words or unusual words are clearly explained. This can be done on the worksheet.*

Choosing resource material

When choosing resource material be aware of the following:

● Pupils find non-fiction more challenging to read and therefore the reading level of the text should be carefully matched to the level of the class. Non-fiction texts that are going to be used without teacher support, i.e. without you reading them aloud for pupils or explaining the text as you go along, should be *two* years lower in reading level than the average of the class.

● Where you are responsible for choosing set books for your class choose wisely. Order inspection copies and get pupils to review them for you. Whatever the age of the pupils you teach they will have something to say about a book you show them – so ask for their opinions.

- Ensure that the layout and look of the book is good and that illustrations and colour have been used wherever possible. Not only do these illustrations aid visual learners but most non-fiction books also benefit from having clear illustrations to support the text.

- Active verbs are easier to read than passive verbs. For example, 'the books were taken by the pupils' is more difficult than 'the pupils took the books'.

- Modal verbs such as 'could', 'should', 'might' and 'may' cause comprehension difficulties for poorer readers in a class.

How do we assess reading age?

Reading ages can be determined by conducting various tests with pupils. Some determine the skill a child has in decoding a text, and by this we mean their ability to read aloud the passage as it is printed on the page. Some tests will not just determine this mechanistic decoding ability but will also seek to ascertain whether the pupil can 'understand' what they have read and at what level this understanding is, i.e. comprehending the meaning contained within the passage, not just reading it aloud.

Currently, there are a number of objective measures of reading ages available. In order to use these tests you need to follow a few basic rules:

- Count the syllables in a word. If you are not sure how to do this, say the word aloud to help you hear the different sounds: delay = 2; different = 3; dissident = 3; laces = 2; aloud = 2; some = 1.

- When counting any dates, symbols or initials count one syllable for each number: 2006 = 4; 6.33 = 3.

- Abbreviations count as one syllable – for instance, km, kg.

- Ignore headings and subheadings.

- Formulae are usually ignored but probably increase the reading age.

Some well-known tests you can use are given below but there are plenty more to be found. Just type in a search for readability tests on the web to get to a relevant site (e.g. www.timetabler.com). Printable versions of all the tests listed here are available on the book's website, at www.pearsoned.co.uk/essentialguides.

Gunning FOG Readability Test

Select samples of 100 words, normally three such samples is adequate.

- Calculate L, the average sentence length (number of words divided by number of sentences). Estimate the number of sentences to the nearest tenth where necessary.
- In each sample count the number of words with three or more syllables. Find N, the average number of these words per sample.
- Then the grade level needed to understand the material $= (L + N) \times 0.4$.
- So the reading age $= [(L + N) \times 0.4] + 5$ years.

This FOG measure is suitable for secondary and older primary age groups.

Flesch–Kincaid Formula

This is a US government Department of Defense standard test.

- Calculate L, the average sentence length (number of words divided by number of sentences). Estimate the number of sentences to the nearest tenth where necessary.
- Calculate N, the average number of syllables per word (number of syllables divided by number of words).
- Then grade level $= (L \times 0.39) + (N \times 11.8) - 15.59$.
- So reading age 5 $(L \times 0.39) = (N \times 11.8) - 10.59$.

Powers–Sumner–Kearl Formula

This is the only one suitable for primary age books and is most suitable for books in the 7–10 age range. It is also suitable for secondary school pupils with lower reading ages.

- Select samples of 100 words.
- Calculate L, the average sentence length (number of words divided by number of sentences).
- Estimate the number of sentences to the nearest tenth where necessary.
- Count N, the number of syllables per 100 words.
- Then grade level $= (L \times 0.0778) + (N \times 0.0455) - 2.2029$.
- So reading age $= (L \times 0.0778) + (N \times 0.0455) + 2.7971$ years.

Many schools assess pupils' reading ages as standard practice. Schools use well-established standardised reading tests like those produced by the National Foundation for Educational Research. By using a standard test schools are able to reassess pupils year on year and see the reading gain made by pupils who may or may not be having reading support of some kind. In this way, schools can also

compare one intake of pupils with another to assess pupil profile. If the intake is markedly different, either with more able readers or weaker readers, then the school can put in measures to take account of this. They could challenge stronger readers further or put in place more support for the weaker readers. The reading ability of a pupil cohort can seriously affect the lesson planning and teaching materials used every day by teachers in a school.

It is important to know the reading ages of pupils in your class so that you can make appropriate materials for them. Below is a list of reading ages of materials that will be familiar to you:

Title	Reading age in years
Financial Times	17½
Times Educational Supplement	17
A Tale of Two Cities (Dickens)	13
To Kill a Mockingbird (Lee)	11½
Lord of the Flies (Golding)	11
Kes: A Kestrel for a Knave (Hines)	10½

In addition, you can look at the National Literacy and Numeracy Strategy's (NLNS) lists of words that pupils should be familiar with from their primary years (www.standards.dfes.gov.uk/literacy/publications/framework/).

However, just because pupils should be aware of these words it does not mean they understand their meaning or how to use them in sentences. The figures overleaf are extracts taken from the Oxford Reading Tree scheme. This gives you an awareness of exactly what a pupil with a reading age of 8 or 9 is likely to feel comfortable reading. You may want to compare this to some of the textbooks or worksheets that you use on a regular basis in your classes.

Using reading levels to group pupils for learning

It is common in primary schools to find pupils grouped according to ability in a class. Sometimes the teacher may put children of similar ability in a subject together on one table so they can support each other's learning. This can be done with reading as well so that able readers can work together on a common text that challenges them. However, it may also be useful to put a *strong* reader or two in amongst less fluent readers, encouraging them all to read aloud within the group. This can work in a primary or secondary setting and allows the teacher to use strong readers to aid the development of less fluent readers.

Grandmother told Wilma about the Jump Up.
"Back home you'd call it a carnival," she said.
"Can we be in it too?" asked Wilma.
"Yes, I should think so," said Grandmother.
"Shall we try and make you some costumes?"
"Yes please," said Wilf and Wilma.

A Proper Bike – average reading age 8

The next day they set off on the picnic. Wilma's dad took them out of town in his car. He put the bikes in his trailer and he put Anneena's bike on the roof rack.
"Where are we going?" asked Biff. "It seems funny to go for a bicycle ride in a car."

Wilma's mum laughed.
"We are going to Kingswood Forest," she said. "When we get there we can ride our bikes and stop whenever we like for our picnic."
"We can't go too far," said Chip, "if Anneena has to ride that old bike."

The Holiday – average reading age 9

Source: Pages from *A Proper Bike* and *The Holiday* by Rod Hunt illustrated by Alex Brychta (Oxford Reading Tree, OUP, 2004), © Oxford University Press, reprinted by permission of Oxford University Press

Knowing the reading ages of your pupils enables you to be flexible about the way you group pupils in your class. It also ensures that you do not ask a less fluent reader to read aloud a passage that is clearly beyond them, thus possibly damaging their confidence immeasurably.

Some teachers shy away from asking anyone to read aloud who doesn't volunteer. It is a sensitive issue and one that you need to feel comfortable about. However, whatever your subject area, you should ensure that reading is encouraged and where possible reading aloud occurs, whether it is by you or volunteers in your class.

What are text types?

Primary schools spend a lot of time teaching pupils the different types of writing that make up the text types found in non-fiction. They are clearly identified and pupils are given a clear formula to use in order to write in that genre.

In both primary and secondary schools we expect pupils to be able to:

- recount (accounts of observations and experiences, visits, anecdotes from everyday life)
- report (produce a factual account or description; this could be of an experiment in science)
- explain (the how and why of an event or occurrence)
- be procedural (give instructions, possibly how to make something in technology or give directions)
- persuade (opinions, promotional literature, advertisements, leaflets, political speeches)
- discuss (how they feel about an event or subject). This will contain balanced arguments and will call for pupils to analyse and evaluate their response to the subject giving a point of view supported with evidence.

What are the main types of writing required by my subject?

The table overleaf will help you to identify what types of writing are used in your subject area and what skills are being developed. Provide examples of the types of writing that are commonly found in your subject in the third column. In the fourth column list any writing tasks within your subject that fit this category. Fill in the final column (Where taught?) and then complete the specific skills column, some of which has been started for you.

Identifying types of writing

Text types	Typical examples or locations in my subject	Key examples in my subject	Writing tasks in my subject	Specific skills within my subject	Where taught?
Narrative	Novels, myths, ballads, short stories, folk tales, plays			Note taking	
Recount	Autobiography, biography, newspaper articles, journals, travel books, blurbs			Comparing and contrasting information	
Procedural	Recipes, rules, instruction manuals			Selecting information	
Explanation	Parts of an encyclopaedia, manuals, sections of many textbooks			Summarising information	
Report	Sections of many textbooks; official reports; sections of reference books			Single sentence, short paragraph, evaluative writing	
Persuasion	Adverts, brochures, political propaganda, editorials			Establishing evidence providing information to support a point of view	
Discussion	Formal essays, opinion pieces, evaluation and analysis			Structuring information	
Other				Writing key sentences using the appropriate connecting phrases or scanning	

Source: Strong (2001, p 134)

What are writing frames?

A writing frame is basically a plan that pupils follow which enables them to complete a piece of work to the best of their ability. The figure below shows the processes involved in using a writing frame.

Next (overleaf) are examples of two writing frames, one simple and one more complex. Pupils find persuasive writing the most difficult of all the text types and therefore these frames cover that genre of writing. Printable versions of these writing frames can be found at www.pearsoned.co.uk/essentialguides.

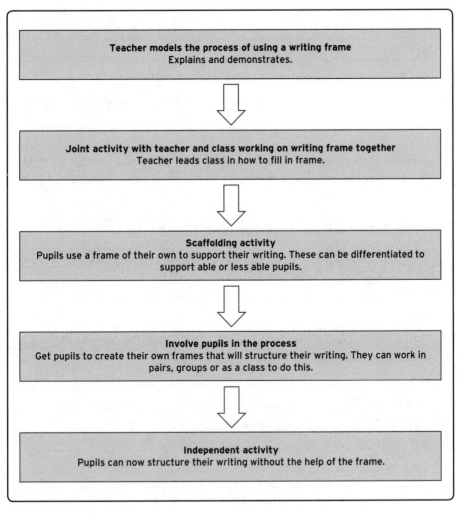

Using a writing frame

Source: Strong (1999, p 87)

Writing frame examples

The task

Write down the advantages (good things) and the disadvantages (the bad things) of keeping animals in a zoo. Explain whether you think it is a good thing or not.

Version 1: A simple writing frame

In my essay I am going to write about _____

I think there are three advantages to keeping animals in a zoo.

First, _____

Second, _____

Third, _____

I think there are three disadvantages to keeping animals in a zoo.

First, _____

Second, _____

Third, _____

However, I think that overall we should/should not keep animals in a zoo because

_____

Version 2: A more advanced writing frame

In this essay I am going to _____

Some people are of the opinion that _____

They also believe _____ because _____

However, _____

On the other hand, there are some people who are of the opinion that ____

They disagree with the idea that _____ because _____

They suggest that _____

They also state that _____

I believe that _____ because _____

In addition, I believe that _____ because _____

To conclude, _____

Writing frames help to improve the quality of a pupil's work by helping them to get organised. However, there are advantages and disadvantages to their use.

Writing frames can help pupils by:

- curing the 'I don't know how to start' syndrome
- providing them with a sense of what they are writing and how to write it
- encouraging them to avoid using repeated phrases such as 'and then ... and then'
- giving them an understanding of the different genres of writing and what each should contain
- encouraging them to work confidently and independently
- encouraging them to achieve their potential by allowing them to express their ideas.

However, writing frames can be a disadvantage, particularly for able pupils, for the following reasons:

- They limit creativity. Writing frames were developed to help pupils write non-fiction. Pupils should be encouraged to use the frames for guidance only and able pupils may want to write without them or use them just for loose guidance. You can help by ensuring that the frames are flexible and varied.
- Pupils can become too reliant on the frame. They should be encouraged to plan their own work using their own frames.
- Like anything, pupils get bored doing or using the same thing all the time, so limit their use.

Why not try this?

This chapter has been about readability, reading ages and writing frames. With that in mind:

- Think about what you have learnt about readability and how you can make resource material that will best match your pupils.
- How could you organise your class more effectively over time by using the reading ages of the pupils to inform your decisions?
- Think about the language complexity of the material that you present to the class both when you are supporting their learning and when they are left to use materials alone, possibly for homework.
- Think about how you can use writing frames to support your pupils' learning and aid them to achieve their potential.

Chapter 8 on lesson planning will enable you to use your knowledge from this chapter in a practical context. Before that, however, let us turn our attention to personalised learning.

Going further

DES (1975) The Bullock Report: *A Language for Life*, London: HMSO.

Johnson, K. 'Readability', available at www.timetabler.com.

Strong, J. (1999) *Literacy at 11–14: A Practical Guide to Raising Achievement Through Whole School Literacy Development*, London: Collins.

Strong, J. (2001) *Literacy Across the Curriculum: Making it Happen,* London: Collins.

www.standards.dfes.gov.uk/literacy/publications/framework

Personalised learning – every child matters

What this chapter will explore:

- What personalised learning (PL) means
- How the quality of teaching is vital to successful personalised learning
- How assessment for learning and pupil data aids PL
- How target setting and pupil tracking improves outcomes
- Pedagogies used in PL schools, including Philosophy for Children, TASC (Thinking Actively in the Social Context) and Learning to Learn

Personalised learning refers to the way that teachers are expected to adapt their teaching techniques to the individuals in the classroom to enable all pupils to attain their potential. Planning for progression and differentiation are the keys to successful personalised learning strategies. Teaching

and learning objectives are shared with the pupils and clear indications are given as to how pupils can progress. In a personalised learning school teachers take account of their pupils preferred learning styles, encourage them to take responsibility for their own learning and use data rigorously to track progress against potential. The classroom environment is positive, encouraging pupils to have high expectations, and praise and rewards are used to support learning. The overall school ethos is a supportive one and promotes high expectations for school success in all areas of learning, valuing the individual and their potential.

> 'Taking a highly structured and responsive approach to each child's and young person's learning, in order that all are able to progress, achieve and participate. It means strengthening the link between learning and teaching by engaging pupils – and their parents – as partners in learning.'
>
> (Teaching and Learning in 2020 review, www.dfes.gov.uk)

What is personalised learning?

The diagram opposite is taken from the National Strategies website and shows the different aspects which contribute to providing a personalised learning framework for all pupils. Each strand is important, but for the purpose of this chapter the focus is only going to be on some of these:

high-quality teaching and learning

target setting and tracking

focused assessment (see Chapter 14)

intervention

the ethos and learning environment within a school.

It will also refer to preferred learning styles, which are covered in Chapter 8, and introduce some new teaching techniques, such as Philosophy for Children (P4C), Accelerated Learning and Thinking Actively in the Social Context (TASC), which have all been proven to engage and promote success in schools.

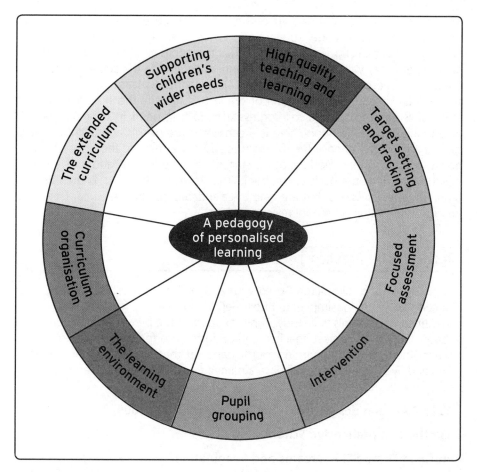

A pedagogy of personalised learning
Source: The National Strategies website, DCFS

High-quality teaching and learning – what is it?

'The big picture' and 'ladders to learning'

Lessons in a personalised learning school are well planned and take account of prior learning. Teachers share with pupils the 'big picture' of learning, not just sharing lesson aims and objectives but also fitting the lesson into the context of a whole learning experience that may take place over a day, a week, a half-term, a term or a year. The older the pupil is normally determines how much of the whole picture is shared at any one time. For instance, in a primary context a teacher may just share what teaching is going to occur that day or week. Teachers will

also share the assessment and success criteria with pupils and in some schools these form part of a 'ladder to learning'. Where the school has been successful in using assessment for learning techniques the pupils will have progressed to a point where they will be confident enough to determine the success criteria for themselves (see pp. 216–7 in Chapter 14). A 'ladder to learning' is a series of statements compiled for each level or grade that identify the skills and content that pupils need to acquire to progress beyond that point in their programme of learning. In some schools there is a consistent use of this approach and each subject is expected to have the 'big picture' visually evident at the front of pupils' books; or if the work is modular at the start of each module. A 'ladder to learning' may be evident at the back of the book. This 'ladder to learning' is then used in progress review sessions that are held at calendared points in the year (see page 265 for information on school review sessions).

Reflecting on practice

An example of a 'big picture' used with a Year 7 pupil in art is reproduced below. In a simplified pupil-friendly format the teacher has identified what pupils will study. Pupils are part of the process and in consultation with their subject teacher and/or form tutor/personal tutor decide where they are on the learning journey and set themselves clear targets. In England by 2010 all pupils will have a named personal tutor assigned to them who may or may not have QTS.

Year 7 Art and design tasks and homework sheet 2009

Cynffig Comprehensive School

Autumn Term: SELF: Dreams and imagination!
8 outcomes (2 are set homeworks)   **Tick!**

1. **Record big 6 week H/W**: 5 min group project on Marc Chagall – show and tell. It should be a PowerPoint presentation. Stick sheets into books and put names on books clearly. Make a colourful intro page in book.   ☐

   Back-to-back game. Describe one of Chagall's paintings to a friend. Finish and evaluate to high standard.

2. PowerPoint presentation on Chagall, Block Busters Quiz.   ☐

3. Mind map in pairs on your dreams, childhood experiences. Use lots of pictures and colour! Title/annotate.   ☐

4. Start six design ideas for your self-portrait based on Chagall's work. No white gaps, use lots of bright colours.   ☐

5. Finish ideas and start your A4 portrait. Use light lines, add paint – light to dark. Use class pictures to help.   ☐

   ➡

6. Continue portrait. No white gaps, use paint thickly. Evaluate in books. (Use guide below.) ☐

7. Complete portrait by today, evaluate in books using the guide below! ☐

Half-term

8. **Second big H/W set: 'produce an A3 completed painting of your dream'.** Add paint and use mixed media (pastels, collage, crayons, pencils, etc.). **Big homework due:** Present H/W to class in groups. ☐

9. Present homework to class in groups. ☐

10. Class presentations continued. ☐

11. In pairs, describe a dream you had to each other, use the mind map to help. Draw in books and write ideas. Use wide variety of art materials like pastels, crayons and paint. ☐

12. Observed drawing of instruments/guitar. Use line, tone and form. Pencil only, no colour, use books. Short evaluative comments on your attempts. Use guide below (line, tone and form). Use word wall to help you. ☐

13. **Big homework** presented to class. Show your A3 dream, tell us more! Start assessments in books. ☐

14. Assessment lesson. Levels, peer, pupil and teacher assessments. Discuss the term's work. ☐

Evaluation of artist's work: What can you see in the work? What colours? What is the scale of the work? What do you think it means? How was it made? What do you like about it? Why did you choose the image/s?

Evaluation of own work: What have you made? How did you make it? What is the scale of the work? Were you pleased with it? What improvements could you make?

Source: Darran Williams, Cynffig Comprehensive School, Bridgend

Teachers now have a lot of information about pupils' prior attainment and they use this to decide not just what they will teach but also the level of difficulty that pupils will be presented with. When planning lessons the pupils' preferred learning styles (see Chapter 8) are very important and many schools audit pupils on entry to determine this. Lessons are designed as part of a continuum and teachers ensure that a range of teaching techniques are in use to suit pupils who are visual, auditory or kinaesthetic learners. There is a high level of pupil involvement, and teaching is not just something done to them but they are also

an active part of the teaching and learning processes. Pupils are encouraged to be active learners and seek out answers for themselves or verify that what they have been told is correct.

Teachers use different teaching/learning methods and will encourage pupils through use of snowballing, pair and share, market place, jigsawing, rainbow, envoy and other pedagogies. (See the website at www.pearsoned.co.uk/essentialguides if you do not know what these techniques are.) All of this ensures that pupils consolidate and take time to review what they are learning and how much they fully understand. Praise is also a very important part of the process and the ethos of the classroom and the school ensures that teaching and learning is taken seriously. Pupils feel valued and know that the school has high expectations of them.

The learning ethos and environment

Within the classroom

The learning ethos and environment must support personalised learning within each classroom, and pupils should be clear about what is expected of them. Progress charts for class groups may be evident on the walls, especially for pupils undertaking external assessment in GCSE, etc. The learning environment should be conducive to being changed to support group or individual learning, and ICT provision and support is often integrated into the classroom. Teachers regularly review and evaluate the quality of their lessons and have clear target outcomes for the classes they teach. The classroom is well organised for learning with key words on the walls and the pupils know that by the end of the lesson learning has to have taken place. Lessons are differentiated even in a subject where setting has taken place. Pupils within any set/class are given clear individual targets in the form of levels or grades and each child is working towards an individual goal. Teachers then assess the pupils' work to ensure that the pupils are performing in line or above these predicted target levels. Regular, rigorous assessment of outcomes is evident with marking used to inform the next teaching steps. Where pupils fall below expectation intervention is swift and ensures limited opportunities to underachieve. Teachers also ensure that support is given to pupils who are identified as vulnerable. They may have individual learning needs or have home issues that could impact on learning, such as being a 'looked-after child' (LAC). The evidence at present suggests that white pupils on FSM are the group most vulnerable, performing half as well as those not on FSM, and their progress should be carefully tracked (see Chapter 5). (The gap between the attainment of boys on FSM and those who are not is 27% on the 5+ A–C index.)

Within a classroom, support assistants may be used to support an individual or a group of pupils. Within the classroom the teacher may organise the

pupils in groups based on prior attainment. In one lesson all able pupils may be put to work together on a more sophisticated task set at a higher level than those in other groups are capable of. In cases like this differentiation is occurring through the task set. In another lesson able students may be placed in groups to act as group leaders in order to lead less able learners and aid their progress. In this way the able student is both working as a lead student and gaining skills in facilitating. In a task that follows work of this kind the differentiation will occur due to the *outcome*. The task set is the same but the pupils' ability will determine how well they achieve at the task. The former example is *task-differentiated* and so the performance of the pupil may be capped at a grade C or B or the level determined by that task and the skills required by the pupil.

Within the school

The school itself is an orderly, purposeful environment that values its pupils and ensures that success is celebrated. Displays and photos around the school should be up to date and celebrate the academic and extra-curricular successes of pupils. Assemblies will support this and pastoral leaders will ensure that pupils in their year groups are aware of where they are against their overall targets for progress. Year group assemblies will at times focus on reviews and identify progress, indicating those who are on track and those who need to be monitored more carefully. Enrichment opportunities will also be provided for all pupils. In some schools pupils are taking GCSE qualifications at Key Stage 3 and beginning AS courses at Key Stage 4. Progress is related to individual needs rather than being age-related – this is often referred to as 'stage not age' learning. The school may use motivational techniques and outside agencies to help build a learning ethos within their school.

Reflecting on practice

BBC Wales has produced a programme called 'Raise your Game' using well-known TV celebrities and sporting stars to help build pupil confidence. Its purpose is to share how these people have had to work to attain success and it stresses the need to be focused, motivated and committed if one is to achieve anything in life. In some instances the BBC team have arranged for these people to visit schools and meet pupils individually and the schools involved have monitored the positive influence this has had on outcomes and learning.

Tracking for success

For personalised learning to be successful pupils have to understand where they are now and how they can improve. Mention has already been made of both 'assessment for learning' and the use of data, and further chapters in this book are devoted to these important topics. However, personalised learning schools make rigorous use of both and in England £150 million has been allocated to embedding 'assessment for learning' techniques into schools between 2008 and 2011. Where schools use data and tracking effectively certain characteristics will be common to all:

● Pupils will know their strengths and weaknesses and know how to improve.

● All teachers will understand the data they have on pupils and use it to inform their lesson planning.

● Pupil progress is regularly reviewed.

● Pupils have regular opportunities to review their progress and discuss this with their teachers, a personal tutor or a learning coach.

● Parents are fully informed of the learning goals achieved and their own child's learning targets.

● Teaching is adapted to suit the individual needs of pupils and teaching, revision and intervention programmes are in place. For instance, some schools have catch-up homework clubs, as well as revision classes during the Easter and Whitsun holidays and sometimes early in the morning prior to a GCSE or A level examination.

● Pupil progress is monitored across the school and in most cases a member of the senior team of the school is a data analyst and oversees pupil progress.

● The process is used across the whole school and ensures that pupil progress is continuous and in line the school's predetermined targets.

Innovation and personalised learning

TASC

In some schools innovative techniques have been used to enhance and support personalised learning. One of these is called Thinking Actively in the Social Context (TASC). It is a learning tactic and is something that can be used easily in a secondary classroom.

TASC was developed by Belle Wallace, a former president of the National Association for Able Children in Education (NACE). TASC is a universal thinking skills framework which allows learners to:

'Work independently yet within an inclusive school policy

Develop skills of research, investigation and problem-solving that can be used across the curriculum

Develop a positive sense of self as an active learner

Develop their strengths exploring and using the full range of their human abilities

Develop skills of self-assessment.'

(www.tascwheel.com/ideas)

Pupils are taught to use the TASC wheel (see overleaf). Where primary schools in particular have used this alongside AFL, significant gains over predicted outcomes have been made. The most important aspect of TASC is that pupils taught how to use this to problem solve can continue to use it independently in their learning across different areas of the curriculum.

Here are some teacher comments about TASC taken from the website:

'The TASC approach encourages Personalised learning, because the children make decisions for themselves. Although the class is working on the same broad project, each group can work on an aspect that interests them and report back to everyone else.'

'The children are able to take ownership of their learning. They use the TASC Problem-solving Wheel to guide their thinking. Their attention span has increased because they are more involved.'

(www.tascwheel.com/ideas)

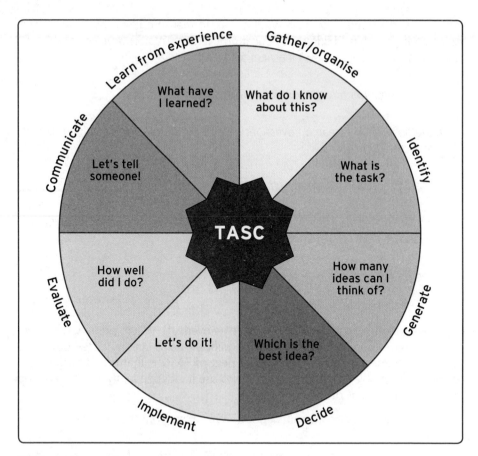

TASC wheel

Source: www.nace.co.uk/tasc/taschome.htm

Philosophy for Children

In other schools Philosophy for Children (P4C) has been used to improve pupils' cognitive skills, and in research studies gains have been found to be made on the latent IQ scores of these pupils (see www.smu.ac.uk). In the past it has been asserted that IQ is static, but the use of P4C and its success in improving cognitive skills has challenged that assertion.

Philosophy for Children (see www.sapere.org.uk) was developed more than 20 years ago by Dr Matthew Lipman, a philosophy professor at Montclair State College, New Jersey. It is an international educational programme taught in many countries around the world, and is described as a thinking skills programme, or a course in critical and creative thinking. It works by building on pupils' curiosity and their ideas about the topics that they are given. Pupils work together in

a 'community of inquiry' to generate questions about a topic; they then work together to generate answers to these questions. In this way, the process of thinking becomes creative, and hence significantly improves the pupils' ability to think logically and analytically about any problems they may encounter.

In this 'community of inquiry' pupils learn to respect, listen to and understand a diverse range of views and ideas. Pupils learn to become more responsible for their own learning and develop the ability to think more independently. They also learn to voice their own opinions and to have confidence in their own convictions and beliefs about the topic they are supporting.

Why not try this?

Go to the book's website at www.pearsoned.co.uk/essentialguides to view a lesson plan for a P4C lesson used in a school where the curriculum has been changed for Year 7 pupils and where P4C is part of the learning to learn curriculum adopted by the school.

Reflect on how you could make use of P4C in your own teaching.

UsefulWebsite

Teachers who deliver P4C lessons undertake training, much of which is provided within authorities. For information go to the website of the Society for Advancing Philosophical Enquiry and Reflection in Education, at www.sapere.org.

Learning to Learn

Learning to Learn is a strategy used in some schools with the express purpose of showing pupils how they learn. It works on the presumption that if children understand both how they learn and what the processes involved in learning are they will work to improve their own learning skills. It encourages pupils to understand and know their learning styles but goes much further than this initial starting point. In schools where this is promoted pupils are taught the importance of eating sensibly, exercising and sleeping. They are shown ways to organise their work and learn through the use of chunking information, linking concepts and ideas or mnemonics. The Learning to Learn strategy is highly sophisticated and in many schools is built into timetabled learning opportunities. In some cases the Year 7 or Key Stage 3 curriculum has been changed to accommodate this.

Learning to Learn strategies include teaching children how to read material, and when to read an article in depth and when to skim read it. Pupils are also taught the importance of organisation and planning, and time is spent improving these important skills that we assume pupils have but on the whole do not. Pupils are also set tasks and then given a choice of ways to perform the tasks, with ideas displayed in a number of formats. They are then asked which they think is the most effective method of presenting their information and findings. In this way the pupils are encouraged to become autonomous learners able to organise and plan their work and make informed decisions about how to tackle their work.

When teaching pupils about Learning to Learn they will also be encouraged to examine their own set of skills and decide whether they are 'word smart', 'number smart', 'body smart', 'music smart' and so on. The aim is to enable them to be reflective learners able to improve on their strengths and turn their weaknesses into further strengths.

Where Learning to Learn is embedded into the school curriculum pupils will have structured lessons where they learn about Edward de Bono's six thinking hats (1985). In some schools these coloured hats are available for pupils to put on and wear to indicate the thinking processes they are using for a specific task.

De Bono (1985) identified six distinct states that the mind is in when it is thinking through issues or problems, which he characterised as differently coloured hats:

● *White* This is a neutral hat and when used pupils consider purely what information is available, what are the facts? It is a time when pupils will gather as much data as they can.

● *Red* This indicates feeling/emotion, an instinctive gut reaction or statements of emotional feeling (but not any justification). However, there is no evidence to support this, it is just a feeling a pupil may have or indeed how others may feel about an issue. For instance, if you were discussing capital punishment you might want to ask how a victim's family would feel. How would a convicted criminal facing a death penalty feel?

● *Black* This is a negative hat and pupils who wear it apply their thinking and logic to identifying any flaws or barriers. Using the same example as above you can indicate what the negative issues could be in adopting capital punishment, and so on. What are the disadvantages of such a course of action, the flaws in the argument? Often when researching a problem not enough time is spent on analysing and thinking about the negatives.

● *Green* This hat is a creative one and pupils investigate as widely as they can to seek out statements of provocation and investigation, seeing where a thought goes. They are encouraged to think outside the normal parameters.

● *Blue* Thinking about thinking. This is sometimes referred to as the 'big picture' hat and the teacher may wear it to outline what they are going to

do and how they will do it. They may also wear it to re-direct ideas if the groups are finding progress difficult.

● *Yellow* This refers to the positives and is the opposite of the black hat above. Pupils wearing the yellow hat look for positive information and evidence to support a point of view.

Reflecting on practice

The thinking hats can be used in all subjects, for example in a geography lesson pupils could be asked to consider the impact of a new motorway being built in an area of natural beauty close to them. They could be asked to consider this from an employment and environmental viewpoint using the thinking hats to help them.

In secondary schools where this is embedded the younger pupils may well wear the hats, or one in a group may wear it to symbolise what part of the process they are working through. The 'thinking hats' provide a tactic by which pupils can fully investigate or think through an issue. The thinking hats technique works well as you can ask groups to use different hats and then share information at the end of the lesson.

Think about how you could use this technique in your own subject area and plan how you would introduce the hats and how you could integrate their use into a specific lesson.

Finally, in personalised learning schools there are planned and staged interventions that will occur if pupils are finding the work too easy or too difficult. In the case of the former, enrichment programmes will be put in place to provide additional stimulus to some pupils. Entering them for examinations is the most simple and straightforward but does require that teachers ensure that progression is built in for them immediately following this. A pupil who takes a GCSE in Year 9 should begin another more advanced course in Year 10 or other avenues should be found to progress their learning. However, enrichment should be an entitlement for all and some pupils in lower ability classes can be given opportunities to take extra qualifications. For example, pupils with SEN taking a hospitality and catering course could complete a level 1 health and nutrition or hygiene course alongside their GCSE. Sometimes pupils fall behind because they are not engaged in the learning process. Initially the class teacher may provide support but this may not be enough and many schools now use learning coaches and mentors to encourage and support learners. In other cases pupils may be given additional one-to-one support or be provided with the learning materials prior to a series of lessons so that they are ahead of the class before a topic is started. This is an effective way of encouraging reluctant learners or those who lack confidence to engage in the learning process.

John Cabot City Technology College
Cabot Competency Curriculum
Lesson plan 5.1 – PMI

Strand: Thinking Methods

Lesson: Four Thinking Skills – PMI   **Duration:** 1 hour   **Resources:**

Competencies to assess
L2 – Thinking methods – OPV, PMI, CAF and APC

Brain Gym
PPT:
Thinking Skills – PMI
Worksheet: PMI Smoking Ban
Computers
Web links
or
Print copies of articles using links

Session objectives
● To introduce students to a variety of thinking methods as tools for researching – PMI, OPV, CAF and APC.
● To introduce what PMI is and how to use it.

Starter
● **Using Brain Gym**
  – Hook-ups (Brain Gym) or positive points (Brain Gym)

Lesson
● **Use PPT:** Thinking skills – PMI

● **Focus question**
  – *Slide 1*: When thinking about thinking skills what could PMI, CAF, OPV and APC stand for?
  – *Pair discussion*: Students to discuss this focus question.
  – *Class discussion*: Collect examples of what the students think PMI, CAF, OPV and APC stand for.
  – *Slide 2*: Answers for PMI, CAF, OPV and APC:
    – PMI – plus, minus and interesting
    – CAF – consider all factors
    – OPV – other person's view
    – APC – alternative, possibilities and choices
  – *Explain*: Students will need to use these thinking methods to prepare for a debate they will be participating in but they first need to have a practice at using these thinking methods.

● **Give it a go – using PMI**
  – *Slides 3 & 4*: What is PMI?
    – Student can take notes on PMI.
  – *Slides 5 & 6*: Fox hunting.
    – Review web links for background information on fox hunting:
      – http://news.bbc.co.uk/2/hi/uk_news/politics/4275753.stm
      – http://news.bbc.co.uk/cbbcnews/hi/find_out/guides/animals/fox_hunting/newsid_1717000/1717812.stm
      – http://news.bbc.co.uk/cbbcnews/hi/find_out/guides/animals/fox_hunting/newsid_3645000/3645188.stm
      – http://news.bbc.co.uk/2/hi/in_depth/uk/2003/hunting_debate_/default.stm
    – Show students a basic PMI on fox hunting.
    – Ask students if they can add to the PMI provided.

→

- **Give it a go – using PMI continued**
  - *Slides 7 & 8*: Smoking ban.
  - Get students to research the smoking ban.
    - Use computer and web links or provide student with hard copies of the articles using links:
      - http://news.bbc.co.uk/1/hi/health/4014597.stm
      - http://news.bbc.co.uk/1/hi/uk_politics/4709258.stm
  - Students to complete a PMI on the smoking ban.
    - Use worksheet: PMI smoking ban.

Extension
- Create a brochure or leaflet for PMI as a reference source to other students.
- Create a word search/crossword on the PMI issue – smoking ban in public places.

Plenary
- **Review PMI**
  - What does PMI stand for?
  - Why would you use PMI to look at an issue?
  - What symbols might represent the letters PMI?

- **PMI teams**
  - Divide students into three teams *or* Designated P/M/I corners – students move to one corner
    - P – plus
    - M – minus
    - I – interesting
  - Students provide one P, one M and one Interesting point for the following topics when selected:
    - Cars
    - War
    - Competitive sport
    - The Royal Family
    - Space exploration
    - Affirmative action
  - Award point for best points raised – therefore award-winning team or winning individual.

Starter
- **Using Brain Gym**
  - Hook-ups (Brain Gym) or positive points (Brain Gym)

Source: John Cabot Academy, Bristol

In the lesson plan above thinking skills are integral to learning for all pupils. At John Cabot College, Learning to Learn strategies are taught to all pupils and empower pupils allowing them to understand clearly how they can best engage with their studies.

Key ideas summary

This chapter has focused on the way pupils learn and the initiatives, of which there are many, that are intended to aid pupils to improve further. These techniques are all tried and tested and have aided pupils to gather the skills they will need to achieve, ensuring that for the most part they will achieve their potential. In the next chapter you will learn about how to plan the perfect lesson. You may wish to think about some of the initiatives you have been introduced to now and think how you could use at least one of these in your lesson

Why not try this?

Consider the following questions:

- Is your classroom a bright, exciting learning environment where pupils' work is valued and shared?
- Do you share the big picture for learning with all pupils?
- How do they know how to improve? How is this shared with them?
- Do pupils know their individual target grade or level?
- Could you devise a ladder for learning in your subject area?
- How do you support the less able and enrich the learning of all?
- Have you used any Learning to Learn strategies?
- When you tell a pupil to revise what advice do you give them about how to do this?
- Does your school use Philosophy for Children or any of the other techniques discussed in this chapter?
- Does it have a learning policy in place?
- What techniques might you want to use in your classroom to improve individual learning?

Going further

de Bono, E. (1985) *Six Thinking Hats*, London: Penguin.

www.bbc.co.uk/wales/raiseyourgame

www.cabot.ac.uk – The John Cabot Academy

www.campaign-for-learning.org.uk – Learning to Learn information

www.edwdebono.com – Thinking hats information

www.nace.co.uk – National Association for Able Children in Education

www.thersa.org/newcurriculum/ – The Opening Minds Programme

www.sapere.org.uk – Philosophy for Children

www.smu.ac.uk – Swansea Metropolitan University

http://nationalstrategies.standards.dcsf.gov.uk/personalisedlearning/

www.tascwheel.com/ideas – TASC wheel

Learning to teach and teaching to learn – planning lessons

What this chapter will explore:

- What makes a good lesson?
- Preferred learning styles
- Starting the lesson: lesson starters and brain gym
- Using mini whiteboards to engage all learners
- Using games to engage learners and consolidate learning
- Using interactive whiteboards in lessons
- How do we use videos in lessons?
- The four-part lesson

This chapter consolidates your knowledge from Chapter 5 by applying it in a practical context. You will learn how to plan and structure lessons to give pupils variety, keep them interested while learning and consolidate their knowledge.

What makes a good lesson?

This question is often asked in an interview for a teaching post especially when the short-listed applicants are new to the profession. It is a question that is intended to ascertain if you have the basic knowledge required to plan and deliver good lessons, time and time again.

The figure opposite shows the constituents of a good lesson. Research over the last decade and a half has changed our view of how a successful lesson should be planned and recent research has concentrated on the preferred learning styles of children. We all learn differently and if you are going to become a successful teacher and ensure that pupils in your class succeed, you need to be aware of preferred learning styles. In addition, schools use data to tell them how individual children are performing in reading and spelling as well as cognitive abilities tests that predict how a child might perform at the end of Key Stage 4.

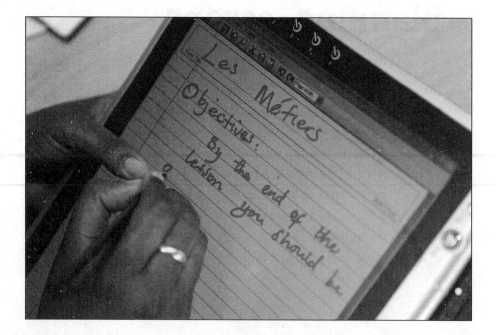

A lot of research has also centred on how boys and girls learn and this has resulted in teachers using different classroom techniques in order to get the best from all pupils.

Even in subjects where pupils are set there will be huge differences in the most and least able in the group. There is clearly a lot of thinking to be done before a teacher plans a lesson suitable for the whole class. Look at the lesson information sheet overleaf. Many colleges and universities produce sheets that may be similar to this, and they are useful in helping with lesson planning. Study both figures carefully and then read the rest of the chapter before thinking about planning your own lessons.

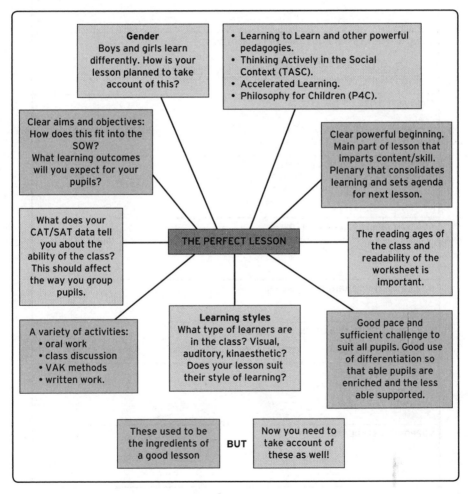

Lesson planning for successful teaching

LESSON INFORMATION SHEET

DATE	PERIOD	SUBJECT	TEACHER	LSA/EMLAS/ANO

GROUP	NUMBER OF BOYS GIRLS TOTAL	TYPE OF GROUP

TOPIC/UNIT OF WORK/learning styles used in this lesson

TOPIC OF THE LESSON AND LEARNING OBJECTIVES

MAIN ACTIVITIES OF THE LESSON

CONTENT OF PRECEDING LESSONS

CONTENT OF LESSONS TO FOLLOW

REVIEW OF THE LEARNING AT THE END

KEY SKILLS TO BE EVIDENT IN THE LESSON

HOMEWORK TO BE SET

SUPPORTED STUDENTS

A sample lesson information sheet

Sample lesson plans from a recent NQT and the lesson information sheet template can be found on the book's website, at www.pearsoned.co.uk/essentialguides.

In Chapter 15 the need for differentiating lessons is also emphasised. It ensures that all learners in the class are catered for and that the able are enriched and the less able are supported.

Preferred learning styles

You will hear people talk about VAK learning methods. Most pupils prefer one of the following learning styles to the others:

- **V is for visual**   These learners need to see the teacher's body language and facial expression. They may prefer to sit near the front of the class. They may also think in pictures and learn through visual displays such as diagrams, illustrated textbooks, overhead transparencies, interactive whiteboards, flipcharts and handouts.

- **A is for auditory**   These learners learn through verbal lectures, discussions, listening to audiotapes, the teacher, etc., talking things through and listening to what others say. Auditory learners interpret the underlying meaning of speech through listening to the tone of voice, pitch, speed and other nuances. Written information has little meaning unless it is also heard.

- **K is for kinaesthetic**   These pupils learn by doing. They prefer the hands-on approach and enjoy actively exploring the physical world around them. They may prefer role-playing or hot-seating exercises.

> **TOP TIP!**
>
> *If you want to know more about planning lessons using VAK methods then look at* The Teacher's Toolkit *by Paul Ginnis (2002). For more on learning styles look at Howard Gardner's* Frames of Mind: The Theory of Multiple Intelligences *(1993).*

Why not try this?

The table below shows you how you can work out what type of learner you might be. It can also be used with your pupils to build up a profile of the preferred learning style of the class.

Read the word in the first column and then answer the questions in the successive three columns to see how you respond to each situation. Your answers may fall into all three columns, but one column is likely to contain the most. The dominant column indicates your primary learning style.

When you	Visual	Auditory	Kinaesthetic and tactile
Spell	Do you try to see the word?	Do you sound out the word or use a phonetic approach?	Do you write the word down to find if it feels right?
Talk	Do you talk sparingly but dislike listening for too long? Do you favour words such as *see, picture* and *imagine*?	Do you enjoy listening but are impatient to talk? Do you use words such as *hear, tune* and *think*?	Do you gesture and use expressive movements? Do you use words such as *feel, touch* and *hold*?
Concentrate	Do you become distracted by untidiness or movement?	Do you become distracted by sounds or noises?	Do you become distracted by activity around you?
Meet someone again	Do you forget names but remember faces or remember where you met?	Do you forget faces but remember names or remember what you talked about?	Do you remember best what you did together?
Contact people on business	Do you prefer direct, face-to-face, personal meetings?	Do you prefer the telephone?	Do you talk with them while walking or participating in an activity?
Read	Do you like descriptive scenes or pause to imagine the actions?	Do you enjoy dialogue and conversation or hear the characters talk?	Do you prefer action stories or are not a keen reader?
Do something new at work	Do you like to see demonstrations, diagrams, slides or posters?	Do you prefer verbal instructions or talking about it with someone else?	Do you prefer to jump right in and try it?
Put something together	Do you like to look at the directions and the picture?		Do you ignore the directions and figure it out as you go along?
Need help with a computer application	Do you seek out pictures or diagrams?	Do you call the help desk, ask a neighbour or growl at the computer?	Do you keep trying to do it or try it on another computer?

What is your primary learning style?

Source: Adapted from Rose (1987)

In schools where teaching and learning is high on the school development plan, pupils' preferred learning styles are identified and the teachers use the data to inform their lesson planning. Where a class has a high number of pupils who prefer to learn kinaesthetically and visually, the teacher may use this information to plan lessons that will better enable these pupils to engage in the learning and attain their potential.

Chapter 16 deals with data in detail and how teachers, departments and schools use data to set effective targets for progress.

Pupils may not fall neatly into one preferred learning style or another. To ensure that pupils all get a chance to learn most effectively, the challenge for the teacher is to plan a series of lessons that include these different learning styles. This is one major way that lesson planning has changed. Now for a lesson to be successful, it should not be viewed as a one-off performance but as one in a series of lessons that a teacher is producing for that class.

The following are some techniques that can be used to make lessons more engaging and easier to recall. Study them carefully in conjunction with the figure on p109 before deciding what is going to go into your lesson and completing your plan.

Starting the lesson

Some schools have adopted a whole school approach to lesson planning in which all teachers follow a similar pattern/structure.

Lesson starters

A popular method is using a lesson starter. Lesson starters are exactly that – a quick-fire beginning to the lesson. Here are some ideas that can be adapted to any subject area.

Lesson starter 1

In a modern foreign language (MFL) lesson get pupils to write down:

- the numbers from 1–10
- the days of the week
- the months of the year
- ten words to describe things to do with a house
- ten words to describe people and their appearance.

→

Get pupils to listen to you when you give them numbers in the foreign language and ask them to add them together, multiply them, etc. This fits in with numeracy work that should be occurring across the school.

When taking the register ask pupils to answer with a word that you have been using over the last two weeks. No one is allowed to repeat a word that has been used before.

When taking the register ask pupils to answer with a word that you have been using – the next person must listen to the letter at the end of the word. Their word must start with that letter.

Lesson starter 2

In an English lesson, take a long word like Constantinople. If the pupils are very young then give them five minutes to find as many words as they can from its letters. If they are older ask them to find as many words with five or more letters. Give a small prize to anyone who comes up with words of seven or more letters, except 'constant'!

Give pupils a list of words with definitions that are mixed up. Get them to match the definitions as this can extend vocabulary knowledge.

As an introduction to a poetry lesson, give pupils a list of key words and ask them to match definitions to a key word.

When reading a story put a list of words on the board that describe a character – this can be adapted for any age or ability. Get them to write down the name of the character.

Lesson starter 3

In a science lesson, put a list of symbols on the board. This can be an interactive board or an ordinary whiteboard. Get pupils to write down the full name for the symbol.

Give pupils a list of key words (e.g. atoms, molecules, solutions) and a list of definitions or constituents. Get pupils to match the key words to the definitions, etc.

Put pictures of laboratory equipment up on the board. Give pupils a list of names which match the equipment and get them to pair these up.

Give pupils a spelling test. Write five words on the board, get them to memorise the spelling and then wipe them off and test them. This can be used as a mini whiteboard activity and or in any other subject. It also brings literacy into science.

While lesson starters ensure that pupils become engaged immediately, thus imposing class control and hence behaviour, they must be used with care:

- If they are used at the wrong time, for example when a start to a lesson is going to be disrupted by pupils arriving later than normal, as can happen after an assembly, they can be more disruptive than beneficial.
- If everyone uses lesson starters pupils will become bored with them. Pupils, like teachers, enjoy variety.
- They can take too long and dominate the lesson so diminishing the main learning intention.
- Preparing lesson starters takes time and effort and sometimes they do not fit neatly with the learning intention.

Chapter 15 has more information on learning intentions, as this is integral to good lesson planning.

TOP TIP!

No matter how you plan your lesson it is most important to:

- *Share the learning intention with the class. It is not a secret.*
- *Explain what you are learning and why.*
- *Explain how the lesson fits with the rest of the work that they are doing. Pupils are entitled to share* **the big picture.**

Brain gym

Another technique similar to lesson starters is something called brain gym, where teachers pose a question that pupils have to problem solve.

Question: If you are in a room with a candle, a wood stove and a gas lamp and you have only one match, what do you light first?

Answer: *The match*

Question: Would you rather a crocodile attack you or an alligator?

Answer: *I would rather the crocodile attack the alligator.* (Read the line again)

Question: Add a single straight line to make this equation true: 5 + 5 + 5 = 550

Answer: *5 + 545 = 550* (You have added a line to + to make it into a 4)

→

Question: You have a barrel filled to the top with water which weighs 150 pounds. What can you add to the barrel to make it lighter?

Answer: *Holes!*

UsefulWebsite

Many brainteasers can be downloaded from the web but permissions may apply in some cases! See www.brainbashers.com for some examples.

There are plenty of brainteasers that teachers can use. They do get pupils thinking and can be good for getting brains activated and ready to learn. However, like lesson starters they can be overused and pupils get fed up when every teacher is using the same techniques. Also, the danger is that in a short lesson too much time may be lost in the warm up and little real time may be left for the learning intention to be clearly stated and delivered. It is better to use all these different techniques little and often – variety is the spice of life!

Using mini whiteboards to engage all learners

Mini whiteboards are today's equivalent of the little blackboards with a few sticks of chalk that you used to be able to buy. Now whiteboards and felt pens are used with a cloth to wipe the boards over. Pupils in a class are given these and the aim is to ensure that all pupils are engaged in the learning activity. No one can escape as they all have to produce the answers and hold the boards up. Mini whiteboards can be used in any subject, as the following ideas suggest.

Mini whiteboards 1

This works for any age, primary or secondary. Depending on what you are doing you can get pupils to:

- Add/subtract/multiply/divide checking that they have sound basic mathematical skills and know their tables.
- Look at a sum on the board with its answer and ask the class if the answer is true or false.

→

- Change a fraction into a decimal.
- Work out the area of a shape that is given.
- Work out the degree of an angle.

Mini whiteboards 2

- Give pupils a time in a foreign language and ask them to write down the time in numbers.
- Give pupils the names of buildings and people, asking them to write down the meaning in English (e.g. school/house/church/station/policeman/teacher/nurse/footballer.
- Ask pupils to write down the meaning of a word that you give them.
- Read out a passage in a foreign language. Ask questions and get pupils to write down one- or two-word answers.

Mini whiteboards 3

- Ask pupils to write down three key words that have been used in the lesson. Choose one of the key words (e.g. photosynthesis) and write down three things about it. Compare what the class has written to see if they have written the same things and then discuss the responses.
- Jumble up a set of numbered pictures that show how species rely on one another for survival. Get pupils to put them in the right order by arranging the numbers of the pictures in the right sequence on their boards.
- Write the definitions of a word on the main board and ask pupils to write down the word being defined on their boards.

Using games to engage learners and consolidate learning

Games are fun and engage pupils but as in all activities they need to be kept under control.

There are many methods that can be used to consolidate learning but it is best when the activity is given a rigid time frame. Like anything new, pupils need more time when they first get to play but this can be reduced as they improve.

Why not try this?

Dominoes for maths

Make cards that have the names of mathematical shapes on them or the shapes themselves. This helps pupils learn the spelling and recognise the shape, so introducing literacy into maths lessons.

Dominoes can be adapted and used in many subjects:

- In chemistry match symbols to the names of elements that appear in the periodic table.
- Match OS symbols in geography to their names.
- Match health and safety symbols in laboratories to their meanings.
- Match the shapes of land masses to the names of countries.
- Match capital cities to countries.
- Match dates to events in history.
- Match fractions to the decimal equivalent.
- Match a sum to the answer.
- Match a definition to a word to improve and extend vocabulary.

Work like this can be used at the end of a lesson to consolidate learning or in the middle of a lesson before a transition to a new task or aspect of the lesson.

Why not try this?

Guess the lesson

Put a word on the board. Tell the pupils that this lesson has something to do with the word on the board and that they will get a maximum of five words or phrases to help them. This is good for oracy work as the pupils have to give a reason to support their answer. It is important that key skills are integrated into all subject lessons.

History

mud   barbed wire   1914   poppy   trenches

Answer: World War I

→

This could be supported by music playing from that era as the pupils walk in and by an interactive video showing clips from World War I. Copies of the poem 'In Flanders Fields' by Dr John Macrae could be given out. The words could also be substituted by pictures.

Jerusalem   quest   pilgrimage   journey   duty

Answer: The Crusades

longboats   Norway   axe   horned helmets   blonde hair

Answer: Vikings

Geography

Play a piece of music with Luciano Pavarotti singing.

Have an Italian flag.

Have a packet of spaghetti.

An outline shape of the country.

Answer: Italy

Why not try this?

Washing lines

These can be used in a lesson to show a sequence of some kind. Stretch a line of string across the room by either getting pupils to hold ends or putting two hooks in the wall and keeping the line ready for when you want to use it.

Mathematics

Give out large cards, each with a number on it. You might want to explore number size for example, so pupils would have to pin the cards on the line in ascending or descending order.

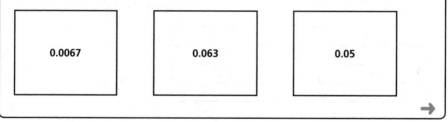

0.0067   0.063   0.05

→

Science

- Use the line to display the most acidic and the most alkaline chemicals or match pH levels to chemicals. Hang up the pH values and put the right chemical next to each one.
- Use the line to show the sequence of events in a reaction between two chemicals and the results and conclusion.

Geography

- Use the line to show a journey from one place to another, especially useful for younger children. For example, 'What would I see if I left school and walked to the post box?' Put the items in order of appearance on the journey.
- Put a set of given countries in order from east to west along the latitude line. Then order them from west to east.
- Biggest countries and smallest countries can also be ordered.

History

Make timelines of events in history or the topic that is being studied. Or consider events in the life of a well-known historical figure.

English

A sequence of events in a story and the plot outline can be hung on the line.

Why not try this?

Can we play a game?

In this game groups of pupils have a set of cards and they are all given an equal share face down in front of them. They must not tell their opponents what is written on their card.

The aim of the game is to get pupils to guess what is being described without using any of the three words written below the main word.

Ocean
Large
Body
Water

Simile
As
Like
Comparison

→

This idea can be used in any subject and can be good for encouraging understanding and knowledge of key words, and ensuring that key skills such as oracy and literacy are being embedded within all subject areas.

Why not try this?

What is the word?

Ask for a volunteer and get them to sit at the front. On their forehead put a sticker that they have not seen. This should be a key word that has been used in the lesson. You may wish to demonstrate by allowing a reliable pupil to choose a sticker that you have not seen from a number that are face down.

The aim is for another person to use questions to find out what the unknown word is. This again ensures that oracy skills are being developed. Extend this further by having a list of definitions, etc. on the board or on a sheet and ask pupils to match a definition to the key word. This is a good way to consolidate learning.

Using interactive whiteboards in lessons

Interactive whiteboards can be powerful educational tools when used well. However, there are still many teachers who have no access to them. Ensure that you have watched lessons where these are being used. In many secondary schools nearly every teaching room has a whiteboard and teachers have made, bought and shared valuable software. They are used to introduce the learning intention by having an example of the day's work on the board for all to see. (See the case study on the website, at www.pearsoned.co.uk/essentialguides.)

There are many ways to use this resource.

Why not try this?

Example from an English lesson 1: Teaching a poetry lesson

● Put the poem on the board without the title. Ask the class to think about what the title could be and to give reasons. To do this they have to think carefully about the content. Ask them to date the poem.

→

- Allow 10 minutes for a discussion.
- At the appropriate time put the title on the board and then the date.
- Begin to discuss the content of the poem and allow pupils to come up and annotate the text on the whiteboard.
- At the end of the lesson save the annotations and print out a copy. This then forms the basis of the next lesson.

In addition, photos can be used to link with the theme of the poem or biographical information about the poet can be built into the lesson. Software is also available for all subject-specific areas of learning. (See the website, www.pearsoned.co.uk/essentialguides, for an example.)

Example from an English lesson 2: For any text

- A PowerPoint presentation was used to introduce the text 'A View from the Bridge' by Arthur Miller. The text is set in the USA and deals with immigrant workers from Italy. It is important to give a lot of background information to pupils so that they understand the context.
- The same presentation was then put on to the school network and in the next lesson pupils were asked to log on and fill in the worksheets that they were given. These were differentiated into 'higher' and 'foundation' worksheets, as this was a Key Stage 4 mixed ability English class.
- Pupils filled in the worksheets independently and were then allowed to work in pairs. This was to allow pupils to share their work.
- Eventually the worksheets were taken in and the pupils' research skills and understanding were assessed.
- All the data compiled by the pupils were collated on to two final worksheets that the pupils were given to keep and use as a reference tool.

How do we use videos in lessons?

For teachers who do not have access to interactive whiteboards, the use of a video can work well in all subject areas to engage pupils and improve attainment. The major TV channels produce some excellent resources that can be used as the basis of many lessons. For example, teachers.tv is an excellent resource that is accessible to all teachers and free. Large schools with their own libraries might have a stock of these. In schools without a librarian there may be someone responsible for recording programmes. LAs have library services, which might also be involved

in supporting learning, and many schools have a funding allocation for books and learning resource materials like videos and DVDs.

In subjects like English literature, adaptations of the texts certainly aid understanding and help to bring the text alive for many pupils. In many cases, world events can be used to support pupils' understanding of the effects of natural disasters on the environment and mankind, and current affairs programmes provide much valuable resource material enabling informed discussions about complex issues.

In some cases teachers may show a video and then re-show it, with pupils being expected to respond via a worksheet, or it may be used as an integral part of a lesson to reinforce a theme.

The four-part lesson

In some schools, as with lesson starters, a standard format for the way lessons are planned has been implemented (see figure overleaf).

Differentiation

Differentiating the work you plan to use in class is important. In all lessons you must expect different pupils to learn at different rates and some pupils in all classes will finish work before the others. If these pupils have completed the work well and you are confident they understand the work then you need to supply them with extension work. This could be an extra written question or an extra diagram that they are expected to interpret. The task is not there to occupy the pupil but should develop their learning further so that you are enriching their learning experience. Pupils like to be challenged!

Differentiation is a term used to describe the way teachers plan work to suit a particular group of pupils. An English teacher could set an essay entitled 'My best holiday'. This task would differentiate by outcome. All ages and abilities of pupil could undertake this task but an A* pupil will write a piece commensurate with their ability. The task differentiates by outcome.

However, a teacher covering circulation in biology may have to alter the materials used to suit pupils of different abilities by altering the readability of the material, the type of tasks they set to test understanding and so on.

The data that schools now provide on pupils and their prior learning allow teachers to group pupils in a class effectively. Teachers use these data in a number of ways. Sometimes they group the most able students together so that they can challenge them with a task that the average pupils in the class might find too

Phase 1

Learning atmosphere established.

Previous lesson is reviewed and the present one is set in the context of the BIG PICTURE.

Clear lesson intentions and objectives are given.

A sense of challenge and excitement in the learning is generated.

Phase 2

New information is provided but in small amounts.

Teacher asks closed questions then open questions that elicit greater understanding.

This part of the lesson is characterised by tasks and activities.

Key words are being used.

Phase 3

Success criteria are being tested.

Have the pupils understood at a basic level and a more complex level?

Oral questioning and written tasks explore this.

Tasks that require thought, understanding and verbalisation of understanding are provided.

Pupils transfer information into a format that suits their learning style.

Phase 4

This phase is vitally important and is, in effect, a plenary session with pupils actively reviewing the learning objectives.

Pupils think about what they have learnt.

The teacher may use questions and encourage pupils to work in pairs to discuss and consolidate their learning.

Pupils may think about what activities they have participated in and what learning techniques have been successful for them.

The plenary should also lead into the next lesson.

The four-part lesson

hard. In this way they can enrich their learning and push them on a little more. However, at times it may be useful to put an able pupil in a group with weaker pupils in order to develop that group and to move them all forward. Pupils learn most effectively from each other and teachers need to harness that and use it to good effect.

Remember that whenever you set a task you must make it time related. In Chapter 4 you should have noted the need for setting time-related tasks. Boys definitely need a tight structure to their learning and enjoy an element of competition in their lessons. You will also need to refer to Chapter 6 on reading ages and readability when you are planning your worksheets. It is important that you make your materials accessible but do not dumb down the work or make it too easy. Your aim must be to extend pupils' vocabulary and learning. Children need to be exposed to a rich language experience in the classroom. This is particularly true of those who have come to this country and are learning the language.

Look again at the figure on p109 and think about what you should be considering when you are planning your lesson. The different ideas given above also provide a teacher with ways to engage the attention of pupils and appeal to a range of learning preferences. Then use the following checklist to ensure that you have accounted for all aspects.

TOP TIP!

Your lesson should take account of all of the following:

- *Clear aims and objectives.*

- *A well-planned lesson that can be delivered in the time allowed.*

- *Good pace and challenge.*

- *Groupings identified (pupils must realise that you are in charge of the layout and seating for the class – no discussion is allowed on this). Use data to group the able together when you want to enrich their learning and set them a challenging task. Put able children with average pupils to bring the whole group performance on.*

- *Seat boys and girls together to improve the oral work of boys and when you want to encourage risk taking – girls can be overly cautious and boys too hasty. Put them together to find a good, balanced approach to tasks.*

- *Variety of tasks – all clearly timed to ensure that pupils remain focused and on task.*

→

- *Differentiation may be achieved through the type of questions that you ask the most able in the class versus the average or less able, or through the written kinaesthetic tasks set and through the groupings you identify (see above).*

- *Learning styles should take into account what VAK methods were used in the last lesson and the teacher should aim to produce lessons that recognise these different preferences.*

- *Ensure that clear learning outcomes and success criteria are identified for the pupils.*

- *Make sure you keep up to date with the latest educational pedagogy by attending good training courses, joining subject-specific teaching organisations and reading teaching-related publications.*

Why not try this?

- The acronym VAK is used to describe different learning styles. What do the letters represent?
- What eight factors should you think about when planning the perfect lesson?
- What is a lesson starter and can you think of one you would use in your own subject and classroom?
- How would you use one of the games suggested in a lesson?
- How could you use photos, videos or an interactive whiteboard in your lesson?
- Plan a lesson that is structured as a four-part lesson.
- How would you differentiate this lesson to suit three distinct ability groups: the most able, the average child and the less able in a year group?

Going further

Gardner, H. (1993) *Frames of Mind: The Theory of Multiple Intelligences*, New York: Basic Books.

Ginnis, P. (2002) *The Teacher's Toolkit*, Carmarthen: Crown House Publishing.

Hughes, M. with Potter, D. (2002) *Tweak to Transform*, Stafford: Network Educational Press.

Rose, C. (1987) *Accelerated Learning*, Aylesbury: Accelerated Learning Systems.

www.brainbashers.com

Storing data and organising lesson plans

What this chapter will explore:

- What data do you have access to?
- How should data be recorded?
- Storing resource materials and lesson plans

In order to become an excellent teacher it is not enough to deliver high-quality lessons. Teachers must be good markers of pupils' work and be able to give good diagnostic feedback to pupils about how they can improve (see Chapter 14). They must also be able to track pupil progress comparing it with the data that they have available to them (see Chapter 15). As a teacher you will have access to a lot of baseline information on any pupils you teach. This chapter is concerned with how you keep that data. It aims to make you a much more effective and efficient teacher, one

able to use the data so that you are both data *and* knowledge rich. Having the data and not using it to best effect makes it redundant! This chapter is also about how best to organise your lesson plans and any resource materials you have produced for future use and ease of reference.

What data do you have access to?

You may be given some or all of the following data:

- reading ages and spelling ages
- Standard Assessment Test (SAT) levels
- teacher assessment from the prior year, reports, etc.
- Cognitive Abilities Test (CAT) results.

All teachers need to keep this important data in their markbooks or in a suitable file. Teachers should also record classwork and homework performance on a regular basis.

How should data be recorded?

All schools should have detailed marking policies and some will instruct you as to whether you should record in levels, grades or marks. However, most have a whole school policy that is interpreted by individual departments. The recording of classwork in a practical subject may be very different from the recording of pupils' work in a maths lesson, for instance. Make sure you record pupil progress appropriately using detailed guidance from your line manager or subject leader. Some schools now insist that only a comment is recorded in a pupil's book and that this comment identifies the strengths and weaknesses of the work. The comment must also identify how the pupil can progress to the next stage of learning. If this is the case in your school or department then it does not mean that you can't record the level, grade or mark achieved in your own markbook.

A markbook of some kind is mandatory for all staff, and teachers must keep detailed records of pupil attainment to inform their report writing and enable them to report orally to parents during parents' evenings. Some schools provide loose-leaf files in a standard format for all areas of learning; others provide purpose-made markbooks. It is useful to have all the data on pupils available in one place and not to have to move between different files.

The figure below illustrates an extract from a markbook showing part of a sample page of data on a pupil group.

Names	Form/Class	M/F	Reading age	Spelling age	CAT verbal	CAT numerical	CAT non-verbal	SAT English	SAT Maths	SAT Science	ILP/EMLAS
Wasima Ali	7A	F	11.6	11.0	100	110	102	5	5	5	EMLAS
Josh Anderson	7A	M	10.6	9.0	94	107	108	4	5	5	ILP

Extract from a markbook

What is an individual learning plan (ILP)?

Some pupils have special needs and these children may need support of some kind. Pupils with dyslexia for instance will have an individual learning plan (ILP). In some schools they are called individual education plans or IEPs.

EMLAS stands for Ethnic Minority Languages Advisory Service. Some children may speak English as a second language and need additional language support. They could well be very able and their language difficulty should not prevent them being in top sets if the school uses a setting system. (See Chapter 5 on poverty and ethnicity factors and how they affect teaching and learning outcomes.)

Some pupils may have a school health plan. These enable a school to put in place a plan for managing children who have individual health care that a school needs to take account of. For example:

- a child who has to be allowed to leave the room immediately they want to go to the toilet
- a child with hearing or visual impairment of some kind
- a child with severe epilepsy or asthma.

TOP TIPS!

These tips are for secondary teachers or teachers in a middle school who teach a range of subjects and have a number of classes for each subject. In your markbook:

● Allow at least five double pages for each year group.

● Trim down the last four pages, cutting off the area where you would put names. This will mean that the names written on the first page are seen whichever page you happen to turn to.

● On the first page write the names and all the current data you have, as seen in the figure on p131.

● Put classwork marks on one page and homework marks on another (see the figure below). This makes it easy to see how well pupils do without class support. It also ensures that you can see at a glance the homework record of a pupil. Compare the marks between classwork and homework. Parents can make a big difference to homework marks! However, children may also be distracted in class and work more effectively at home.

Names	Homework marks with dates		
Wasima Ali	Classwork marks with dates		
Josh Anderson			
Charlotte Bedwell	Student data including individual learning plans		
Hannah Davies			
Rhys Davies			

Adapting your markbook

● If you are a teacher with no form of electronic marking and you have a number of different classes, record attendance on a →

separate page. This is an important piece of data and can affect pupil performance significantly.

● Keep one double page for making notes. An English teacher would make notes about oral work, spelling, punctuation skills, quality of imaginative writing, persuasive writing and so on.

● Make up your own shorthand to help you remember certain pieces of work for good or bad reasons! You may wish to refer to these marks/grades/levels in a comment for a report. For example: ND = not done, EXC = excellent, M = merit awarded, D = detention given, → average, ↑ better than average, ↓ lower than average, TBF = to be finished, and so on. Leave a column next to the level/grade/mark to enable you to do this (see the figure below).

ENGLISH	C	L	A	S	S	W	O	R	K	06
Names Year 10 / 2	CW Comp 2005 /20		Writing /20		Oral work					
Wasima Ali	16	A (M) ↑	14	B–	14	B–				
Josh Anderson	13	C–	TBF		15	A ↑				

Example of a 'shorthand' system

● Add up the marks or look across at the levels or grades awarded for a period of time – a half-term for instance. Award an average for that period of time. It is useful to do this from time to time to see the rank order for the class. In this way you will not overlook a bright child who is quiet and does not demand your attention and yet is near the top of the class. It is often the case that the ones you think are doing well and demand your time are not the best! Some schools have a reward system. Use this as a reference for awarding rewards/merits, etc. (See Chapter 14 for more on rewarding good work.)

● Some teachers use computers as markbooks and put the data on to an Excel spreadsheet. This has obvious benefits for ranking the class, etc. However, computer data is not easily accessible in the middle of a busy lesson. Data in a markbook can be used easily →

to match a pupil to their progress in order to facilitate discussions about progress as you teach the pupil in the lesson.

- *You may want to put exam/test and term grades on a separate page. Record the level of examination that a pupil is to be entered for: higher/intermediate/foundation or the appropriate level.*

- *Record the identifying numbers of the books that pupils may have on loan from the department or learning area so that you can get these returned at the appropriate time.*

- *Remember that markbooks should be used at parents' evenings and that pupils' books should also be in evidence so parents can see the quality of learning and marking.*

- *See page 266 for how to prepare for a review day.*

Reflecting on practice

One school's use of its website

In Eirias High School, Colwyn Bay, a maths teacher, Patrick Morrow, now puts his classes' classwork, homework and test/examination results on to his website. Pupils have a password and they can only access their marks. In this way they are able to see how they are performing. For each piece of work the average mark awarded to the class is shown. This means that if they scored 4.5 on a piece of work and the average is 3.7 then they may have done well. If the opposite is the case then the pupil needs to improve in that area of learning. Pupils can relate their progress to that of the rest of the class. Pupils who miss work can also access lesson and resource material, which they download and use to catch up on.

Patrick Morrow is also keen to show attendance and can show how poor attendance often affects performance in that area of learning – highlighting depressed scores. This is very obvious in a subject like maths where topics are studied sequentially and end-of-topic assessments show how poor attendance might have affected the ability to do well in this area.

See www.pearsoned.co.uk/essentialguides for more on how attendance affects performance.

Storing resource materials and lesson plans

Over the course of your teaching career you will amass a lot of material. In order to be efficient, and not have to repeat work unnecessarily, organising this material is essential. Here are some ideas.

A lesson planner

Many schools provide these. Some make them in-house and they are customised to suit the school. The advantage of a purpose-made planner is that it may include important calendar dates as well as lesson times, important whole school policies, LEA contact numbers and so on. Bought lesson planners come in A4 and A5 sizes and enable you to keep lesson notes. In your first year of teaching you may want to make more detailed plans to supplement these. Some teachers keep a file for each academic year as well.

A year file

Divide this into the classes you teach, or divide the file into subjects or learning aspects. In each space keep detailed lesson plans. You should also keep copies of any worksheets in a poly pocket and date it. In this way you can keep spare work ready for anyone absent on a specific day for a specific lesson. This system ensures that you always have 'spare' worksheets for those who missed the work or who mislaid the worksheet. It also avoids disruptions that can cause behaviour difficulties for relatively inexperienced teachers.

At the end of each academic year file your materials using the method suggested below.

The big files and IT backup

An English teacher can organise files neatly according to literary texts they will have taught that year:

- *Romeo and Juliet*
- *Lord of the Flies*
- *Carrie's War*
- *Charlotte's Web*

Does your subject lend itself to this? Can you organise your work into topics? If so you could adapt the suggested idea to suit your subject(s).

Put all the information in envelope wallets that are clearly labelled on the outside. On the cover, list the sheets that are contained inside. Use poly pockets to divide up the contents of the wallet so that you can see at a glance the resource material available to you. Save all work produced on a computer on to labelled discs/CDs, etc., so you don't lose material owing to computer failure. Many teachers now use small portable flashdrives. These are not without risks. Portable external hard drives are very useful and a more robust backup system. Look at the examples below for suggestions on how to organise lesson topics from Key Stages 2 and 3.

Geography Key Stage 2

My town

History of the town

Why towns grow up in locations, e.g. crossroads, sources of rivers

Map of the town

Pictures of different types of housing

List of streets

Worksheets marking route from home to school

Science Key Stage 3

Worksheets on different types of soil

Lesson starter video clip from the internet

The rock cycle

Notes on sedimentary/metamorphic/igneous rocks

Game to help pupils remember

Diagrams

Large lever arch files are useful for storing one-off items such as exam papers, SAT papers/tests/assessment tests. Divide the file by subject/year group taught. On the divider list the contents – this means it is easier to see at a glance what the file contains. Again put worksheets together in one poly pocket. This makes it possible to see quickly if you have just a few or enough ready for a class. Over the years it is easy to forget just what you have produced and finding an already tried and tested good worksheet is a pleasant surprise for a busy classroom teacher! Many

schools now use or have a VLE (virtual learning environment) where staff are able to store a lot of material electronically in a private area that is password protected and backed up on a school server. This makes storage easy, but remember that most teachers move from school to school to secure promotion, so ensure that you also have hard copies of your work.

Finally, look carefully at the good practice of experienced teachers around you and ask them how they organise their work.

Why not try this?

Having read this chapter, reflect on the following questions:

- Do you have a markbook?
- What additional information has been made available to you about your pupils?
- How are you storing this data?
- Is it ordered as well as it could be?
- How does your mentor store data on pupils?
- What materials have you already prepared for lessons?
- How have you ordered and filed this material?
- Is it going to be readily re-useable?

Using classroom supports to maximise pupils' learning

What this chapter will explore:

- What type of support staff will you find in classrooms today?
- What can you expect teaching or classroom assistants to do?
- Establishing best practice
- How classroom assistants and support staff will be used in future

This chapter looks at the variety of support that is available in many areas of the UK. Many schools have particular requirements and this is reflected in the amount and type of support staff they use. Remember that each school is different. The chapter then discusses the best ways of working alongside all additional adult classroom support.

What type of support staff will you find in classrooms today?

Many teachers will find that they have with them a support teacher (ST) or a teaching assistant in the classroom either on a full- or part-time basis. An ST is a member of staff who may be employed by the local authority to support the learning of children with specific needs. One common use of an ST is to support children who have English as an additional language. These teachers have got specific expertise and will work on a one-to-one basis or with a group of children to improve their language skills and allow them to engage fully with the school curriculum.

Another common use of STs is with pupils who have specific educational needs like dyslexia. These teachers usually come from a special needs background and will come into mainstream classrooms to support average ability or able pupils who have been identified as having specific learning difficulties. These children can cope well in the mainstream, have a good level of understanding and with support will access GCSE and GCE qualifications.

Finally, STs may also be members of staff who have spare contact time and this needs to be used effectively to support those pupils who are identified as needing extra help.

Over the past ten years the number of teaching assistants (TAs) or classroom assistants (CAs) who have no formal teaching qualification has grown considerably. This is due in part to the number of initiatives that have been introduced, such as the NLNS. Another valid reason is the inclusion into the mainstream of pupils with very many widespread needs. Recently, the workforce remodelling ongoing in schools and the reduction in administrative tasks that teachers are allowed to carry out has meant a further increase in the use of support staff.

The specific titles of TAs vary. In one school they are given one title that may be different from the school next door where a TA is doing exactly the same job. In order to provide some clarity it is more useful to suggest the range of roles and responsibilities that assistants may carry out by looking at a fictitious case study.

Case study

How High Cross Secondary uses its support staff

The following describes the way in which TAs work alongside other staff in High Cross School. Their titles were carefully selected to suggest the types of work they do and areas of the school they work in.

➡

Learning support assistants (LSAs) (pupil)

These are attached to individual children who have statements of educational need. These pupils have help on a one-to-one basis for a designated number of hours a week depending on the assessed need of the child. The LSAs know what work the child is doing and visit the same subject lessons on a timetabled basis. Where LSAs are attached to individual pupils, if a pupil is not in school the LSA is not required officially on that day. LSAs (pupil) normally move through the school with the named pupil. Where pupils have needs caused by physical or mental disability the LSAs usually have a higher degree of training and this is specific to the needs of the pupil. Some LSAs will be able to change catheters for children for instance.

Learning support assistants (group)

These are also employed by High Cross School to work with children who do not have an individual statement but need some form of extra support that has been identified. This is normally referred to as School Action. These LSAs may have specific subject expertise – where this is the case they will be used in this subject as support where possible.

It is likely that although one member of staff is specifically employed to work with a named child they will in fact end up supporting the group of children who sit near the named pupil. Working with one is difficult to achieve as other pupils who sit near the pupil or who are friends will also ask the LSA for help if they need it. This is common practice.

Behaviour support assistants (BSAs)

These assistants work with pupils who are identified as having specific learning difficulties that are more closely allied to their behaviour than their ability. In some cases pupils may have low ability and poor behaviour. These assistants work with the pupil and support learning. They may be involved in counselling the pupil about poor behaviour and will be used to remove a pupil from the room if their behaviour threatens to disrupt the whole lesson and get them into trouble. Some of these BSAs will have attended further training devised to help them cope with those whose behaviours can be challenging.

Pastoral support assistants (PSAs)

These assistants work closely with the head of year in the school. They will support the work of the head of year in carrying out administrative tasks, phoning parents, tracking attendance and putting up displays. However, this is only part of their role. Pupils who have been recognised as needing support

➡

for a number of personal reasons – e.g. bereavement, being a school refuser, underachievement – are identified. The PSA works with these pupils either in the classroom setting or takes them out in small groups and manages and supports their learning. In some cases, they help pupils who have been absent for a long time to catch up. They work with the subject/class teacher to ensure that the pupil attains their target levels or grades as identified by data held by the school. This support will be timetabled and the target pupils may change as and when pupils have progressed significantly enough to no longer need additional support. Many of the pupils who have needed support so far in High Cross School have been boys and this is at a ratio of 5 boys to 1 girl, which is close to the national norm.

Curriculum support assistants (CSAs)

These work with subject leaders on a rota basis. They also support the curriculum area by organising photocopying, putting up classroom displays, helping to make subject-specific lesson materials such as flash cards and carrying out routine administrative tasks. In addition, the CSA may have expertise in numeracy and literacy and will help deliver the strategy to small groups of identified pupils under the direction of the class teacher who plans the lessons. Some of the school's teaching assistants also help with peripatetic reading groups and run spelling workshops first thing in the morning.

Cover assistants (COAs)

Workforce remodelling has reduced the amount of time that a classroom teacher can be asked to cover for absent colleagues. In order to ensure that classes are taught effectively when teachers are absent a team of CAs has been employed. They are not qualified teachers but have completed accredited training. Teachers who know that they will be away at meetings or on courses prepare the work in advance and will talk it through with the CA. If they are away due to illness, the line manager will provide work or will go to a bank of work ready prepared by the absent teacher for just such an occasion.

Cover support manager (CSM)

The CSM is in charge of organising the cover team on a day-to-day basis. The manager is responsible to the deputy headteacher who line manages the team. The latter is in overall charge of the continuing professional development (CPD) of all staff and manages the CPD budget and the budget for staff cover. The CSM completes day-to-day administration tasks and returns supply teacher information to the local education authority so that supply teachers can be paid centrally. The CSM along with the deputy headteacher

→

organises additional training for the cover team and the CSM regularly covers classes for absent staff, as do the rest of the team.

Learning coaches (LCs)

These classroom assistants work with individual pupils in the school. Every pupil in the school has at least an hour's interview with a learning coach to discuss their progress and to identify any issues that they need help with. Detailed records are kept and where necessary individual pupils are targeted for extra help and support and a further series of meetings. The LCs work closely with heads of year, with subject leaders where necessary and with PSAs. LCs can arrange meetings with parents when necessary but need to discuss this with the line manager in charge of pastoral issues for that area of the school.

Time is set aside where possible for all CAs to meet to discuss issues relevant to them. The school organises regular inset for the support team based on needs identified by the team itself or identified by the inclusion manager. The inclusion manager is similar to a Special Educational Needs Coordinator (SENCO), but in this school is responsible for all pupils including the most able, the deaf, the autistic and all who may need extra support. The inclusion manager is supported by an assistant and the senior learning support manager (who is not a teacher), the deputy headteacher and headteacher. All TAs who work directly in a classroom-based environment are encouraged to help make materials where time and deployment permits. They are also encouraged to help differentiate materials where appropriate. CAs at High Cross School are not all paid on the same salary scale and the salary reflects the amount of training they have had and the level of responsibility they are expected to undertake.

What can you expect teaching or classroom assistants to do?

Ask if the school has a general job specification for CAs; this will suggest what teachers can expect a CA to do. Workforce remodelling has meant that job specifications should now be in place and where CAs are paid on different levels the reasons for the differential will be explained. If a job specification is not available ask the SENCO for an indication of what exactly the school expects a CA to undertake. This will ensure that you are not asking them to do something inappropriate or that could cause resentment.

Read the job specification that follows. This will give you some idea of what a typical CA might be expected to do and suggests the expectations schools have of TAs.

Teaching assistant's generic job specification

This job specification may be amended at any time following discussion between the headteacher and member of staff, and will be reviewed annually.

Purpose

To support/enrich the teaching and learning of pupils in curriculum areas, pastoral areas and classrooms and maintain positive attitudes towards learning, achievement and behaviour.

Key areas of responsibility and tasks include the following:

- Strategic direction and development of year group/groups of pupils/ individual pupils

- In cooperation with and under the direction of the headteacher, deputy headteachers, SENCOs and, where appropriate, the curriculum and pastoral coordinators and class teachers to:

  - support the vision, ethos and policies of the school and promote high levels of achievement

  - support the pastoral or curriculum teams, SENCO and class teachers to deliver the development plans in operation in those areas

  - contribute to strategies that positively impact on teaching, learning, behaviour management and attendance in collaboration with key personnel, including those mentioned and the attendance officer and Education Welfare Officer (EWO).

Teaching and learning

To:

- Assist the teacher with delivering good-quality lessons

- Deliver good-quality lessons prepared by the teacher where appropriate

- Prepare lesson material and resources to support learning where appropriate

- Use ICT effectively to support learning activities and develop pupils' competence and independence in its use

- Assist the teacher with the development of suitable classroom resources and, where appropriate, mount displays to enhance the learning environment

→

- Support the teacher in managing the behaviour of named pupil(s)
- Work with the class teacher to identify valid learning targets for individual pupils
- Work with the class teacher to deliver the individual educational plans for pupils who are targeted for classroom support
- Work with the class teacher to ensure effective use of time and provide clear structures for learning by maintaining pace and focus and ensuring that pupils remain on task
- Work with the SENCO and class teacher and other designated staff to assess a pupil's changing needs on a regular basis
- Use specific specialist skills such as behaviour management training, counselling skills, dyslexia training, etc. to support the needs of pupils to ensure positive outcomes for their learning
- Support the classroom teacher by working together to use a variety of teaching approaches and a range of strategies to help their learning needs
- Develop knowledge of a range of learning support needs and develop an understanding of the specific needs of the pupil(s) to be supported
- Work with small groups of pupils to deliver literacy/numeracy/computer-aided learning or other specific lessons as determined by link staff and with the agreement of the SENCO
- Support the physical needs of pupils ensuring that effective teaching and learning can occur
- Develop a supportive relationship with pupils in order to promote effective teaching and learning
- Mentor specific pupils, supporting them and helping them to learn effectively.

Monitoring, assessment, recording, reporting

To:

- Keep a record of the teaching and learning of pupils in their care
- Monitor pupil progress
- Contribute to the reporting process to parents and other staff about the learning of pupils
- Aid in the assessment of pupils where applicable and to contribute to the routine assessment systems
- Track the progress of named pupils in consultation with relevant teaching staff

→

- Assist the teacher in assessing pupils' work
- Assist in setting challenging targets for pupils
- Be familiar with reading and using school data as and when applicable
- Administer and assess/mark tests and invigilate exams/tests.

General

To:

- Take on specific tasks related to effective teaching and learning and support for pupils
- Operate within the stated policies and practices of the school
- Establish effective working relationships and set a good example through their presentation and personal and professional conduct
- Endeavour to give every pupil in their care the opportunity to reach their potential and meet high expectations
- Contribute where appropriate to the corporate life of the school through effective participation in meetings and extra-curricular activities necessary to the life of the school and specific individual pupils
- Participate in performance management processes and use the process to improve professional and personal effectiveness
- Contribute to the out-of-school learning activities where appropriate within guidelines established by the school
- Line manage other teaching assistants where appropriate
- Hold regular team meetings with managed staff
- Undertake recruitment/induction/appraisal/training/mentoring for other TAs.

It is important to identify why the classroom assistant is in your classroom. If the CA is there for an individual child then the teacher needs to be aware of the reason. Children who are supported will have ILPs and these need to be used by the teacher and the CA to support the pupil's learning. The CA may have worked with the pupil for a number of years and will have a good understanding of the problems that prevent them from learning. It is useful to find out as much as you can about pupils with support from the CA.

Make an effort to get to know the CAs you work with. Where possible try to arrange a meeting so that you can negotiate the ground rules for working as a team with pupils in the classroom. This can be difficult if you work with a number of different CAs but is important.

The following list is an example of *specific* activities that CAs might be expected to undertake in any classroom situation:

- Read materials aloud to the pupil explaining any words that are difficult or that the pupil does not understand.
- Ensure that the pupil is able to use specific equipment and materials available and give help where appropriate.
- Assist the pupil in any areas of weakness or difficulty (e.g. spelling, reading, behaviour, handwriting and presentation).
- Restate the task if necessary to allow the pupil to engage with it.
- Help the pupil to focus on work and ensure task completion.
- Help pupils who have specific physical disabilities to learn effectively.
- Work with small groups of pupils either in the classroom or, if the school policy permits, in another workspace on specified tasks set by the class teacher.
- Liaise with the class teacher about individual education plans.
- Help to monitor and track progress and contribute to class teacher reports.

Establishing best practice

Tensions can arise if there has been no discussion about how to manage situations that may arise in the classroom. The class teacher is in charge of overall discipline and therefore should support the CA if the latter has difficulties with poor behaviour. In some cases the CA may remove a poorly behaved pupil or pupils at the discretion of the class teacher. The CA is there to support the learning of a child or a group of children, and in some cases may have specific expertise with behaviourally challenged children. However, even though it is important that the teacher and assistant learn to work together as a mutually supportive pair of adults, the class teacher needs to retain ultimate responsibility and take decisive action where it is called for.

'A day in the life of a classroom assistant' can be found on the book's website, at www.pearsoned.co.uk/essentialguides.

Liaising about work

The class teacher is also the professional in charge of the teaching and learning room and as such will plan and deliver the lesson, and this will be part of a scheme of work (SOW). Therefore, sharing the SOW and the lesson plans and materials

beforehand is important. Providing a pack of the materials that you are going to use during that week or over the course of a half-term makes it much easier for the CA to direct the work of the pupil or pupils they are helping. The CA, with their knowledge of their pupils, will be able to suggest ways of adapting the work to suit the pupils' needs. Part of their job specification, depending on their status and salary, might well be to help differentiate the teaching materials to make them suitable to the needs of the pupils they support. Even when the CAs are not able to differentiate the written materials, they may want to find other resource materials to support their pupils' learning.

A CA may read the materials with the pupil, explaining any difficulties and restating the task if this needs doing, possibly simplifying the language and the task if this is necessary. CAs should also ensure that pupils are on task and might be involved in checking and correcting work. In some cases, CAs will be involved in assessing pupils. They may help them to complete exam papers, observe them in lesson situations and contribute information to behavioural and learning reports that could be used by an educational team.

Establish with the CA their expected role in the classroom and if necessary use the school job specifications as a basis from which to work. In many schools the SENCO will line manage the CAs and will be able to help staff develop an acceptable system for working as a team.

Liaising about behaviour

As well as managing the work, the CA and the teacher need to discuss how they will manage the behaviour in the classroom. It is usual for the teacher to retain whole class control but to delegate some level of responsibility to the CA, who is the one sitting next to a pupil or group of pupils and as such is in a position to know what is happening in that area of the room. It is important that the teacher delegates some responsibility to the CA, allowing and indeed expecting them to manage the behaviour of the pupils nearby. However, the teacher will need to step in to manage serious breaches of discipline and show that they support the CA. One of the most common issues that can arise is when a supported pupil refuses to work for the CA or is rude to them. It is important to listen to the CA and support them when this occurs. On rare occasions it may be necessary to separate the pupil and CA, seeking help from an on-call system or the SENCO.

Classroom assistants are familiar with the school rewards and sanctions systems and should have some autonomy to use them. The class teacher should reinforce this practice. The pupils in the class need to know that both adults in the room have power and the teacher needs to be seen to support the CA. Pupils can be very good at playing one adult off against another as they do sometimes with parents! In all cases of indiscipline you must find out exactly what happened and be fair and consistent in the application of sanctions.

Establishing ground rules

In some cases the CA removes pupils from the class during the lesson and it is important to establish that the CA will take control of the behaviour of those pupils while they are with them, ensuring that pupils follow school behaviour rules. The ground rules should also include the following expectations of CAs:

- Like teachers they should have high expectations of the pupils and show respect for their social, cultural, linguistic and religious differences.
- Treat pupils with respect, ensuring the development of the learner.
- Work as part of a team.
- Ensure that pupil's health and well-being is protected in line with legislation.
- Provide support for teachers, pupils and the school.
- Act as role models using language and behaviours that are commensurate with their duties in the school and with young people.

Some teachers work with pupils with profound learning difficulties and may have two or more CAs in the room. Where this occurs it is important to seek advice from line managers and from the SENCO about best practice in this situation. Make time to see others teach who have experience in this type of situation. New teachers are not expected to know everything and making use of mentors and their expertise is vital. Teaching is like skydiving: it is better to get it right first time if you can; or at least live to fly another day!

The future for classroom assistants and support staff

In future, schools will undoubtedly use TAs in more and more diverse ways. The continuing professional development that is already in place for teachers will be further extended and assistants will be further involved in school-based training as well as training provided by specialist deliverers. The challenge will be to use all assistants so that they effectively and significantly support the teaching and learning that goes on in school to improve standards.

> 'Teaching assistants play an important part in the implementation of the NLNS by supporting teachers and pupils in the classroom ... Section 10 inspections show that the presence of teaching assistants improves the quality of teaching. This improvement is most marked when the teaching assistant and teacher work in close partnership or when the teaching assistant is following a tightly prescribed intervention or catch-up programme.'

(Ofsted, 2002, pp4–5)

Why not try this?

Consider the following questions:

- How many teaching assistants are there in your school?
- What roles do they fulfil?
- Does your mentor have any that work alongside him/her?
- How do classroom assistants record the work that they have done with pupils in your school?
- Does the classroom assistant meet with the teacher to discuss the work that will be done prior to the lesson or is this done informally in the lesson?
- Note any effective classroom practice involving teachers working alongside classroom assistants.

Going further

Dragonfly Training Ltd, 'How to maximise the effectiveness of teaching assistants in schools', available at www.dragonfly-training.co.uk.

Lee, B. (2002) 'Teaching assistants in schools: the current state of play', National Foundation for Educational Research LGA educational research programme, Local Government Association, Research 34, Slough: NFER.

Ofsted (2002) 'Teaching assistants in primary schools: an evaluation of the quality and impact of their work', HMI report 434, 23 July, London: Ofsted.

Part
3

Behaviour management

Chapter

11

Behaviour – let's start at the very beginning

What this chapter will explore:

- What is a behaviour policy?
- What strategies can be used to prevent poor behaviour? The educational behaviour plan
- Promoting positive learning: sanctions and rewards
- Preparing to face a class
- Body language, voice and eye contact
- First steps in achieving class control

The next two chapters deal with one of the biggest issues facing teachers today – that of controlling the behaviour of unruly pupils. This chapter outlines how schools manage pupils' behaviour and apply consistent measures to ensure that all staff play a part in this. It also explains how

exclusions work and why certain pupils may have educational behaviour plans. It is intended to get you to think about how you will prepare for taking control of a group of pupils. No matter how good the school or how academically bright the pupils are, they all have the capacity to wreak havoc and chaos when confronted by a teacher who clearly does not know how to control a class. This is where you can start to get it right!

Why is this important?

Remember that good teachers develop their management skills over time and very often reflect on a poor lesson in order to ensure that it improves the next time. This chapter and Chapter 12 are not intended to be fully comprehensive; they are a starting point. In order to become a good classroom manager you will need to seek advice constantly, watch good classroom managers at work, read extensively about strategies you could use and objectively review your own practice. You will also need to understand how schools work in relation to managing behaviour so that you have an overview of where you will fit into this.

Before you go any further it may be useful to look at a checklist of possible reasons that prevent pupils from learning in a classroom:

- poor attitude to learning
- low self-esteem of a pupil or a whole class
- poor classroom management of the pupils
- ill-prepared lessons with a lack of clear instructions for pupils to follow
- lack of differentiation of work: it is too easy or hard
- lack of variety within work
- poor attitude and relationship of a teacher with a class
- lack of consequences from poor behaviour
- boredom.

If you know the likely causes then these can be avoided or strategies put in place to minimise them.

What is a behaviour policy?

Most secondary schools and an increasing number of primary schools have written policies on behaviour. This should go some way to ensuring a consistent approach throughout the school to such an important issue. A *behaviour policy* outlines the discipline procedures that are in place for dealing with all pupils in the school. It should explain the standard operating procedures of the school and it will be explicit about how pupils should behave in class and the expectations the school has for them. It also suggests the code of conduct for staff and, in some cases, lays down basic rules for the way that a classroom should be kept (e.g. all chairs placed under desks at the end of a lesson). It could also indicate how pupils might be expected to enter and leave classrooms. In some schools pupils are still expected to stand when any member of staff enters the room. It might refer to rewards and sanctions and to on-call staff or time-out procedures. It will refer to a list of behaviours that might occur in your classroom and suggest ways of dealing with them in a structured and hierarchical fashion.

Some schools have a three-strike system:

1. The first strike is a verbal warning for poor behaviour, failing to follow instructions, being mildly rude/answering back, etc.

2. The second strike will result in a written punishment or a punishment meted out by the classroom teacher.

3. The third strike is a formalised detention that is recorded. This will occur in a lunch hour, after school or even on a Saturday morning in some cases.

The on-call system

More extreme poor behaviour could result in an on-call where another teacher is called in to intervene. An on-call system is common in a secondary school. It is where senior staff and members of the pastoral team are on an on-call timetable/ rota and will be available to support any staff who may require help with a difficult pupil or class at that time. The on-call system also means that if there is another type of emergency where staff might need support there is someone available. This on-call system might occur formally in a large primary school but in many smaller schools primary staff work closely and informally to support each other.

An on-call member of staff will normally remove the pupil from the classroom and either place them with another teacher in the department (normally the head of department or faculty) or take them to a designated place. In some schools pupils are made to sit outside the office of the senior member of staff on call where they carry on with work given to them by their subject teacher. Pupils referred to the on-call teacher in this way will have some form of standard punishment, such as an automatic after-school detention. This should be recorded so that a behaviour profile of a pupil is being developed. The punishments are progressively harsher as the offences get worse. However, for extreme rudeness to a teacher or repeated failure to follow instructions that seriously undermine the teacher an internal exclusion, fixed-term exclusion or a request for a parent to visit the school is more common and teachers will not be expected to go through the three-strike system.

The time-out system

Time-out refers to a system agreed amongst the staff, whereby a child may be allowed to leave the classroom and stand outside for a five-minute cooling-off period. Though this does occur there is a legal issue in that you are responsible for a pupil who is timetabled to be with you at a specific time. Imagine the extreme scenario where the pupil runs off and gets knocked over by a car – you may find yourself responsible. In cases like this it is important to check through procedures carefully with a line manager.

In some schools the term 'time-out' is used to refer to a punishment whereby pupils are internally excluded from their normal class(es) and they spend the day being supervised by a senior member of staff or staff on a rota. This system is used for poor behaviour that is not deemed bad enough to warrant excluding a pupil from school totally. For many pupils this is a greater punishment than a formal exclusion – in an internal exclusion they miss out on the social side of school and just do the work bit! They will be prevented from mingling with friends at breaks and at lunchtime. For some pupils, who may have parents who cannot control

them, this is a far worse punishment than a day spent at home watching telly or cruising the streets.

Exclusions: fixed-term or permanent

There are also specific rules and regulations that cover the exclusion of pupils from all schools whether it is for a fixed amount of time (fixed-term exclusion) or permanent exclusion. Most local education authorities insist that they are informed about exclusions and the school must send them a standard form indicating the name/age of the pupil, length of exclusion and reason for exclusion. No school is allowed to exclude a pupil for truanting. Over the course of the academic year there is also a fixed amount of time that a school can exclude a pupil for, unless they are permanently excluding them when this restriction does not apply. At present, pupils can only be excluded in an academic year for a total of 45 days cumulatively. The LEA has to be notified about exclusions especially for those who have already had over five days of exclusions in one academic year. The governing body will also be involved and there is one sub-committee of the governing body that is delegated to deal with all issues to do with behaviour and exclusions within a school.

Excluding pupils permanently is not easy, but pupils can be excluded immediately for a number of obvious reasons – arson attacks on the school, attacks on teachers and other pupils, dealing drugs on the premises and other similar serious offences. In reality, a pupil is excluded for a number of incidents that cumulatively suggest the school has done all it can to retain that pupil but that all intervention strategies have failed. When excluding pupils in this way schools realise that it is important to ensure that all exclusions, interventions and strategies have been tried and that a clear record of exclusions and reasons has been retained. In addition, the methods the school has adopted to help the pupil remain in the mainstream will have been rigorously recorded.

Excluding a pupil should not be taken lightly but it is important to realise that these pupils can seriously undermine the ethos of learning in a school and send out the wrong message to other pupils on the cusp of behaving badly. A pupil who is excluded is often unlikely to find another school to take them and sometimes will fail to find a place in a specialist behaviour institution, such as a pupil referral unit, due to the pressure on places. They are also unlikely to attain formal qualifications and are much more likely to end up in prison. A study found that 42% of young offenders sentenced in courts have been excluded from school and a further 23% were truanting significantly (Audit Commission). This is why permanent exclusion should not be taken lightly; nor should bad behaviour that seriously prevents pupils who want to learn from learning. Pupils who have been permanently excluded can appeal against the exclusion, which is why carefully recording all information regarding all pupils is vital.

What strategies can be used to prevent poor behaviour? The educational behaviour plan (EBP)

Most pupils want to learn and will be frustrated by those in the class who try to prevent that happening. Schools have a number of ways of dealing with pupils who behave poorly on a regular basis. The obvious strategy is to talk to the pupil about their behaviour, indicating what it is they are doing wrong, why it will not be tolerated and suggesting clearly the sanctions that the school will use to bring them back into line. It is also important to suggest to pupils that the final outcome will be a permanent exclusion. Parents need to play a significant part in this discussion. They can be invited to a meeting in school and an agreement might be made whereby the pupil is put on a daily report. This report will indicate to a parent how the day has gone and whether the pupil has attended all lessons. Some pupils find getting to a lesson the most challenging part of it; others find behaving in the lesson and remaining on task challenging.

Each teacher a pupil comes into contact with, as well as non-teaching staff, will record comments. The report with comments is taken home for parents to read, sign and return. Pupils are normally given a daily report but schools implement whatever programmes best suit them. The school might also ring the parent to request that they remove the child from school for part of a day when things are going badly; an extended form of time-out that may have been discussed prior to its need.

Referral to an educational psychologist and the EBP

In some cases the school may decide that a referral to an educational psychologist (EP) is advisable. When this occurs it is important to call a meeting of the pupil, parent, EP and relevant staff to put in place an EBP that will be followed. This is similar to a contract that is negotiated between all parties. Although schools try to avoid exclusions, if a pupil is seriously undermining the ethos of the school there may be no alternative. If an exclusion is to be successful the school has to show that it has put in place strategies like this to support the pupil but that, despite these, the pupil has failed to conform to the demands of the school.

It is important that the pupil understands the seriousness of an EBP and that it is not a normal occurrence within a school, but something that has had to be devised and implemented for them exclusively. In some cases where pupils are behaving so badly that they are at the point of exclusion, it is normal to limit the timetable of the pupil to a few days or sessions a week. This puts a lot of pressure on the family, who have to arrange transport to and from school at inconvenient times, but may be essential, as the child cannot behave for sustained periods of time at that stage of the EBP.

While this is one way of managing a serious behaviour problem within a school, pupils do not have to see an EP to have an EBP. Some pupils who have emotional problems caused by their home circumstances coupled with poor behaviour may also have similar plans and may be involved with Social Services through family group conferencing or with other groups who support pupil learning.

Read the school behaviour policy

The above information is intended to give you an overview of how behaviour problems may be dealt with in a school. In most schools the majority of children come to school ready to learn and will cause few behaviour problems. Before you begin in your school it is important to read any behaviour policy and make sure that you are fully aware of any rewards or sanctions that are in place. Discuss fully with your line manager how pupils who misbehave are dealt with. In a secondary school each department may operate its own detention for pupils who misbehave or fail to complete homework, as well as being part of a whole school system. Primary schools, especially large ones, may also have similar systems to those in secondary schools to ensure that order and good behaviour are maintained.

Schools that are successful in terms of achieving the best results for their pupils and enabling them to attain their potential will have clear and established behaviour policies that will be applied consistently by the staff. Pupils therefore have a clear idea of what is expected of them while they are in school and clearly get the message that poor behaviour is not allowed to interfere with learning.

Promoting positive learning: sanctions and rewards

Many schools have realised that they need to do more to encourage pupils to want to learn. Some have adopted a system called promoting positive learning (PPL). This system relies on mutual respect between staff and pupils and on staff working positively with pupils to ensure good learning outcomes. Staff involved in the system are encouraged to use positive praise to reinforce good behaviour and ensure that maximum learning occurs. As a guideline, it is suggested that in any lesson a teacher should be trying to use positive praise three times more often than they use negative reprimands or comments. In schools where this system has been adopted staff have agreed rewards for attendance, sustained good effort and good learning outcomes. In a primary school these could be stars on a chart in the classroom, in a pupil's book and so on. It may also be a merit/star based system where pupils gain so many merits/stars, which will entitle them to a small reward of some kind (e.g. free pens, pencils, entry into a prize draw). In some secondary schools funding has been sought and this finances end-of-term merit draws for a bike, DVD player and so on. This is sometimes coupled with a commendation

system where teachers/departments identify pupils who have worked well and these pupils receive a letter home to their parents highlighting their achievement. However, many schools have found that pupils like the commendations but not the publicity that accompanies it!

As is the case with so many systems, schools will adopt and adapt a system that best suits their own ethos and needs. In one secondary school the merit system is used for the first three years and then in Years 10 and 11 pupils are awarded credits in card form. The subject teacher signs these credits and the pupil hands them in to their head of year. At the end of each term there is a prize draw so the more credits a pupil has, the higher their chance of winning the star prize. Star prizes have included a holiday for four to Disneyland, Paris, as well as a chauffeur-driven limousine for the end of Year 11 leavers' ball.

Pupil planners

Pupil planners have also become popular in secondary schools as a way of keeping parents informed about behaviour and merits gained. Pupils are given a planning diary for the year – usually a weekly diary with additional room for comments which parents and form teachers sign every week. In it parents record reasons for absence and teachers record merits awarded or information about behaviour, concerns about homework and so on. These planners can also be purpose-made for the school and a school calendar of events is normally included as well as information for parents about school policies. Many schools include the home/school agreement in planners as well as information regarding the school's expectations about the conduct of its pupils.

TOP TIP!

The home/school agreement is a statutory contract between pupils/parents and the school outlining what each party agrees should occur throughout the year. Ensure that you are familiar with its content.

Planners are a useful way of keeping in touch with parents to share any concerns a teacher has about a pupil's progress.

Preparing to face a class

Having familiarised yourself with the school behaviour policy, found out as much as you can about the class you are about to teach and prepared the lesson well, you are now ready to think about entering the classroom. However, you are not quite in the door yet!

Some experienced teachers suggest introducing a set of rules and regulations over the first few days or lessons with a class. It is important that all teachers think about what is going to be appropriate in their class. Teachers who teach a practical subject might impose different rules from others who do not. Think about how pupils will enter and exit your lesson. How will you start the lesson and how you will end it? Try to make that a standard routine. Good practice suggests that the opening of a lesson should involve a clear statement of the learning intention which could be written on the board, given to each child on a piece of paper or merely stated. Good practice also suggests that a plenary session at the end of a lesson to consolidate the learning is important. Planning a lesson to include time for a good introduction and a good summary is going to be an important contributor to instilling good classroom management. However, in the first lesson it is important to make your expectations explicit to pupils.

Here are some rules that are important in any lesson. They should be shared with pupils and could form the basis of your code of conduct. These rules are available on the book's website, at www.pearsoned.co.uk/essentialguides, to download and customise for use in your own class.

Rules for sharing with your class

Pupils must:

- turn up with the necessary equipment
- behave appropriately at all times without nudging each other or distracting others from working
- enter and leave the classroom in an orderly fashion
- sit down and get equipment and books out ready for learning to begin
- not speak while the teacher is talking
- not shout out
- not make sounds that are distracting whilst others are working, like whistling, tapping pens, etc.
- not answer back
- do what the teacher says – if a pupil is asked to move, then they should follow that instruction, as there will be a reason for it
- complete learning work to the best of their ability
- complete homework on time.

The teacher is in charge of the teaching and the organisation of the classroom – pupils need to be clear about this.

Clearly outline the sanctions that you will use if pupils do not comply. This may include a reference to school sanctions. Knowing the school behaviour policy, and reminding pupils that you know it, sends out a powerful message about how efficient and prepared you are. Finally, behave well as a teacher and as you would expect others to behave.

Body language, voice and eye contact

Now having prepared your lesson and thought about what rules and regulations are appropriate, it is important to think about what impression you are likely to have on a class. First impressions are important. Imagine if you went to a doctor's surgery and the doctor was dressed in a scruffy pair of jeans and dirty crumpled shirt, there were documents strewn everywhere and your notes could not be found. What impression are you gaining of their expertise and professionalism? Imagine if when they talk to you they mumble a lot, repeat themselves and do not maintain eye contact – what would you think? The way a teacher dresses, addresses the class and their body language tells pupils of all ages a lot about them.

Conducting a lesson is very much like giving a performance and needs initially to be practised. Try starting your lesson looking closely at yourself in a mirror. Look at your body language. Do you look confident? Imagine that you are looking at a class of 30 pupils spread out in a room. Keeping control is about having eyes everywhere and that is why getting used to scanning a room as you speak is vital to success. Immediately you are able to spot the pupil who is not listening to you and by looking at them intently for a few seconds, until you have their attention, you will be able to say to them without uttering a word, 'I have you in my sights, watch it.' Eye contact is a powerful tool. Practise holding that gaze and think about what else needs to happen when you make eye contact. Your facial expression is going to change slightly. You are going to be conveying your annoyance/disappointment/displeasure that someone is not listening to you. Practise that look while looking in a mirror. Earlier it was suggested that you clearly announce to the pupils your rules and regulations. Where teachers are good classroom managers these rules become a woven part of the fabric of a lesson and pupils are overtly reminded of them when the need arises.

You will also need to practise using your voice. Good classroom managers rarely shout – bad ones do it all the time, to no effect. Teachers must have a good, clear voice and the intonation of the voice needs to be varied. Many well-known politicians have used a voice coach to retrain them into how to change a monotonous voice that can be boring and non-effective into a powerful tool for persuasion. In the case of a teacher, the voice is used to impart information and to maintain control: it needs to be clear and loud, and teachers have to project their voices. (This need to project the voice and the strain it puts on vocal chords is the reason why new teachers suffer so much from sore throats and husky voices in the first year or so of teaching.) It is the change in tone, coupled with eye contact and, if necessary, an additional verbal direction that tells a child that they have overstepped the mark. Raising the voice is unnecessary when a teacher knows how to change the tone of their voice successfully.

> **TOP TIP!**
>
> *If you are currently in training, then it is helpful to work with other new teachers to practise starting lessons and using eye and voice control. Discuss with each other how successful you feel you have been.*

First steps in achieving class control

Make sure that you have what you need for your lessons:

- a lesson plan
- worksheets/resource material – plenty of these and copies of worksheets from previous lessons if this is not the first lesson with the class
- a register of names
- a contact if you need help or support in the lesson
- spare equipment for pupils who may not have a pen or pencil
- spare paper and exercise books
- a list of your own rules and regulations.

If you are a newly appointed teacher and have a classroom of your own remember that in addition to all the above you will want your classroom space to give out a powerful message about the type of teacher you are. Interesting posters, key words and teaching materials kept in an orderly fashion are all important in creating the right impression. Finally, areas on the wall that are ready to showcase pupils' work are essential. Pupils of all ages like to see their work displayed: it suggests to them that their work is valued and that you care.

The next chapter is about how to avoid certain situations developing in your classroom as well as how to cope with the ones that you can't avoid.

> **Why not try this?**
>
> Before you read the next chapter consider the following questions:
>
> - Have you read your school's behaviour policy?
> - Has the school got one or is it an informal system operated in an *ad hoc* fashion?
>
> →

- What have you learnt about the exclusion process in the school?

- Why is exclusion a step that should not be taken lightly?

- Are there any strategies referred to that you feel might work well in your classroom?

- What rules are going to be important in your classroom?

- Think back to when you were in school. Who were the teachers who made a good or bad impression on you? What did they do to influence you in this way? What lessons can you learn from their practice?

Going further

Audit Commission (1996) 'Misspent youth', available at www.audit-commission.gov.uk.

Behaviour management – teachers rule, OK!

What this chapter will explore:

- The cardinal rules of classroom management
- Why is the first lesson so important?
- What else matters in your classroom?
- How to cope with the 'hard' class
- Using a notebook to record misbehaviour
- Mentoring pupils who need help
- Tackling pupils who bully teachers
- Consolidating what you have learnt

This chapter will help you win the battle of the classroom, take control of your pupils and establish an ethos where learning can take place. No matter how fantastic your lesson plan and how well you have differentiated

the materials for your class – without discipline and good standards of behaviour it will all amount to nothing! As well as giving you clear guidelines about how to cope with your initial meetings with classes the chapter outlines some common misdemeanours that can occur. Look at the scenarios and how they have been dealt with. These are intended to provide you with clear strategies that have been tried and tested and have proven successful. Now begin by reading the cardinal rules.

The cardinal rules of classroom management

Try to be in the classroom before the pupils. Where possible, stand by the door and wait for the pupils to line up outside the classroom. The benefit of this is that it allows the teacher to control the entrance to the classroom and the way pupils enter the space. Do not block the entrance allowing just a small space for pupils to squeeze by, as some staff do: this is intimidating and pupils resent it. Instead greet the pupils confidently, then stand back telling them clearly to line up sensibly and then enter the classroom and sit quietly at the desk. In some schools pupils might not line up outside the room but come straight in. Whatever is the norm, teachers must control that entrance, as it is part of implicitly stating that the space belongs to them and the behaviour within it is subject to their control. Allow the pupils to come in but make sure that they enter in an orderly manner; any nonsense should be dealt with firmly.

Rule 1

The first rule of any classroom is not to allow any misdemeanour to go unnoticed or unchecked. If teachers let the small things go, the big things will occur all the more quickly and be twice as hard to eradicate. In a secondary teaching practice, student teachers will have a variety of classes to work with from different year groups, whereas in a primary school a teacher may work with a class for an extended period. Primary teachers may already be in the class with the normal classroom teacher and the transition from the usual teacher taking the class to the ITT student taking it may not be as evident as it is when pupils are moving from one class to another and the school day is timetabled rigorously. However, it might not be as necessary to establish such rigorous control in a primary classroom where pupils are in closer proximity to their normal class teacher and know this. In a secondary school, passing on information about misbehaviour to the normal class teacher is sometimes delayed because of the timetable and the movement within a school day around the school. This could mean that a class plays up a new teacher, feeling that punishment is further away, or indeed that they may get away with it.

Rule 2

Pupils are normally keen to see how new teachers perform and will want to settle so that they can weigh them up. At this point the teacher may want to introduce themselves formally by writing their name on the board. The second rule is never to enter into a dialogue about where you have taught or not taught before. If you do, you will need to lie – if they think you are new and inexperienced they are quite likely to treat you accordingly. In addition, the pupils will know that you can be distracted away from the classroom task and they will have displaced the lesson plan with one of their own. If the class does not seem ready to settle then that is your cue to ask them to face the front, stop talking and listen. If this does not work the first time, then you will have to use a sterner, louder and deeper voice tone. In most cases this will be enough.

The next step is to share with the class your individual classroom rules. By establishing your rules early you suggest to your class that you are an efficient classroom manager.

Rule 3

The third rule is one of the most important rules to establish – punctuality. Late pupils can seriously damage the start of any lesson and undermine the classroom discipline that teachers are trying to instil (see p172 for detailed advice on how to deal with latecomers). A very good deterrent to lateness is to punish pupils by keeping latecomers behind during lunchtime or a breaktime. If a pupil was 5 minutes late then the teacher can 'fine' them 10 minutes. Do not do this the first time but warn them that this will happen if they are late again.

If lateness persists then increase the punishment and take the matter further.

TOP TIP!

Remember that any punishment that a teacher suggests will be given must be carried through. Pupils who are threatened but not punished will soon become more and more disruptive as they know you bark but don't bite!

Rule 4

The fourth rule has got to be that pupils do not talk when the teacher is talking. You must be able to teach without a background of noise provided by pupils.

What if pupils call out in your class?

What do you do when pupils persist in calling out in your lesson or even talking across the class to one another?

Action

Re-establish firm rules about pupils who call out or hold conversations across the room. Some pupils will do this and will blithely ignore the teacher. Explain that the first person who does this will be punished. If you know this is a continuous problem and you do not think you can deal with it alone then ask for help. This may be by arranging with your mentor to remove the first offender from the class. This acts as a huge deterrent. Do not send the pupil out of the room but send a trusted pupil with a note to your mentor. Arrange for them to pick up the pupil.

The reasons

The presence of the mentor lends you further credibility and gives out a powerful message that you are in charge and you have others to support you. If you don't know who called out or made noises explain that the whole class will be kept in if the offender is not identified. It seems unfair but it is the only way to impose your will on the class and eventually the children who are innocent will force the offender to own up.

The sanctions

In addition to the child being removed it is important that you impose your own sanction. As the child is removed explain that you will expect them to return to see you and state a time.

> **TOP TIP!**
>
> *For younger children a few, short, simple rules will normally suffice, but it is still important that they are stated and that you draw your line clearly.*

Rule 5

The fifth rule is that you must clearly assert that as the teacher you are in charge. This gives *you* the right to decide where pupils sit. You can explain how this might

work. Sometimes you may allow them to sit in friendship groups, you may group them according to tasks in specific groups or you will move pupils who are not on task to prevent them disrupting others. This rule is one of the most important as pupils very often react adversely to being told to move or sit with other pupils they are not used to. However, if you remind them enough that you are the teacher and that this is your right – due to your role – then they are more likely to comply. The classroom teacher must have the sole authority to determine who sits where in any classroom without question. The younger the class the less likely it is that you will have to be too strident in outlining your rules.

Rule 6

The sixth rule should be that pupils answering questions learn to put a hand up and not to shout out. Pupils who are allowed to shout out will soon use this as a weapon against the teacher and oral work becomes a nightmare. Again the message has got to be one of orderliness and structure.

Why is the first lesson so important?

During the first lesson it is important to show that, as the teacher, you are aware of the rules that normally apply in the school and its sanctions and rewards. Knowledge of this kind is power and it suggests to pupils that the new teacher is part of the organisation. This association with the establishment confers power on you that pupils will understand. In Chapter 11 you were asked to think about the rules that you would establish in your classroom; now is the time to include any of those in the list of cardinal rules suggested above. For example, another useful rule to apply is that pupils only move around the classroom when they have permission from the teacher to leave their seats. This avoids a lot of poor behaviour erupting simply because pupils are out of their seats to cause mischief.

In the first lesson it is also important to tell pupils what they can expect to learn over the week or weeks that you will be teaching them. It may be necessary to link your scheme to a summative assessment, such as an external examination that they may be working towards.

Schools operate different systems and some schools will insist on all teachers starting their lessons with a lesson starter (see Chapter 8). The advantage of this is that all pupils come into the lesson and work immediately. This can be particularly effective with a disruptive class or in a school where behaviour is an issue. It is a useful tool for young teachers to use with difficult classes. In some schools teachers use brain gym (see Chapter 8) to get pupils ready for undertaking the learning task for that lesson. Whatever the system operating in a school it is important to ensure that once the lesson starter is completed or the brain gym finished the learning intention is clearly shared and that pupils are ready to start on the main part of the lesson.

In the sections below, we discuss some important behaviour management scenarios that the new teacher may encounter.

What if pupils are late?

What do you do if pupils arrive late to your lessons?

Action

Do not stop the lesson except to say, 'You are late and I will need to find out why at the end of the lesson. Sit down please.'

The reasons

If you stop to find out where latecomers were then you will stop your other pupils learning. It also leaves the latecomers in a vulnerable position as they know that at the end they will have to account for where they were. Remember to tackle them or they will think they can do it again.

You are giving an overt message to all – lateness is unacceptable.

The sanctions

If it is the first time and there is a valid reason just remind them that lateness disrupts the lesson and it must not happen again. If it has happened before then you need to impose some sanctions in line with school policy or have some of your own ready:

- Write in a pupil planner for a parent to see.
- Give the pupil some extra work – this may be lines.
- Keep the pupil in for twice the amount of time they were late.
- If this continues report it to your line manager and seek help.

Note: In all cases the pupils need to see you act and impose sanctions; not rely on a line manager who has already established their position.

What if a pupil is passing a note?

What do you do if you spot a pupil passing a note to another pupil?

Action

Take the note away from the child but *do not* open it. Just say that you will not have people passing notes in your lesson. Tell the pupil that you will speak to them at the end of the lesson. The pupil will probably want to know if you will give the note back. The answer – 'I will think about it, depending on your behaviour for the rest of the lesson.'

The reasons

If you read the note it is likely that you will have to deal with the consequences so it is probably better to avoid this. If you tell the pupil that you will think about it then the pupil will avoid any further disruption as they know they will not get the note back, and if you read it they could be in worse trouble.

The sanctions

A verbal warning may be enough to ensure that this does not happen again. Sometimes it is useful to hold certain things over pupils by saying, 'If you are caught doing something like this again the punishment will be twice the normal, as you have been warned.' In this way you are almost forcing a pupil to behave for a while. In a difficult class this can be very useful.

What if your class has not done their homework?

What should you do if pupils have not done their homework by the deadline you have set?

Action

In all cases the class has to have some form of punishment for failing to do something that had to be done.

The reasons

This is a real test of your resolve. If the majority of a class have failed to do homework then you have to act appropriately. This scenario can seriously impact on your effectiveness in the long term.

The sanctions

A good sanction is to try to find a time when you can keep the whole class behind for a while. This might be at a breaktime or lunchtime depending on when a lesson occurs. If it is a primary class it is easier to find a time as they are normally in one place and can be kept in more easily. A secondary class may have a different subject before break or lunch. If the timetable does not give a convenient point when the whole class is together then it will have to be told to return at a specific time you have set. In order to ensure this is taken seriously by the class it is worth stating that their form teacher or pastoral coordinator will also be told about the detention and if they fail to attend then a more serious sanction will be given.

A letter could also be put into an exercise book with a space for a parental signature, or you can use the planner to inform parents of your detention.

What if a pupil you teach is on report?

What do you do when the pupil presents the report card to you at the beginning of the lesson?

Action

Sign it with the highest mark/grade/comment you can and say that you expect them to live up to that comment or you will change it.

The reasons

It suggests that high standards of behaviour are expected in your lessons as the norm. Pupils live up to the expectation if you have faith in them: if they don't the sanction is predetermined!

The sanctions

There will not normally be any because most children will want to live up to your high expectations of them. If, however, despite you writing a great comment they then disrupt the lesson, change the comment and let the person who has put them on report do the rest. Reports are usually monitored on a daily basis and the reporter and their parents will see any adverse comments and act accordingly.

What if you ask a child to move and they refuse?

What should happen if a pupil refuses to obey an instruction?

Action

Pupils have to realise that you are the lead professional in the classroom and will decide where people will sit. Remind the pupil that one of your rules is that you decide seating arrangements. Do not shout but say this very firmly and indicate with your eyes and facial expression that you are not happy. Remind the pupil that you have asked them to move and that you are not discussing it or negotiating but telling them to move. The next statement is: 'I am waiting – this is your final warning. You are now wasting my teaching time and the other pupils' learning time.' If the child refuses to move then you need to state that they are now in serious trouble and will be punished. If at this point the pupil *does* move, ask them to stay behind at the end of the lesson. At that time explain that though you were pleased they finally did act as you had expected them to, you do not expect that type of behaviour. Suggest that you are not going to punish them at this point but you are recording the incident and if there is a repeat of it, then serious actions such as contacting home and detentions will occur. However, if they do not move and your school operates an on-call system, now is the time to say: 'You are already in serious trouble with me and will have to complete a punishment – but this is your last chance. If you still fail to obey instructions then you will be punished by the on-call teacher.'

The reasons

Sometimes children have bad days, as we all do. A child may refuse to act straight away and occasionally it is possible to get them to review a hasty decision and move. When they do this you are in a win–win situation as you can now praise their good sense but also use their first poor reaction to you in the future, if necessary. You do not always have to punish there and then. It is useful to say that if they continue to behave and there is no repeat of this situation you will forget about it (e.g. after the next half-term). If they behave badly again then both misdemeanours will be recounted! In the case of the pupil who flatly refuses, they have to learn that there are rules and that they have to obey them. They will need to be encouraged to comply with a teacher's reasonable request to sit where instructed.

The sanctions

If your school has an on-call system now is the time to use it. If it does not, then you will need to get your line manager to work with you. The child should really be removed from the class and an example made of them. The parents should also be informed as refusing to follow an instruction like this is a serious breach of discipline. The child may also be expected to complete a detention for you personally and in some cases they may be kept out of mainstream classes all day or even sent home. When pupils behave this badly the individual class teacher should be able to rely on whole school support from middle and senior managers.

What else matters in your classroom?

Teachers who are firm but fair and have a sense of humour are those who are most likely to win the hearts and minds of pupils. Some books on behaviour suggest that you have to make a choice between being scary and firm, or firm but fun. The reality might be somewhere between the two where a good classroom manager is firm initially, so that they establish clear boundaries and do not suggest that they can be manipulated. They may even show a hint of the scary if a pupil misbehaves. Finally, with good structures in place a teacher can introduce a little more of their personality into the teaching to show a sense of humour and a more human aspect. This comes with a health warning. If a teacher comes across as too funny initially this can be confused with being easy-going and a pushover. A teacher's job is not to try to be top of the popularity stakes. Teachers whose classrooms are orderly, safe places, where the ethos is laden with teaching and learning, and where pupils are treated with respect and can succeed, will win those stakes hands down. Pupils like teachers who teach and to be where the pupils learn!

Other things to consider:

- Be fair and unprejudiced. Pupils know when a teacher is 'talking down' to them or feels that he/she is superior.
- Motivate pupils by showing that you want them to succeed inside and outside your classroom and care about them as individuals, but don't be too familiar.
- Don't make unfair comparisons between one class and another, or one pupil and their sibling or friend, or be influenced by others who do.
- Apply the same sanction for the same misdemeanour.
- Don't back a child into a corner so that a confrontation is inevitable.
- Don't lose your temper. Most good classroom managers shout at some point for effect – not because they are 'really' mad! Most good classroom managers would be worthy Oscar winners.

- Use your head to manage, not your heart, and remember that you are the adult and should behave accordingly. What pupils want from you is an expert who is in control of the class and sets boundaries.

- Show through your lesson planning and marking that you are working hard for the good of the pupils. They are more likely to play up a teacher who is making no effort.

- Convince pupils that increased good behaviour will be in their own interest.

Good clear transitions make a difference

Lessons can go wrong when teachers are moving the pupils on from one learning task to another. It is important to make it very clear that you are moving forward. It may be that pupils have written some answers and now you want them to mark the answers as a class, or for pupils to work in pairs to assess their work. With younger classes, or when you are still establishing yourself, it is useful to halt the lesson and ask all pupils to stop what they are doing and face the front ready for the next instruction. Once the instruction has been given it is important to ensure that all pupils know what they are expected to do and a question like 'Is everybody clear what we are doing next?' is posed. There is a joke that suggests that teachers stand out in a crowd because they are the only ones to repeat an instruction three times. Hopefully, twice should be enough!

TOP TIP!

Don't forget that setting timed tasks is important for keeping pupils focused and on task.

What if a child is caught using a mobile phone in the classroom or listening to an MP3 player?

What do you do when a pupil is texting or talking on a mobile, or using headphones?

Action

Some schools have rules that apply to this and you will have to follow them. Normally it is expected that the object is taken away from the pupil. This can cause problems:

- If a teacher confiscates an object and it is stolen from their possession – from a drawer that they put it in for instance – then that puts the teacher in an awkward position.
- Many pupils can become quite confrontational if they think that their property is being taken away.

The reasons

The pupil knows that you are alert and that you do not miss anything going on in the classroom. This in itself gives a powerful message about your control. If you state that you are going to do them a favour this time but in the future you will show no mercy then you are being human/fair, but you are also warning of the potential consequences while avoiding the confrontation that might have occurred. However, if the pupil ignores your warning then you need to come out the next time with all guns blazing!

The sanctions

If it is the first time, give the pupil a verbal warning. Suggest that if the object is seen in the classroom again or is being used then a school sanction will follow. The object will be taken and because they have been warned beforehand this sanction will be increased.

What if a fight breaks out in your classroom?

Sometimes, with the best discipline in the world, pupils will be overtaken by emotion and a fight will flare up.

Action

If there is a problem as the pupils enter the room and before anything starts then insist that pupils sit far away from each other and warn them about your classroom rules. Later in the lesson try to find out discretely from each of them what the problem is. Prevention is better than cure. If necessary, involve another member of staff to ensure that when they leave your room to go elsewhere they will not fight.

The reasons

Your aim must be to ensure the safety of your pupils. If it is too late for that you will need to get between the pupils and break up the fight. If this proves impossible then you will need to send for support from a nearby classroom. If the pupils are older then you will normally find that other pupils will be there to help.

The sanctions

For such a serious breach of conduct someone in authority within a primary or secondary school normally applies the sanction. This could be a deputy headteacher or a pastoral coordinator in a secondary school. In a secondary school, sanctions can include fixed-term exclusions. The term will be determined by the pastoral coordinator in consultation with a senior member of staff and will depend on the severity and reasons for the fight.

What if a child truants your lesson and you find out?

What do you do when you realise a pupil is missing?

Action

Do not let pupils get away with it. You should be omnipresent and omnipotent. Good classroom managers know everything there is to know about a pupil's behaviour.

If a school suspects that a child is truanting they must inform the parent or guardian straightaway. If it fails to do this and a pupil is then injured or worse, then as the school is *in loco parentis* it could end up in court.

The reasons

You are in charge of the pupils on your register at the time you are supposed to teach them and it is important that you check who is in school and who is absent. Schools sometimes operate a system where pupils are registered in every lesson and internal truancy can be picked up. Pupils who are in school often like to let a teacher know about other pupils who are not.

The sanctions

Most schools operate a standard punishment for truancy with parents being informed, and often in a secondary school a detention or report system is implemented. It is important that you as the class teacher show that you feel they have let you down.

Dealing with persistent truanters

Dealing with pupils who persist in truanting can be very time consuming for staff and very stressful if you are concerned about their well-being. Three methods have been used effectively:

- Insisting that a parent/guardian accompanies their child to school and walks them from class to class to ensure they get there safely. Parents who are supportive will do this and those who are not may be persuaded when you remind them that it is their duty to ensure that their child attends school. Usually the warning that this will occur can be enough for some pupils.

- Warning a pupil that if they leave the premises and the school is not aware of where they are and feels they are at risk then the school will report the child as a missing person to the police. This is very effective.

- Using the educational welfare officer to support school sanctions and liaise with parents.

How to cope with the 'hard' class

In your career you will inevitably come across a class that is particularly difficult. This can be because the class has learnt how to work really well together to disrupt. In a class of this kind it is normally difficult to pick on one individual who can be disci-

plined seriously enough to make an example of them. This is usually because pupils have become adept at moving the disruption around the class so that no single person is wholly responsible. In a situation like this it is difficult to break the cycle. Normally, it is the golden rule *not* to punish a whole class for the misdemeanours of a few but in this situation it might be the only way to stop the nonsense.

As a new teacher it is important to ensure that you have discussed any problems of this kind with a line manager. Discuss the problem pupils and the sanctions that have been put in place already to try to ensure better behaviour. It is important that there has been a strategy to encourage the class to comply and that any pupils have been punished where possible. In a school with a three-strike type system this might mean that pupils have already had some form of low-level sanction. The trouble with a class like this is that because the pupils move the disruption around the room constantly, what you are left with is a persistent low-level disruption that becomes a disaster zone for the teacher.

In a situation like this the teacher has to confront the class and discuss what has been decided to bring them back into line and ensure that learning takes place. This should be done with a line manager present for support and to give your plan more organisational backing. Before meeting the class, think about how the meeting might be handled. There are two options:

- A closed meeting – where you as the teacher are going to be autocratic and 'close down' the meeting so that you talk and they listen.
- An open meeting – where the class is allowed to put forward views of their own. However, this needs very tight handling so that they do not dictate the terms.

If the class is lacking maturity and is really difficult then the closed option is preferable.

Follow these steps:

1. Explain to the class that their behaviour is unsatisfactory and that it is disrupting their learning.
2. Explain that it can't go on and that the whole class is on probation.
3. Pick out the pupils who usually disrupt and explain that if their misbehaviour continues their parents will be contacted.
4. Explain to the class that you are now going to treat them as a team. The team has to work together to ensure that learning takes place, and that it hasn't happened. Learning is going to take place from now on – or the team will be punished.
5. If necessary, and as an example, arrange to have one of the key troublemakers removed from your class. They will be allowed back only when they can guarantee their improved behaviour. Explain this to the pupil concerned in private; but the class will soon know who is moving and it will act as a warning to others.

I OWN MY OWN BEHAVIOUR

NAME OF PUPIL

CLASS

TEACHER   SUBJECT

DATE

In this lesson I broke the following class rules

....

....

....

Pupils in my class could not learn for ...... minutes because I broke our class rules.

I did this because ....

....

....

....

In the next lesson I will do the following to make sure I do not do this again

....

....

....

....

If I do not behave in the next lesson then my teacher is going to

....

....

....

SIGNATURE OF PUPIL ....

A sample behaviour declaration sheet

6. Go over the class rules that you have established and re-establish them, ensuring that you all agree what will happen if they are not followed.

7. Think about reorganising where pupils sit to ensure that no pupil is next to someone who is likely to get them into trouble. This can be negotiated; but at the end of the day you are the teacher with the ultimate say.

8. If necessary, arrange for known difficult pupils to be put on report for that lesson. A report can be very simple and will allow you to put down a few comments about behaviour/attitude/amount of work completed/punctuality, etc. This can be done through a line manager or pastoral coordinator, or through your NQT or ITT mentor.

9. Ensure that the class realises that if the behaviour does not improve then you will have no option but to punish the whole class. This may seem unfair but what happens is that the behaving pupils then become your allies in that they do not want to be punished. They will call it unfair and complain and your answer will be, 'I sympathise and understand but I have warned you what the consequences will be.'

Give the pupils who are the main troublemakers the 'I own my own behaviour' sheet shown opposite to fill in (a printable version of this sheet is available at www.pearsoned.co.uk/essentialguides). This makes them focus on what they have done wrong and how they have broken the rules. If they do not fill it in correctly then photocopy their response and send that to their parents with a covering letter. This action often prompts a focused response from pupils.

The form can be adapted to suit any age group and on the bottom you could include other sanctions/punishments that the pupil might get if they continue misbehaving.

Some schools already have behaviour referral forms and teachers may be expected to use them. However, it does not prevent you using the upper part of the form as a way of getting the pupil to face up to what they have done.

Using a notebook to record misbehaviour

Bill Rogers, in his book *Cracking the Hard Class* (1997), suggests that teachers keep a notebook in which they list those who have misbehaved in a lesson. Then ask them to stay behind at the end of the lesson to discuss their behaviour. Following up interventions is the most important thing any teacher can do. If you work in a school that has a cover team in place then this strategy can work well for them. If they all keep a notebook they can periodically compare names and identify pupils who are causing trouble on a regular basis. A strategy can then be put in place to deal with these pupils; this might be designed with the help of a mentor, line manager, pastoral coordinator or senior member of staff (e.g. a deputy headteacher), depending on your school's structure.

When you keep pupils back it is important to think about how you will handle the situation. Pupils of any age can be surly and aggressive when they are kept behind. If you go in all guns blazing you will end up with a classic stand off which neither you nor the pupil will win. Relationships will take time to mend and further sanctions will be needed, depending on how the pupil has behaved.

You should also remember, when keeping pupils behind, to leave the door open and ensure that you follow protocols for seeing pupils alone.

Start off by explaining that you know that their breaks are precious but that you enjoy a break as well. Explain that if you did not care about the class and their progress you would not be prepared to give up your time so readily. Finally, explain what you will expect from the pupil in the next lesson and get them to agree to this. If you are using a notebook or making notes in a teacher's planner, which some schools provide as a standard document, then make sure you record this agreement. Keeping a record means that you can refer to it when writing a report on a child. It also means that you have your own record of class behaviour that you can refer to. Sometimes when you refer to a list of pupils who have misbehaved it is surprising to see who has got the most recorded misdemeanours.

What if you tell a pupil to stay behind and they refuse to follow the instruction?

How do you respond when a pupil defies you?

Action

Do not follow the pupil down the corridor but make a note that you need to see that pupil.

The reasons

If you do follow them, tempting as it is, it is likely they will not accompany you back and you will be in a situation that you cannot win at that time. You cannot manhandle a pupil physically and other pupils will see you with a pupil who is refusing to do as you ask – not at all good for your reputation.

The sanctions

Find out where the pupil is going to be at a time when you will be able to visit them. Go to the class and ask the teacher if you can see the named pupil. Teachers are normally supportive of other staff and will rarely refuse. Take the pupil outside and state that you were disappointed that they did not stay behind,

as now they are in more trouble for failing to follow an instruction that you had given. If your school uses planners, record the information in the planner. Get the pupil to have this signed by a parent. Fill in a behavioural referral form (if they exist in your school) because the pupil's failure to behave initially and then to follow your instructions needs to be shared with a line manager either verbally or in writing. Explain to the pupil that a detention is owed and that you will expect it to be done. (If pupils fail repeatedly to abide by the rules, exclusions can be put in place that are sanctions for not one misdemeanour but an accumulation of smaller ones.)

In the next lesson after the follow up it is important that the class realise that you did see the pupil and that you have carried out your sanction. This is so that they are aware that you are committed to ensuring high standards of behaviour in your classroom.

Teaching pupils and managing classes is hard work. Establishing firm classroom rules takes time and a lot of effort. However, allowing the pupils to get away with things is in the end demoralising, stressful and eventually utterly exhausting. Trust in the fact that your efforts will pay off and classroom discipline for good classroom managers becomes easier as their reputation precedes them.

What if a pupil comes back from a senior member of staff to apologise to you for previous poor behaviour?

It is often hard for pupils to admit that they were wrong and for them to apologise can be a big thing.

Action

As a lead professional, however the teacher feels within, the right thing to do is to accept the apology and to suggest that in the future you trust there will be no repeat of the behaviour you have just witnessed.

The reasons

The idea of a pupil thinking that they can carry on behaving badly and that an apology can get them out of it is something that cannot be tolerated.

The sanctions

If the behaviour and the apology are events that are being repeated for the second or third time then hoping for improvement is clearly a waste of time.

This needs to be discussed further and a strategy put in place. The whole issue of their behaviour has to be confronted and the sanction taken to a higher level. Pupils need to see the stakes getting higher as their behaviour fails to meet the required standard.

Mentoring pupils who need help

Mentoring schemes are common in some schools where they are used proactively to help targeted pupils with their learning. They are used for pupils who:

- need behavioural support to help them concentrate, control anger and/or focus on learning tasks
- have an education behaviour plan and some or all of whom may have had some form of outside agency intervention from an educational psychologist. Pupils with a diagnosed disorder such as attention deficit hyperactivity disorder (ADHD) may also be on medication.

Mentors meet with mentees to discuss what has gone well and what might still need working on. They can arrange for pupils to be supported in areas where they may be likely to behave badly, also ensuring that when things do go wrong there are strategies in place to limit the potential for damage on individual and class learning.

Some schools use staff (teaching or non-teaching) to help pupils manage their own behaviour and therefore improve the level at which they engage with learning. This can work well.

Tackling pupils who bully teachers

Though it is rare, it is true that there are pupils who are quite capable of running a terror campaign against a teacher. When this happens there is normally an identifiable group who between them intimidate the teacher concerned. Bullying of staff should be treated with the same degree of rigour that a school treats pupil bullying. Incidents of bullying should be logged and the culprits have to be brought to justice. Pupils can be guilty of all sorts of misdemeanours. They may knock on a door or classroom window on a regular basis, they may snigger or laugh as the teacher walks by, they may name call and, in severe cases, physically intimidate the teacher. The teacher may actually teach the pupil or they may not. Whatever the circumstances the teacher and the bullies can be brought together and the teacher then has an opportunity to explain to the pupil(s) the harassment that is being caused. A record of the meeting should be kept and the

sanctions then clearly spelt out. Many schools refer to the bullying of teachers as psychological harassment and this is what it is. If the harassment persists then the teacher should expect that the matter is dealt with at a higher level with parents being called into the school and governors becoming involved. In some cases the teacher may be too upset to meet the pupils face to face and in such cases a senior member of staff will see the pupil(s). There should always be a time when progress can be assessed, and the situation should be monitored on a regular basis for an extended period of time to ensure that the pupils realise that there is a zero tolerance to this type of harassment in your school. Like pupils, teachers have a right to feel safe, secure and valued in a workplace.

Mentoring the teacher

Mentoring can also work for teachers who may feel that they need help in coping with a difficult class or pupil, for example if they feel pupils may be starting to bully them. Here the teacher may have additional classroom support. An experienced teacher may work alongside the teacher, coaching them as to how to get the best out of the class. This can be an effective way of learning the tricks of the trade before a situation becomes threatening. In other cases the class teacher could discuss scenarios that may occur – such as being bullied by pupils – and, working with an experienced colleague, examine how best to deal with this in the future.

Consolidating what you have learnt

Managing pupil behaviour is a skill that is acquired over time and most teachers build up a repertoire of responses that they have used successfully. However, no teacher would ever say it was an easy skill to learn and it is certainly a skill that has to be used for the whole of a teacher's career. Managing behaviour is a bit like ironing – the pile gets smaller and the minute you think you have finished you have to start all over again! The following information may help to consolidate what has been discussed in this chapter.

TOP TIPS!

In my classroom I could:

- *Plan lessons well, differentiating them to suit the needs of the pupils.*
- *Control the classroom entry and exit and any movement around the room.*

- Ensure that pupils are aware of the classroom rules and refer to them regularly so that they become part of the classroom ethos.

- Ensure that all sanctions threatened are carried out – otherwise pupils will not take classroom management seriously.

- Have a zero tolerance policy on disrespectful behaviour to anyone in the class – everyone deserves respect.

- Be assertive and confident in the classroom and look carefully at the scenarios and responses highlighted in this chapter.

- Seek help and advice if there are problems with a class.

- Strive not to lose my temper with pupils. (If the lead professional can't control their temper, how are pupils supposed to learn to control theirs?)

- Aim to gain credibility from other staff by being able to control the class and carry through sanctions.

TOP TIPS!

In my department or area of the school we could:

- Have a clear departmental policy for behaviour.

- Share explicit rules/rewards, sanctions with pupils.

- Support people within the department or teaching area when they are having difficulties by removing pupils where appropriate. Assisting through mentoring if necessary as the lead professional.

- Share good behavioural strategies and practice.

- Share innovative teaching techniques and good lessons – this can help reduce poor behaviour.

- Have a reference library of books that support good practice on behaviour management and teaching and learning.

- Develop staff through good staff development and inset. Encourage applications for grants, etc.

- Inculcate a no-blame culture so staff feel they can ask for help.

- Encourage staff to share responsibility for behaviour in their class and not pass it up without taking initial responsibility.

Sanctions for everyday misdemeanours should start with the classroom teacher.

- Support staff by team teaching, lending them status through association by visiting classrooms to ensure good discipline.

- Send letters home to pupils who regularly make an effort and/or achieve well.

TOP TIPS!

In my school we could:

- Have a strong discipline policy supported by rewards and sanctions.

- Ensure the SLG supports colleagues and is involved in taking high-profile detentions.

- Raise money for rewards.

- Provide a mentoring system for staff who have problems.

- Implement mentoring systems for pupils who have behaviour problems through a strong pastoral system.

- Put behavioural referral mechanisms in place both within school and outside through pastoral teams, senior staff and through the educational psychological service.

- Have zero tolerance of pupils who persistently prevent learning.

- Have clear hierarchical structures of sanctions that are consistently applied.

- Have individual behavioural plans in place for pupils who need them.

- Have contract systems/on-report systems/withdrawal systems/ internal exclusion systems in place and supported by senior staff.

TOP TIPS!

In my school I could:

- Promote an ethos of learning where all lessons are differentiated and where teachers use innovative teaching techniques.

- *Promote sharing of good practice in behaviour management.*

- *Promote mutual respect within the school for the opinions of pupils and staff.*

- *Have a school council that is funded, meets regularly and is chaired by pupils.*

- *Put in place clear communication structures to disseminate information about pupils who present a challenge.*

- *Promote a 'no blame' culture so that staff who find some pupils and classes challenging feel they can ask for help.*

- *Present staff with behavioural strategies to help them with classroom management.*

Why not try this?

- Think about when you were in school and about the advice you have come across in this chapter.

- Think about those teachers who influenced you and whom you rated as good teachers. What was it about them that made them good?

- Think about the strategies you have read about and choose the top five that these teachers might have used.

- What structures did the school have in place to ensure that pupils behaved and that teachers were supported when they were having difficulties? Were they obvious to pupils of the school?

- What aspects of your practice could you improve based on the information in this chapter?

Going further

Cowley, S. (2001) *Getting the Buggers to Behave*, London: Continuum.

Rogers, B. (1997) *Cracking the Hard Class*, London: Paul Chapman Publishing.

Dix, P. (2010) *The Essential Guide to Taking Care of Behaviour*, 2nd edition, Harlow: Pearson Education.

13

Promoting inclusion in our schools

What this chapter will explore:

- What are the main policies?
- What is an enrichment programme?
- What is a school council?
- What is a charity committee?
- What are buddies?
- What are peer mentors, student counsellors and mediators?
- The Children's Commissioners for England and Wales

This chapter looks at the concept of inclusion and how schools endeavour to comply with the law to ensure that all pupils within the school, regardless of gender, ethnicity or ability, are given the opportunities and environmental conditions conducive to their achieving their educational

potential. We look at special educational needs policies for those less able pupils as well as those identified as being gifted and talented, and how schools have established student councils and charity committees to ensure that all pupils have a voice and to promote citizenship. An extension of this is seen in the way schools now train buddies and peer mentors to act as a support to those pupils who may need additional help. Finally, this chapter looks at a problem that at one time or another all schools will confront, that of bullying.

What are the main policies?

Pupils are all different and therefore the support one child may need to succeed will differ markedly from another.

Equal opportunities policy

All schools by law must have an equal opportunities policy (EOP). This is normally based on a policy that the local education authority will have issued as a standard to schools. Schools will then adapt that policy to reflect their own school ethos and the type of children it has to educate. An EOP should be seen as a working document. It should highlight how the school treats its pupils fairly, giving parity to all. These days it ensures that girls and boys have equal access to all areas of the curriculum and all subjects.

An EOP ensures that all minorities in the school are catered for and outlines how the school will do this. For example, it may refer to children who are in foster homes and are referred to in documentation as 'looked-after children'. Similarly, it may suggest the intervention strategies that are used to aid these pupils. These pupils often need a lot of extra support and help to compensate for the problems they have had to endure in growing up.

All schools should have clear strategies for support. An EOP should also highlight how the school promotes inclusion of all races, religions and creeds within its moral, spiritual and cultural curriculum.

Special educational needs policy

Another policy that should be in place if we want to be fully inclusive is a special educational needs (SEN) policy. This policy outlines how all children who are

less able and those who are more able will be supported. Most schools now realise that pupils who are very clever also need specialist support and a special programme of study if they are to succeed. These children are often referred to as 'gifted and talented'. Many schools put in place 'enrichment programmes' to cater for their special educational needs. An SEN policy will also outline how a school will support children with specific learning difficulties like Asperger's syndrome, autism, dyslexia and dyspraxia.

Anti-bullying policy

If schools are to be fully inclusive then all pupils must feel safe and protected and this means that schools cannot tolerate bullying of any kind.

By law, all schools must have an anti-bullying policy. All schools will at some time have instances of bullying and it is vital that these are dealt with efficiently and effectively and that schools have clear strategies for dealing with this issue. When a child alleges that they are being bullied the school must ensure that this is logged and all strategies used to overcome the bullying are also recorded. It is also vital that a school investigates allegations rigorously and deals with them. Legally, if a child thinks or perceives that they are being bullied the school has an obligation to treat that child as a victim and to deal with the situation accordingly.

TOP TIPS!

To ensure that bullying is dealt with effectively:

- *Record all instances and allegations and investigate them rigorously.*

- *Ensure that pupils understand that bullies and bullying will not be tolerated. Assemblies can be used to overtly show pupils the school's attitude to bullying.*

- *Ensure that when bullying is alleged and it is proven that the bully is punished.*

- *Make sure that the bully realises that if they then involve other pupils and get them to intimidate the victim too they will be punished further, as will the new bullies.*

- *Ensure that parents of bullies and victims are kept fully informed of all investigations and sanctions taken.*

→

> - *If the bullying is persistent then more action will need to be taken.*
> - *The victim can keep a small book to record all instances of bullying and all witnesses should be named in the book.*
> - *Mediators or outside agencies may need to be called in to help deal with serious bullying, to help the bully and the victim and to put an end to the bullying once and for all. The local education authority may have experts in behaviour support or PSHE teams and these will be able to help. The police can also be involved, particularly if the bullying occurs outside school. In some instances, school mediators and pupil counsellors can get involved and this may help.*

What if a pupil or pupils is obviously disrespecting or bullying another pupil in your class?

Action

Do not ignore this at any time. You are the lead adult and professional and you must bring an end to this behaviour. Explain that in your classroom everyone is entitled to respect. You will not tolerate name calling of any kind. Tell the offenders that you expect them to stay behind at the end of the lesson.

The reasons

It is important that the offenders realise that what they have done is bullying. All schools have an anti-bullying policy and sanctions for bullying should be explicitly stated in it.

The sanctions

You must follow the school sanctions. In addition, you may wish to bring the offender and the victim face-to-face. The aim of this is to get the offender to face up to what they have done and be told how this made the victim feel. This is more effective if you can get the victim to explain to the bully how they feel. If you feel that this is beyond you then ask for the help of a more experienced member of staff.

Racial incidents and those of bullying should be logged. Every school has a designated person in charge of dealing with racial incidents and pastoral coordinators or senior staff who will deal with bullying.

Staff inclusion

In a fully inclusive school staff deployment will also reflect this ethos. All teachers in a school, department or team will have an opportunity to teach all abilities irrespective of age but dependent on expertise, experience and qualifications. Where setting or banding is used staff would expect to have a fair range of classes and groups and not just be given lower sets that will not give them a range of experiences. In real terms, inclusion is all about giving pupils *and* staff opportunities to develop within a caring environment that values every individual within that organisation.

How can you tell that a school is fully inclusive and promotes equal opportunities (EO)?

- Boys and girls will have equal access to all courses and subject areas in a secondary school. Boys will be encouraged to take English at A level, as well as food technology, health and social care; girls will be encouraged to take physics, construction and resistant materials classes.
- Schools will monitor the progress of boys and girls and where there is an attainment gap will put in intervention strategies to improve performance.
- All pupils will have access to the resources of the school.
- Pupils of all abilities will take part in school musicals, sport and school trips.
- Pupils of all abilities will have equal access to exam opportunities.
- Able secondary students could take GCSE examinations early.
- Able students start AS courses pre-16.
- Looked-after children achieve at a higher level than the national average.
- Children from ethnic minority groups achieve at a higher level than the national average.
- Pupils who are very able are 'enriched'.

What is an enrichment programme?

Many schools have realised that in the same way that they cater for the less able they must recognise and cater for the most able. Some schools have taken to implementing an enrichment programme. Schools identify pupils who are very able in particular subjects. They then try to develop this ability by providing extra opportunities within that subject area. These opportunities are often negotiated and might vary from subject to subject.

Reflecting on practice

How an enrichment programme works in one school

In one school, teachers identify very able students in their subject. Each subject is given a calendared week for enrichment activities to ensure that work is spread across subjects and throughout the year. The enrichment programme runs through Years 7, 8 and 9. Pupils who are very able across all the subjects are allowed to choose their favourite three subjects to be 'enriched' in, but it is rare for a child to need to be targeted in every subject.

Other initiatives used with pupils

- A history department gave a group of Year 7 pupils a range of well-known stories from history to read. They then looked at the *Horrible Histories* and chose to write their own horrible history based on one of these stories. These were then published and sold. A copy was sent to Terry Deary, the author of the original *Horrible Histories*.
- A music department took Year 7, 8 and 9 pupils off timetable to work on a composition of their making and to perform it.
- An RS department got Year 7 pupils to produce a PowerPoint presentation for other pupils explaining the different religions that they had studied in Year 7.

What is a school council?

Many staff and headteachers have realised that schools and pupils have changed over the years. Pupils are now more mature, informed about their rights and have, through their subjects and personal, social and health education (PSHE) lessons, been encouraged to voice their opinions about issues of concern to them.

School councils have 'empowered' pupils, enabling them to have a say in the running of their school. Where a school has a flourishing school council it meets regularly, has democratically elected members, a budget and will in many cases act as a forum for consultation and discussion. Primary and secondary schools alike have set up these councils. Each year group will have a year council and representatives from the year group will sit on the school council. A school council is a really powerful way of promoting inclusion in a school. Pupils regularly discuss issues to do with behaviour, litter, the canteen food, teaching and learning. In many schools the school council plays a part in interviewing short-listed candidates for posts including those of heads and deputies.

School council members might be asked to represent the school at internal and external events. Pupils involved in these events gain valuable social and inter-personal skills.

Although school councils are now well established it has been suggested that they should be made statutory in all schools. They work best when they are well supported by the school SLG and have some autonomy of their own. This might not happen if they are foisted on schools.

However, school councils face problems:

- Finding a focus for meetings and identifying projects that the school council can be involved in.
- Ensuring that in council meetings discussions are fed back to year groups.
- Ensuring that the school council is more than a talking shop and that it maintains a high profile.
- Ensuring that the school council members and their work is known to all.

In order to counteract some of these problems the following initiatives have been tried:

- Having a school council noticeboard that has photos of the representatives on it and highlights projects they are involved in.
- Putting a copy of the agenda up in all classrooms with the minutes of the meeting to follow.
- Having assemblies given by school council members who update pupils on the work.
- Organising and running one 'Big Project' every year that is determined by the school council. This could involve making over one area of the school, organising a merit trip, etc. These are given a high profile within the school and progress is regularly reported on.

(See www.pearsoned.co.uk/essentialguides for a case study on Langdon School, London.)

School councils are helping to make a difference to schools by empowering pupils but they cannot work in isolation.

> 'What has become clear is that for a school council or other system of pupil representation to work, it must be embedded in a total school ethos of democracy, equity and concern for pupil and teacher welfare and performance.'

(Davies, 1998, p 27)

As part of a whole school approach to inclusion it has been shown that instances of poor behaviour and exclusions have been reduced where school councils exist.

What is a charity committee?

Many schools also have a charity committee whose purpose is to raise funds for good causes. These committees have always been successful as they have a designated purpose and function and their outcomes can be clearly measured. Encouraging pupils to think of others is an important way to promote citizenship in a school and helps pupils to feel good about themselves and the work they are doing. In some schools, each year group identifies a charity that they will raise money and awareness for – this is a good way of encouraging competition between year groups and consolidating a year group identity at the same time.

Pupils in some schools have:

- sponsored the education of a child in a developing country
- raised money for local children's wards
- raised money for local disabled groups
- raised money for Children in Need and Comic Relief
- sponsored a Guide Dog for the Blind
- sponsored animals in danger through national organisations
- raised money for disaster funds
- raised money for Macmillan coffee mornings
- organised visits and fundraising events for children affected by disasters such as Chernobyl and the Tsunami.

In addition, many charity committees have provided meals on wheels to local old age pensioners, delivering them a hot meal and sandwiches two or three times a week. Students have also helped maintain gardens for those who can no longer manage the work themselves. These initiatives enable a link to be made with the community and encourage the young and old to mix in a way that is mutually beneficial.

In some schools there is an annual commitment to provide parties for the local MIND group or local old age groups at Christmas. Pupils involved in ventures like this are regularly given responsibility for the organisation and fund raising that is expected. This obviously allows pupils to develop good people skills and problem solve in ways that will be of long-term benefit.

Involving pupils in charity work encourages them to be good citizens and not be self-centred and selfish. It also encourages pupils to feel good about themselves and their school and can be used to market the school positively. Charity work allows pupils to practise inclusion in a practical way outside school.

What are buddies?

It has long been recognised that moving to secondary school can be difficult for some pupils. Schools have trained pupils to be 'buddies' for children entering their school. In some schools two schemes could operate: young pupils act as buddies but older buddies will get more training and will in the latter years in school become mediators, mentors or counsellors.

Buddies are trained to support and help new pupils to integrate into the life of the school. Trainers may be teachers with a high degree of PSHE experience or advisors from the LEA. Pupils are also trained to identify problems which they are not able to help with and report those to a member of staff for further intervention. The role is a responsible one and pupils who are trained are made very aware of this.

Buddy schemes have proved to be highly successful and have helped pupils who might have found starting or moving school so traumatic that they would have become school refusers. Buddies continue to act as a support mechanism for pupils and offer help on organising work, doing homework and preparing for examinations. They may act as an early warning system for pupils at risk of being bullied.

A personal account of being a buddy can be found on the book's website, at www.pearsoned.co.uk/essentialguides.

What are peer mentors, student counsellors and mediators?

Peer mentors act as a support to fellow pupils. They are similar to buddies and are paired with a pupil for a specific reason. In one case mentors have been used to support students moving from secondary education to tertiary education. Pupils identified as needing support were in danger of dropping out of education completely or had specific learning needs that needed supporting. The ethos of a college is very different from that of a school and many past pupils had found this transition difficult. This was for a range of reasons including disability and weak English skills (when a pupil had moved here from overseas). Some pupils mentored had had home tuition in the past and other students had been involved in crime. It is possible to see that pupils being mentored could have a range of problems that needed to be addressed and that support was crucial if they were to succeed. However, using other pupils of similar age was seen to be far preferable to using adult staff and was more likely to be successful.

Mentors have worked well in all school sectors, not just in a transition situation. Mentors support students by acting as role models and support advocates, helping their mentee in a number of ways, for example giving pupils help with their reading and writing, study and IT skills. In nearly all cases there has been a marked positive change in the behaviour and motivation of pupils. Mentors have also benefited as the course that they have undertaken as a preparation for being mentors has in some places been accredited. (An introduction to counselling course has been accredited through OCN at level 2. An introduction to mentoring skills is accredited at OCN levels 1 and 2.)

Pupils can also act as mediators/counsellors and help solve problems that can occur between pupils in any school. In all cases, pupils will undergo training and there will be a member or members of staff, depending on the size of the mentoring/counselling/buddy programme operating within the school, who will meet regularly with the buddies, etc. to oversee their work and check that they are working within set parameters.

Mentoring programmes can also involve teachers within a school who will work with pupils on a one-to-one basis to support their learning. Many pupils who are on the C/D borderline will be targeted in a school for support.

A case study on mentoring at Gorseinon College can be found on the book's website, at www.pearsoned.co.uk/essentialguides.

The Children's Commissioners for England and Wales

Both England and Wales now have a Children's Commissioner. The aim is that the commissioner speaks up for children's and young people's rights. The commissioner's remit depends on the country but it has children and young people at the heart of the job. Young people as well as adults interviewed the Welsh and English commissioners, playing a part in their appointments. The role of commissioner has at its core a set of values, which is to ensure that children:

- are safe from harm and abuse and get the opportunities and services they need and deserve
- are respected and valued
- have a voice in their communities
- know about rights and the UN Convention on the Rights of the Child.

The commission also undertakes to look into things that affected adults when they were young. Through the work of the commissioner and the teams they employ, young people are being more fully included in the decision making that goes on in England and Wales. The aim is to promote inclusion, not just in schools but also within society, so that decisions that affect young people are taken in an informed way and are influenced by those who will be most affected.

Why do we have a Children's Commissioner in Wales?

Children's organisations in Wales campaigned for a commissioner for children for over ten years. Politicians in the National Assembly for Wales were also keen on the idea. They wanted someone who would speak up for children's and young people's rights and help to protect them.

In early 2000, Sir Ronald Waterhouse published his report 'Lost in Care' after a long inquiry into child abuse in children's homes in North Wales. He recommended that Wales should have a Children's Commissioner to try to stop such things happening again. This speeded up the campaign and legislation was passed by the UK government in Westminster to create the post and give it the powers that it required.

The fully inclusive school

To be fully inclusive a good school must have a sound and consistently applied equal opportunities policy in place. This will ensure that boys and girls are treated equally, and that all pupils irrespective or race, background or religion are treated

with respect and supported where it is appropriate to do so. This might manifest itself in the case of a school where there is a high percentage of traveller children. When a school is inspected the inspectors will check that all minority groups within a school are being treated equally and that appropriate support is being given. For example, some schools have groups of traveller children who may attend for short periods of time. The school has to demonstrate the care and support the school gives to the children and how it enables the children to 'catch up' on work they may have missed. They might also look at how the school supports those pupils who have a protracted absence due to illness.

It is important that schools support all groups in a school equally. For example, if a school was seen to have a large discrepancy between the attainment of boys and girls, the inspectors would want to see that the school as part of its equal opportunities responsibility was doing something to reduce the gender gap. Where a school has not reduced a gender gap or has failed to even identify the issue, then they are not being inclusive and are actually failing in their duty of care to a significant group. Inspectors will want to look at the many different groups that a school may be catering for and schools are now also expected to be self-reviewing. This means that they montior how they are doing and if they have a rigorous self-evaluation strategy in place, then issues such as these will be identified and targeted for improvements to take place. The local authority also has a responsibility to promote inclusion and will be analysing statistics for all its schools to try to identify issues that need to be addressed. For example, they may monitor the performance of 'looked-after children' against national norms or the performance of boys versus girls and so on.

An inclusive school will have a strong special educational needs policy that will refer to the more and the less able. Inclusive schools promote citizenship and normally have school councils where pupils are allowed to have a say in the running of the school. In many cases school councils and pupils are now involved in the appointment of staff to the school. Finally, inclusive schools take issues like bullying seriously and realise that if a child perceives that they are being bullied then it is incumbent on the school to investigate and support the child fully. Where a school is fully inclusive then pupils will feel respected and cared for and the ethos tends to be positive and will strongly support learning.

Why not try this?

Is your school or one you are familiar with fully inclusive? Look at the questions below and then make a judgement.

- Does your school have an EOP and an SEN policy?
- How many strategies to promote inclusion have been used in schools that you are familiar with?

→

- How does your school ensure that gifted children are enriched?
- How does the school support the less able?
- How does the school support pupils who are lacking in confidence?
- How does the school promote racial and cultural equality?
- How does your school prevent bullying or deal with cases as they occur?
- Does your school have a school council?
- How effective do you think inclusion strategies have been?
- How do you know?

Going further

Davies, L. (1998) *School Councils and Pupil Exclusions*, Birmingham: School of Education, University of Birmingham.

www.nagty.ac.uk

Part
4

Assessment for learning

Assessment for learning – marking for success

What this chapter will explore:

- Why we mark and assess pupils
- What is an assessment policy?
- Formative and summative assessment
- Assessment for learning: the research evidence
- Sharing the learning intention and developing self-assessment
- Questioning and formative assessment
- How might a teacher manage the mark load?
- What gets in the way of using formative assessment in the classroom?
- Putting it into practice

Preparing a good lesson and delivering it well is important and goes part of the way to ensuring that effective learning has taken place. However, it is not the whole of the story. This chapter is about how you know that learning has occurred through your assessment practices. Recent research has highlighted the need for good diagnostic marking and feedback to pupils. This enables them to progress to the next stage of learning. Marking closely and understanding what has been learnt and what hasn't helps to inform future lesson planning. Read this chapter carefully as it signposts everything that a good teacher needs to ensure that lesson intentions are shared, meaningful targets are set for improvement and effective learning occurs.

Why we mark and assess pupils

Delivering a good lesson is only 50% of teaching. To be most effective good teachers assess pupils' work on a regular basis. Assessment for most teachers involves the reading of work that is in a written format, for a minority it involves the assessment of practical outcomes such as in a drama/physical education/ technology-based context. All subject areas when studied at a higher level will include a significant written element to the course.

Marking, when completed regularly, allows a teacher to form a picture of individual pupils in a class, assessing strengths and weaknesses of the individuals as well as the class as a whole. It is important to remember that whether you teach in the primary or secondary sector, classes that may on paper appear to be similar in ability year on year, can in fact vary markedly in behaviour and attitude and this can significantly influence how you teach them and their responses to the teaching. Marking outcomes should be recorded and stored carefully as these will be used to report to parents at parents' evenings, and in interim and end-of-year reports (see Chapter 9 for more advice on how to keep detailed records on pupils).

What should marking a piece of work tell you?

- That the work is complete and the pupil up to date. If not, why not? Is it due to absence, poor organisation or disaffection?
- Whether a pupil is underachieving as determined by available data.
- Quality of the work.
- Strengths of a written piece.
- Weaknesses of a written piece.

- What a pupil needs to do to improve.
- The level or grade at which a pupil is working.
- Whether the teaching was effective and significant learning took place.
- What a teacher needs to do to improve the delivery of that lesson.
- What a pupil needs to do to improve their learning outcomes.
- What the next lesson will need to contain to ensure a successful continuation of learning.
- The literacy, numeracy and IT skills a pupil has in written work – key skills are now important in all subjects.

Marking pupils' work on a regular basis is the only way to get to know them and their capability. Teachers who base their opinions on classroom contribution will fail to recognise able children who are not confident enough to contribute in front of a whole class. Similarly, they are likely to overestimate the ability of some pupils who, though confident orally and who are knowledgeable, may not have completed class written work or homework, and may possibly have less well-developed written skills. Marking work regularly gives a teacher the full picture and ensures that the able are enriched, the less able supported, under-achievement is eradicated and lesson planning takes into account the needs of all learners.

It is a firm belief amongst good teachers, as well as inspection teams, that it is the job of the classroom teacher in the first instance to tackle underachievement in any classroom. In every classroom there may be an underachieving pupil who despite a teacher's best efforts will need intervention from a person other than the class teacher. They may need to be referred to a line manager within a secondary school department or to a deputy headteacher.

Assessing pupil outcomes is also vitally important as it informs good lesson preparation. When a teacher does not mark/assess they are not aware of how successful or unsuccessful their teaching is. They may repeatedly teach a lesson that leaves the pupils ill-informed about a topic. For this reason alone marking/assessment provides essential feedback to all teachers (see the figure overleaf).

With the emergence of new teaching and learning techniques it is now possible to assess pupils' learning in a classroom through good questioning techniques or through the use of mini whiteboards. Not to be confused with interactive whiteboards these are small, wipe-clean boards similar to the old chalkboards that young children were once given to play with at home. These boards allow all pupils to answer questions and to get involved in the lesson. The teacher asks a question and each pupil writes the answer on their own board, holding it up when asked to do so. The boards can be wiped clean so they can be used over and over again. In this way, assessing the effectiveness of what has been taught occurs quickly. However, although this is a useful assessment tool it cannot be used all the time, assessing as it does recall and content-heavy learning. It has

more limited use in assessing understanding where longer, more complicated answers cannot be easily shown in this way.

Having said that it is important to mark regularly, it is also important to be realistic. Teachers will never have the time to mark rigorously everything pupils do so compromises will have to be made. (The Top Tips! section on p 222 contains ideas about how to manage your mark load.

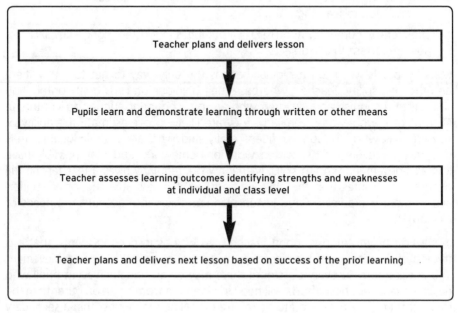

The assessment cycle

What do we mark?

Marking allows the teacher to determine how successful their teaching has been and how much learning has taken place. Marking can involve looking at or listening to:

- classwork
- homework
- written work
- project work
- oral work
- practical work

- tests
- examinations.

Some teachers and educationalists have suggested that the word 'work' should be replaced by the word 'learning'. Referring to classwork in this way emphasises the purpose of the task not the process of doing. It relates the classroom activity to the process of learning more clearly.

Assessment should always involve the teacher in making a judgement about what learning has occurred. The feedback can be oral or written but it should help a pupil to progress.

What is an assessment policy?

Most schools have assessment policies. These cover all aspects of assessment including marking, setting of examinations and the way they are conducted, reporting procedures, tracking pupil progress and so on. An assessment policy will outline how a school will mark and record marks and will try to ensure that there is a consistent approach where possible. In a secondary school there may be standard proformas that will need to be filled in with any assessments made on a pupil. These may be used in parents' evenings and aid in reporting progress to parents. It is a statutory obligation of all schools to provide one full report on a pupil's progress in one academic year and it is common for interim progress to be reported on in a parents' evening. Most schools also provide parents with a half-

yearly report, though this may include grades/levels without full comments. It is also a statutory requirement that schools inform parents of pupil levels at the end of each Key Stage. This external pressure on teachers to present levels or grades for pupils can pose difficulties when trying to use assessment in a formative way.

The assessment policy may suggest how frequently written work will be assessed and whether a mark, grade or level is awarded. In a primary school, assessment may be consistent across year groups, subjects and throughout the school with every teacher marking all work out of 10 or 20, or awarding levels or grades. However, this consistency is not found as often in secondary schools with an assessment policy; individual heads of department determine how work is marked. This is because external assessment by examination boards may be reflected in their individual marking systems. For example, in English departments it is common to mark out of 20 because grading at GCSE is structured this way, and so many English departments mirror this. In science departments marking of practical work or projects may be out of 8 for similar reasons. Therefore the assessment policy in a secondary school will allow for greater flexibility and, although assessment is going on, the awarding of levels/marks/grades may differ from subject to subject.

Many schools insist on departments or class teachers having portfolios of evidence of the work undertaken throughout a Key Stage or year. These portfolios provide a benchmark against which new teachers can check that their assessment is accurate and that they are awarding the right level, mark or grade for a piece of work. These portfolios of evidence are also used to provide models of learning/ exemplars of standards for pupils to learn from.

However, in many schools there has been a move away from putting marks on a page to one of putting formative comments after a piece of work that are intended to highlight strengths and suggest how improvements can be made. Teachers are using assessment to identify clear targets for improvement. This does not mean that teachers are not recording progress in markbooks; they are just not sharing the mark with a pupil, only a diagnostic comment.

Therefore marking serves a number of purposes:

- It informs the teacher about the pupil's progress.
- It informs future teaching plans.
- It informs a pupil about the progress they are making.
- It can be shared with parents to indicate progress being made.
- It can be used as part of the school statistics to indicate how a cohort of pupils is doing and influence future planning (if assessment suggested that a year group was weaker or stronger than usual then the school may take action to support this group).
- It can inform an outside agency who may be involved with a group of pupils.

Formative and summative assessment

Formative assessment is a term used to describe assessment that is intended to bring about an improvement both in teaching (to meet the needs of the pupils) and in learning (as it gives pupils information about how to improve their work). A teacher who marks in this way will give pupils specific information about the strengths and weaknesses of the piece of work, identifying for them clear targets to enable them to move from one level of work to another. Formative assessment occurs throughout a course and is meant to bring about improvements in final outcomes. Summative assessment occurs at the end of topics or Key Stages and is a final assessment of the work of pupils.

Assessment for learning has become embedded in much good practice as the research work of Dylan Wiliam and others has become better known. It has already been suggested that good teachers mark pupils' work regularly and use the knowledge they gain from this feedback to inform their future lesson planning. Marking allows you to see what learning has occurred and to judge the quality of your teaching. Marking will tell you whether pupils have understood key elements of work and whether you need to review it, teach it differently, or whether you can move on. It will allow you to decide on the strengths and weaknesses of individuals in every class you teach. Through marking, the teacher is determining what will happen next and what learning needs to follow. Teachers need to build on what has been learnt and confidently progress to the next stage. However, if pupils fail to understand some work or fail to absorb the content suffi-ciently then moving on could be hazardous. Assessment must lead a teacher to be better informed and should result in improved future lesson planning. It must be regular, thorough and ongoing, and feedback to a pupil is vital.

Marking is *not* about putting red ticks on a page; it is about diagnosing what is good and what is less good about a piece of work and determining how improvements can be made. This applies to whatever age group you teach. Where a teacher identifies strengths and weaknesses in this way then formative assessment/marking is occurring.

See the book's website, at www.pearsoned.co.uk/essentialguides, for a case study on Heybridge High School.

Assessment for learning: the research evidence

Black and Wiliam (1998) conducted an extensive survey of the research literature surrounding assessment and posed three questions:

- Is there evidence that improving formative assessment raises standards?

- Is there evidence that there is room for improvement?
- Is there evidence about how to improve formative assessment?

The results of their survey are now widely known and the answer to all these questions is a resounding 'yes'.

In their review of 20 studies on classroom assessment of children with mild learning difficulties Black and Wiliam found that formative assessment, when used as an intervention strategy, produced significant and often substantial learning gains. The studies they looked at ranged from pupils aged 5 to university undergraduates and covered a number of subjects in different countries.

The gains were measured by comparing the average improvement in pupils' scores on tests (A) with the range of scores for typical groups of pupils on the same tests (B).

The ratio of A divided by B is known as the *effect size*. The formative assessment experiments produced typical effect sizes of between 0.4 and 0.7. Black and Wiliam (1998, p 4) give the following examples to illustrate some practical consequences of such large gains:

- An effect size of 0.4 would mean that the average pupil involved in an innovation would record the same achievement as a pupil in the top 35% of those not involved.
- A gain of effect size 0.4 would improve performances of pupils in GCSE by between one and two grades.
- A gain of effect size 0.7, if realised in the recent international comparative studies in mathematics (TIMSS-Beaton et al., 1996), would raise England from the middle of the 41 countries involved to being one of the top five.

Is there evidence that there is room for improvement in assessment procedures?

Due to the work of Black and Wiliam and that of others it is true to say that in many proactive learning institutions the value of formative assessment has been recognised and steps are being taken to improve the quality of assessment. However, Black and Wiliam identified three difficulties that are still prevalent today despite the spread in the use of formative assessment throughout the UK.

First, in relation to effective learning:

- Teachers encourage pupils to learn at a superficial level and the emphasis is on learning content and not necessarily developing greater understanding.
- Teachers use questioning techniques that are not discussed within the school and are not critically reviewed to ensure that they are getting the best out of

the pupils. (The use of good questioning techniques will be referred to later in this chapter.)

- Teachers were sometimes found to emphasise quantity and presentation of work over quality.

Second, in relation to having a negative impact on a pupil's learning:

- The giving of marks and grades or levels was emphasised *over* the giving of useful advice or identifying the strengths and weaknesses of a piece of work.

- Assessment became a means for comparing the performance of pupils against one another so that the emphasis was on competing with each other and not on the individual improvement of each pupil's performance. Assessment feedback, in effect, acts as a demotivator for those pupils who consistently achieve at a low level.

Third, in relation to the managerial uses made of assessment:

- Teachers are often able to predict pupils' results on external tests because these tests replicate the type of tests teachers use in school. However, often they know too little about their pupils' learning needs and how they can boost individual performance.

- The collection of marks to fill up markbooks and records is given a much higher priority than the analysis of pupils' work to determine learning needs, and too little use is made of assessment made by prior teachers.

Can we improve formative assessment?

The above and other research has suggested that merely adding comments to pupils' work and diagnosing strengths and weaknesses is not going to be enough to bring about the significant improvements that are possible. Real improvements will only come about when a range of strategies is used that change the culture of the classroom and the attitude of pupils to their own learning.

Research has also shown that a number of pupils are content to 'get by', and for formative assessment to work this classroom habit has to change. Pupils have to want to learn and the ethos of the classroom has to focus on what each pupil has to do as an individual to bring about their own success through learning targets. The ethos has to move away from a culture of competitiveness and comparison with others in the classroom to one where each pupil sees the relevance of the advice on what they can do to improve. It is therefore important to inculcate a culture of success where each pupil succeeds at a level that is right for them at this point in their learning, and equally a culture where pupils understand the need for them to work appropriately to bring this about.

'A number of pupils do not aspire to learn as much as possible, but are content to get by, to get through the period, the day or the year without any major disaster, having made time for activities other than school work … formative assessment invariably presupposes a shift in the equilibrium point towards more school work, a more serious attitude to learning.'

(Perrenoud, 1991)

Sadler (1989) pointed out that two things had to happen for formative assessment to be successful:

'Firstly, pupils had to realise that there was a gap between "the desired goal" and his or her present state (of knowledge and/or understanding and/or skill). The second is the action taken by the learner to close that gap to attain the desired goal.'

(Sadler, 1989, p14)

Sharing the learning intention and developing self-assessment

Once children have improved self-esteem and know they can achieve they then need to develop self-assessment strategies. Alongside this they also need to develop their ability to assess their peers. Self-assessment has been achieved with children from five years upwards and it has generally been found that pupils are able to assess each other honestly and reliably, and if anything are almost too brutal in their assessment. However, in order to do this well they need to be aware of the learning outcomes that are intended and need to have a clear picture of what they are doing and why. Therefore it is vital that teachers share with their pupils what the learning intention is. Shirley Clarke (2001) in her book *Unlocking Formative Assessment* states that the learning intention needs to be displayed visually for every lesson. She even suggests writing it down for children who are not able to read at that level at that time. She supports this by stating:

'Imagine you are learning a new language and the teacher is speaking that language throughout the lesson, so most of your understanding is derived from the spoken word. Imagine the teacher writes one of the words she says on a flip chart and points to it, again saying the word. The word stays on display for the whole lesson. What are you most likely to remember about the lesson, even if you could not actually "read" the word?'

(Clarke, 2001)

Here are some further examples of that strategy at a secondary level. Pupils are encouraged to come up with success criteria for their learning, although teachers, in some instances, might think it better to create these themselves when the context is too complex.

Lesson aim

To write an interesting and engaging first paragraph for a short story using ideas that we have gained from our prior research on what makes a good introduction.

Success criteria

The paragraph engages the other pupils on your group ... they want to read on.

It is well structured and uses powerful descriptive language.

It is punctuated accurately.

Lesson aim

To understand why adaptation occurs in nature.

Success criteria

You will understand what the term adaptation means within biology.

You will be able to explain why species change over time and the possible causes.

You will be able to use examples to support your understanding and put this into a PowerPoint presentation that you will prepare for a younger audience.

It is vital that pupils realise the link between what they are doing and why they are doing it. Learning becomes less a set of exercises that are unrelated, seeming to be just work for the sake of it, and more a series of lessons that will lead them to fully understanding something. Learning has moved from ritual to something planned and meaningful.

Encouraging self-assessment

Once pupils have understood the learning intention the next step is to ask them how they will know they have achieved it. For young children the teacher may need to guide them by writing down a list of success criteria on the board and asking the pupils to choose the ones that they will most need to achieve. In this way, the pupils

play some part in deciding what the success criteria are and become used to deciding these for themselves, albeit with the teacher prompting. For older children this may not be necessary as they may be able to deduce their own success criteria.

The next stage in the self-assessment model is to ensure that pupils are able to judge their own learning against the success criteria. This should lead them to be able to fill in a self-assessment sheet like the one shown below. What do you learn from this self-assessment sheet about the way assessment is being undertaken in this classroom?

SELF-ASSESSMENT SHEET ENGLISH Date 21st May

The learning intention was
We were learning how to write a great beginning for a story and to use better vocabulary.

What I think I did well
I liked the first sentence I used because I tried to use more unusual verbs like pounced instead of jumped. I think the opening paragraph made sense and the punctuation was good. My friends thought that it sounded exciting and wanted to find out whether the tiger did anything bad to the boy. Miss liked it and highlighted in blue some of my best words. She said it was my best yet.

What I think I can improve on
The description of the boy was not good because it is hard to describe in words what people are like. I think that I need to look at the books we used to help us when we were researching how real writers do this.

What I can improve on
I think that I need to make the description of people better.

My learning target
Research how to write about people some more.

A sample self-assessment sheet

From the self-assessment shown it is clear that:

- The pupil has understood the learning intentions.
- The pupil has understood prior learning about paragraphs.
- The teacher has clearly told the pupil what was good and has used oral feedback while assessing the pupil's work.
- The teacher has clearly shown the pupil what was good via the written assessment.
- The teacher, pupil and the class have agreed what the marking will mean, how the blue highlighter will be used and what it means.

- The pupil has also been involved in peer assessment where another pupil, Luke, has helped her to review her work and checked it for basic spelling and punctuation errors. The pupil has then decided that one of her other targets has to be to improve spell checking.

In the example above the pupil has determined the target for herself, but training is needed for classes who are unfamiliar with setting their own targets. In the same way as a primary/secondary teacher might help a class to determine the success criteria by giving them a number to work with, a teacher can do the same with targets. While assessing a piece of work a teacher unfamiliar with AFL can easily identify a number of evident strengths and weaknesses. Then the teacher can write a list of strengths on the board and a list of areas for improvement. A class can then be asked to look at the lists and pick out items that they think best suit them as an individual. In time the need to write the lists on the board decreases as the class becomes confident and 'trained' in self-assessment and target-setting techniques.

Questioning and formative assessment

Teachers can learn a lot about the learning outcomes of a lesson by using some very well thought out questions. However, all too often teachers ask questions that are very simple to answer and test superficial knowledge only. In addition, too little time is given for pupils to answer the question, sometimes with a waiting time of only 1–2 seconds. Research (Black et al., 1998) in formative assessment has suggested that this is not long enough. Questioning that could be a rich source of discussion and aid the consolidation of learning for the whole class does not occur. Questioning becomes dominated by closed-type questions that at worst demand a yes/no answer and at best ask for recall of facts.

Research (Black et al., 1998) has shown that it is very difficult for some teachers to change how they ask questions in a class and how long they wait for an answer. They have got into a habit, which takes time and resolve to break out of. It is important to leave enough time for pupils to think out an answer and even to allow time for pupils to consult with a partner:

> 'Increasing the wait time can lead to more pupils being involved in question and answer discussions, and to an increase in the length of replies. One particular way to increase participation is to ask pupils to brainstorm ideas, perhaps in pairs, for two to three minutes prior to the teacher asking for contributions. Overall a consequence of such changes has been that teachers learnt more about the pre-knowledge of their pupils, and about any gaps and misconceptions in that knowledge, so that their next moves could address the learners' real needs. To exploit such changes it is necessary to move away from the

routine of limited factual questions and to refocus attention on the quality and the different functions of classroom questions. An example is a use of the "big question": an open question, or a problem-solving task, which can set the scene for a lesson by evoking a broad-ranging discussion, or by prompting small group discussions, so involving many pupils. However, if this is to be productive both the responses that the task may evoke and the ways of following up these responses have to be anticipated. Collaboration between teachers to exchange ideas and experiences about questions is very valuable. The questions then become a significant part of the teaching, with attention focused on how they can be used to explore and then develop pupils' learning.'

(Black et al., 1998, p 6)

Consolidating learning is one of the most important class activities and is often given too little credence. For new teachers beginning a career, starting with good habits and sound practice seems sensible.

This chapter so far has been about assessment and how teachers can use marking to really inform their own teaching and help pupils to improve. It has also been about the research that has occurred in this area in terms of formative assessment. You should now know:

- why teachers mark
- what they mark
- how an assessment policy will determine your assessment strategy in the classroom
- what formative assessment means and what other strategies need to be in place to ensure maximum benefits for all pupils.

Look at the figure below to see what should be in place for formative assessment to have its maximum impact.

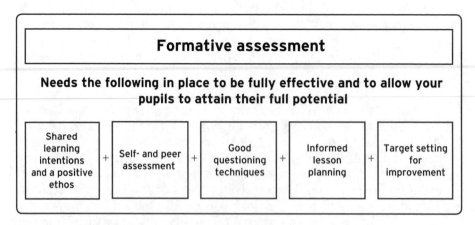

Formative assessment

Needs the following in place to be fully effective and to allow your pupils to attain their full potential

| Shared learning intentions and a positive ethos | + | Self- and peer assessment | + | Good questioning techniques | + | Informed lesson planning | + | Target setting for improvement |

Achieving the most out of formative assessment

How might a teacher manage the mark load?

This section suggests how to balance the demands of marking against all those other demands made on busy classroom teachers. It will also suggest how to deal with obstacles that prevent teachers from using formative assessment within their own classroom.

TOP TIPS!

Many new teachers complain about the workload of preparation and marking and ask how they can best balance the two. These tips on deciding what to mark and how to mark it in a busy teaching day may be of help.

- *Teachers cannot mark every piece of work rigorously.*

- *You should decide which learning tasks are going to be the most important indicators of learning and ensure that those are the ones rigorously marked.*

- *The teacher does not have to mark every piece. Pupils can be provided with marking guidelines or exemplar. Marking their own work teaches them the criteria that are important for success and is a learning tool in itself.*

- *Take books in regularly to ensure that work is up to date and pupils can see that you are keeping an eye on them and checking for continued progress.*

- *Record marks in your own markbook or teacher planner (see Chapter 9).*

- *Ask other more experienced colleagues how often they take books in for marking and seek advice on balancing preparation and marking load.*

- *Identify what you will mark on a daily, weekly or fortnightly basis as being the most important and share this with the pupils.*

How do you choose which tasks to assess rigorously?

To do this you need to think about the SOWs. With a mature class in a secondary school where the teacher has contact for much less time than a primary teacher

the most important tasks may take a few weeks to complete. Therefore, it may be possible to determine what will be marked over a half-term period with all of the classes taught. An example would be an English teacher with a Year 10 class. They may, over the course of a half-term, complete the following:

- an imaginative essay
- a coursework assignment
- a comprehension as examination practice
- a set text with associated tasks
- language assignments intended to improve basic skills as well as additional other smaller assignments
- oral work.

TOP TIPS!

To help manage your marking, consider the following strategies:

- Peer assessment strategies could be used to assess the imaginative essay or the comprehension. Pupils could be given mark schemes for the comprehension and examples of essays that are very good, average and below average. Pupils could then compare their work against the criteria and models. Marking their own work makes pupils aware of the success criteria needed for specific tasks. These success criteria are transferable, as pupils will need to complete more imaginative essays and comprehensions. In most subject areas there are similar tasks that are repeated, and where pupils learn the success criteria needed then this will improve pupil attainment. In terms of formative assessment, once the pupils have assessed the work they could then determine their own targets for the future by comparing their finished work with the mark schemes or exemplar.

- The coursework assignment will need to be marked by the teacher at some point and most teachers will want to see how pupils are doing when completing such important work.

- Language assignments could be marked by a class with model answers being provided. As a rough guide, it is important to mark books every fortnight and over a half-term three significant assignments are marked rigorously and detailed comments added for upper secondary school classes in a core subject.

➜

> ● *New teachers are not alone and it is important to use the expertise around, asking fellow staff how they manage the marking workload and how often they assess pupils' work rigorously.*
>
> ● *Other assignments may be read through briefly and a date and initial placed at the end to show it has been looked at. It is important that parents and your line managers can see that you are looking at pupils' books and assessing outcomes.*

Assessment is not just about awarding a mark, grade or level. Remember that there are a number of reasons for marking a pupil's book and assessing the quality of learning is only one of them. It is also important to see that pupils are keeping up to date and that there are no learning gaps. Some teachers suggest that class teachers mark books on a rota basis, marking all books but only assessing one-third of the books rigorously with diagnostic comments being added. From an organisational point of view this does not seem as easy a system to handle as the former but all teachers are different and ultimately it is for the individual to decide on the best system for them.

What gets in the way of using formative assessment in the classroom?

You may not be able to use formative assessment in a classroom because it is not in line with the school assessment policy or that of the department or line manager. There are still those who are sceptical about putting comments and not marks on a book, who know little about formative assessment or who do not feel it is necessary in their school, possibly because other initiatives are in place that better suit that organisation. In addition, there are those who run large departments or groups of people who feel that marks on a page provide them with a quick way of ensuring that pupils are learning and schemes of work are being covered. This is not the place to comment on whether this is a good thing or not.

Formative assessment is not just about the effectiveness of comments versus marks and many of the strategies for its success discussed in this chapter can of course be used. It should also be stressed that because formative assessment may not be used formally in your school as yet, it does not preclude you from using it. Many line managers would welcome someone in their school who is keen, interested and able to offer new ideas. If you want to try out any initiative in your

classroom it is worth discussing it with your line manager, who 99% of the time is likely to be fully supportive and interested. It is also worth remembering that if you are going to do something like this then pupil and parent support will be needed and information about the pilot and its reasoning shared. All stakeholders will need to help you evaluate its success at the end of the trial period.

Another reason why formative assessment can be problematic is to do with the nature of schools and the need for summative assessments to be made to inform reports. Summative assessment is used to assess pupils in order to rank them in year groups and for organisational reasons. Teachers using formative assessment often perceive a tension between the use of formative assessment and the organisational emphasis on summative assessment. The reality for teachers is that formative assessment has to work alongside summative assessment. One way of dealing with this is suggested in *Assessment for Learning: Putting it into Practice* (Black et al., 2003). Teachers involved in the project identified in this text tried to work out effective strategies for using formative approaches to summative tests.

What could you do to ensure that pupils use formative assessment to aid their learning for summative testing?

Some teachers found that despite using more active methods of learning in their classrooms pupils, when left to learn for tests, reverted to a passive role of reading over work. The teachers tried to restructure pupils' learning by getting them to identify clearly what they were confident about and what they felt needed more work. They used a traffic light system of red, amber and green to do this. These then formed the basis of a revision plan. Pupils were asked to identify questions on an examination paper that tested their red areas and then work with books and in peer groups to ensure they could answer those questions successfully.

Another innovative idea came out of research studies by King and Foos (cited in Black et al., 2003). This study showed that where pupils are trained to prepare for examinations by generating and then answering their own questions these groups performed better than other groups who had not prepared in this way. Preparation of test questions calls for and develops an overview of the topic being studied.

A third innovative idea was to use the examination or test itself as an opportunity for formative work. This would work particularly well with mock examinations or tests conducted as part of a programme of study leading up to a final external examination of some kind. Teachers and pupils could look at questions that were done poorly and concentrate on improving the pupil response to those questions in particular. Peer marking of test papers can also be used. Pupils can then come up with a set of criteria for future success.

These ideas suggest that formative assessment and summative assessment need not be seen as being poles apart and challenge the view that they are so different

that they have to be kept apart. Teachers have always been realistic about the heavy demands made on them to use summative assessment for a number of reasons and these innovative approaches reduce the tension often found between using summative and formative assessments with the same pupils.

Putting it into practice

The final section of this chapter is intended to show how teachers can use the information gleaned from the chapter within the classroom, the department and finally the whole school.

TOP TIPS!

In my classroom I could:

- *Mark work regularly, tracking individual pupil progress and class progress.*

- *Use the assessment information to identify pupils who need enriching, support or who are underachieving.*

- *Keep detailed records in line with school policy to use to inform written reports and oral reports to parents.*

- *Ensure that underachievement is dealt with. First, outline what a pupil has to do to catch up, then the sanctions that will be implemented if this does not occur, and set a deadline for this to be done. If the deadline is exceeded inform line managers and parents for further intervention to take place. Use the department or school policy to suggest strategies that can be used or seek advice. Record all interventions made with dates for reference.*

- *Use assessment information to inform future lesson planning as this is vital to success.*

- *Use questioning techniques as suggested above.*

- *Use the reference list at the end of this chapter to help become better informed about assessment for learning.*

- *Indicate always the learning intentions of the task.* →

- Encourage pupils to identify success criteria for their learning on the specific learning intentions – 'How will I know I have succeeded?'

- Encourage a positive 'can do' ethos in the classroom.

- Use self-assessment and peer assessment strategies.

- Encourage pupils to set their own targets for learning improvement but help them initially.

- Encourage pupils to take responsibility for their learning.

- Use summative tests in a formative way as outlined above.

TOP TIPS!

In my department/school area I could:

- Have a clear assessment policy.

- Outline how often pupils should be assessed and whether teachers should be using formative assessment techniques.

- Ensure that lesson intentions are shared with all classes as standard practice.

- Inform parents about how teachers assess in this department/ area of the school.

- Use self-assessment and peer assessment strategies.

- Introduce proformas for pupil self-assessment and target setting.

- Introduce proformas for staff to fill in prior to parents' evenings that are standard and show that assessment records are being kept. (Parents are entitled to know what level or grade their child is working at and will probably ask for this information.)

- Discuss what constitutes good questioning in the classroom.

- Share good practice.

- Monitor the pupils' books for evidence of formative assessment strategies being used by all staff and to ensure the assessment policy is being consistently applied.

Although as a newly qualified teacher you will have no control over what happens in the whole school, the following suggests what should or could be in place to ensure consistency of marking and assessment. Formative assessment has been proven to improve standards and the following is something that all schools should be working towards. Many proactive schools are using both formative assessment and proven teaching and learning strategies like the standard sharing of lesson intentions to improve standards.

While on a teaching practice or in your school, you could use the final 'Top Tips' as a checklist.

TOP TIPS!

In my school I could:

- Ensure that there is a clear agreed assessment policy that is understood and shared by all.

- Ensure that parents are aware of how teachers assess pupils.

- Investigate formative assessment strategies and, if necessary, introduce a pilot in the school to see how it would best fit the organisation. Encourage staff to take ownership of the initiative, adapting it to the individual needs of pupils, staff and the organisation as a whole.

- Ensure that pupils are encouraged and that there is a positive ethos working in all classrooms and that pupils are not disaffected.

- Ensure that learning intentions are shared and that self-assessment, peer assessment and target-setting strategies are in place as standard practice.

- Ensure that monitoring of assessment is ongoing and consistent throughout the school at all levels.

Why not try this?

- Think about what you have learnt about marking and your own particular circumstances in your classroom and subject area:
  - What will marking tell you about each pupil?

– What will you be marking?

– How do you know how to mark a pupil's work?

● Have you seen an assessment policy and do you understand it?

● Does your school use formative assessment strategies or are they interested in finding out more?

● Do they use any of the strategies identified in this chapter for improving learning outcomes?

● What are the three most important things that you can take away from reading this chapter?

Going further

Black, P. and Wiliam, D. (1998) *Inside the Black Box: Raising Standards Through Classroom Assessment*, Slough: NFER Nelson.

Black, P., Harrison, C., Lee, C., Marshall, B. and Wiliam, D. (1998) *Working Inside the Black Box*, Slough: NFER Nelson.

Black, P., Harrison, C., Lee, C., Marshall, B. and Wiliam, D. (2003) *Assessment for Learning: Putting it into Practice*, Maidenhead: Open University Press.

Clarke, S. (2001) *Unlocking Formative Assessment: Practical Strategies for Enhancing Pupils' Learning in the Primary Classroom*, London: Hodder Murray.

Gardner, J. (ed.) (2006) *Assessment and Learning*, London: Sage.

Perrenoud, P. (1991) 'Towards a pragmatic approach to formative evaluation', in P. Weston (ed.) *Assessment of Pupils' Achievement: Motivation and School Success*, Amsterdam: Swets and Zeitlinger.

Sadler, D.R. (1989) 'Formative assessment and the design of instructional systems', *Instructional Science*, 18.

Beaton, A., Madaus, G., O'Leary, M. and Kellaghan, T. (1996) 'The consistency of findings across international surveys of mathematics and science achievement', Third International Mathematican and Science Study.

www.assessment-reform-group.org

Pupil data – what is it and how is it gathered?

What this chapter will explore:

- What data can we gather on children from birth onwards?
- How this data impacts on secondary education and learning plans
- Why do we use data?
- How can you use data in your classroom?

Primary schools and secondary schools are now using extensive data which gives them a lot of information about the children they are teaching. This gathering of information begins on entry to primary school at a very young age and continues throughout a pupil's school life. All teachers are now expected to use this data to help inform their target setting and lesson planning for all pupils in their care. Interviews often ask new teachers what data they would expect to have available on

pupils in their class and how they would use it. This chapter is intended to ensure that you know what data may be available and that you use it with confidence and full understanding of its importance.

All primary and secondary schools now use data to provide them with more information about the pupils they teach. The data are gathered from a variety of sources and carefully analysed to enable schools to plan their teaching and learning and set individual and group targets for their learners and their school improvement/development plans (SIPs/SDPs). In addition, schools will have set targets in consultation with their local education authority. The data will show whether those targets have been met. It will also allow a school to check its results against other schools by using benchmarking data. Some schools will be more advanced than others in using and analysing these data. In primary and secondary schools it is now common to find a teacher who is also the assessment manager. This person will be the school 'expert' on data and will interpret this information for others when it is necessary. They could also lead any training that is needed for other teachers in the school. Data are obtained in a number of ways and it is vital that schools are not just data-rich but knowledge-rich as well.

What is benchmarking?

Benchmarking is when your school performance is compared with that of another school with:

- similar numbers
- similar intake
- similar socio-economic location
- similar ability children, i.e. a comparison of the numbers of pupils on a statement of educational needs register.

The benchmarking data provide a powerful tool that measures how well your school is doing in relation to others like it. Inspectors use this data a lot. If a school is doing well it is normally adding value to its pupils and will be in the 'upper quartile' for most categories assessed by the benchmarking.

What data can we gather on children from birth onwards?

Anyone who has been involved with a new baby realises that there is a normal developmental line that can be referred to. This suggests the age at which we

can expect a child to do certain things. In the case of all children we can divide this data into three broad categories – physical, mental and social – and this has long been recognised. People who work with children with special needs refer to this type of profile to see where these specific children are developmentally on the spectrum.

In 1998, it became statutory for local education authorities to develop baseline schemes for assessing their young pupils. Some authorities opted to develop their own assessment profiles and some adopted already available schemes. It was felt that this form of assessment should be approached in a certain manner:

> *'An effective baseline scheme will allow access for all pupils to an assessment process in which they can demonstrate what they know, understand and can do in a variety of learning contexts. Any scheme should, therefore, be based upon teacher assessment over a period of time. This will allow children to demonstrate their skills and understanding and provide a foundation for subsequent teaching and learning.'*
>
> (The Association for Achievement and Improvement Through Assessment, 'Baseline assessment')

What are the golden rules for gathering data on young children?

It is important that a data profile is gathered over a wide range of activities and learning contexts that we expect pupils to encounter. In addition, the Association of Assessment Inspectors and Advisers recommends the following:

- The profile should be completed by the end of the first half-term.
- The profile should be based on observation, as well as discussion and questioning.
- Further more detailed evidence should be used to support these occurrences.
- The child should be unaware that they are being assessed.
- Pupils should be encouraged to use their first language.
- Fair access to all pupils should be allowed.
- The profile should help the discussion about learning that should occur between the teacher and the parent or guardian.

The profile should be criteria based. If you look at the profile on pp233–4, the criteria that a child is being assessed by are clearly identified. Criteria-based assessment promotes a consistency across the teaching staff, ensuring that they are in agreement about what they are measuring as they assess the child.

The assessment, when it is complete, should help staff plan the learning programme for the child more effectively. For example, 'This pupil can already do this and in order to get to the next level they will need to do ...'

The following pages feature the Birmingham Profile, an example summary of a very comprehensive profile that a teacher would complete over time.

This example is just one profile for gathering data on pupils compiled by one authority but there are other similar ones available. As the pupils grow older the emphasis on physical skills and personal development is replaced by information that has more to do with subject/skill-based learning. It is important that information is transferred through the school effectively. An effective transfer is one where all the knowledge about a child and their learning programme is successfully passed on to a new teacher, thus ensuring that the child progresses with their learning without 'slipping' back in any way. This also ensures that the teacher knows the new pupil and thus can plan a course of study that will present this pupil with a challenge appropriate to their educational needs. The data set developed in a primary school forms the basis of what secondary school transfer teams use to assess and place new pupils into the secondary sector and therefore it is important to know how this is gathered.

What other data can we expect to come across in secondary schools today?

Most people will be familiar with the term SATs or Standard Assessment Tests. However, although it is sometimes suggested that these existed throughout the United Kingdom this was never the case. For instance, they were never used in Scotland. Look at your curriculum authority's website to see how pupils are assessed at the end of the Key Stages in your nation. Most nations still insist on some form of end of Key Stage teacher assessment even if standard national tests are no longer in existence.

The following are the most common forms of data that a new teacher will encounter:

● *Standard Assessment Tests (SATs) levels*   On entry to a secondary school the information on pupils that has been gathered at primary level will be transferred. This will include assessment of the pupils in English, maths and science, and a level has to be awarded. This has until recently been assessed by a SAT conducted nationally. However, although some parts of the UK no longer have tests or did not have them in the first place, LAs will still want teachers to award a level to pupils to identify how they have done over the course of the two Key Stages or will want to see some form of summative assessment of their primary experience. This data will be used by the LA and the secondary school to set targets for teaching and learning outcomes.

Summary Profile: Pre-Level One and Level One

Child's Name: ....

Date of Birth: ....

	Physical skills personal/social	Oral language	Reading	Writing	Mathematics	The process and language of science
Pre-Level One	a) Engages in range of physical activities confidently ☐ b) Plays with other children in the classroom and in the playground ☐	Can follow short sequences of instructions in classroom situation ☐ Responds appropriately to such questions as 'Where …?' 'What's s/he doing?' 'What's this for?' 'Who …?' 'Which?' ☐	Listens to and shows understanding of simple stories through comments made and response to questions ☐ Plays I Spy using initial sounds ☐	Regularly chooses to use pencils, crayons, paint, scissors etc. ☐	Sorts into sets and names common attribute ☐ Matches and counts accurately groups of objects up to five ☐ Names and recognises at least five number symbols ☐	Can name five senses and knows their functions (e.g. ears to hear, eyes to see) ☐ Interested in new experiences ☐
Level One	Shows flexibility and co-ordination in running quickly, rolling, skipping, catching etc. ☐ Is co-operative member of the class ☐ Carries out daily routines without help ☐	Listens and contributes to conversations about current and recently experienced play and work activities (will ask questions) ☐	Regularly chooses to look at books ☐ Has established range of early skills ☐	Attempts to write 'stories' and to read back to self/other people ☐ Controlled use of pencil and crayons ☐	Can add and subtract numbers to 10 using apparatus ☐ Compares and orders objects for length, height, weight, temperature etc. without measuring: understands and uses appropriate language. Willing to predict ☐	From observation makes models and drawing of people, animals including main parts/features. Can describe ☐ Understands and responds to 'When?' 'Why?' 'How?' 'What might/will happen … ?' ☐

233

Summary Profile: Three to Five Years

Child's Name: ....

Date of Birth: ....

	Physical skills	Self-help and independence	Eye-hand co-ordination	Social development/ play	Listening/ understanding	Communication
By 3 Years	Can walk ☐ run ☐ jump ☐ climb ☐	Can, with help, toilet ☐ dress ☐ eat ☐	Plays purposefully with crayons, bricks, jigsaws etc. ☐	Play mainly physical; may not involve other children but likes to have them around ☐	Responds to simple questions and instructions ☐ Joins in a variety of listening activities with adult help e.g. action rhymes ☐	Indicates needs and wants using words and gestures ☐ Talks to familiar adults ☐
By 4 Years	Regularly and confidently engages in physical play e.g. balancing along walls and benches, climbing, pedalling ☐	Without help, makes good attempt to toilet ☐ dress ☐ eat ☐	Establishing correct use of scissors ☐ crayons ☐ paint brushes ☐ construction toys ☐	Actively involved in play situation with other children e.g. making simple models sequenced domestic play; still needs some adult involvement ☐	Shows understanding of simple stories (through comments made and response to questions) ☐ Can concentrate to carry out a range of listening activities in a small group ☐	Can hold simple conversation about recent past and familiar future events ☐
By 5 Years	Developing early 'games' skills e.g. skipping, throwing, catching ☐	Manages own possessions and carries out daily routines without help ☐	Shows controlled use of tools and materials ☐	Plays complex fantasy/ imaginative games with other children. Welcomes occasional suggestions from adult ☐ Shows concentrated involvement in jigsaws, drawing, painting, making models etc. ☐	Concentrates and responds to more complex listening activities e.g. group stories and discussions, early phonic games ☐	Uses language for wide range of purposes ☐ ☐ to direct self and others ☐ ask questions describe and explain events

- *Reading and spelling test scores*   These can be reading and spelling tests similar to those produced by the National Federation for Educational Research (www.nfer.ac.uk). Many primary schools and some secondary schools conduct reading tests on each year group annually. If a school compares these results year on year it can make judgements about its intake based on prior performance of years with similar/stronger/weaker results.

- *Predicted grades or levels* based on prior attainment.

- *Target grades/levels* set by teachers.

- *Internal assessments*   These can be tests or examinations and will be reported on to parents once a year.

- *Pupil self-assessment*   If pupils are to take greater control over their learning they have to learn to assess where they are at present and how they might improve in future.

- *Tracking grade sheets* allow teachers to see how pupils are doing across a range of subjects and provide a 'snapshot' of total performance at different times of the year.

- *Cognitive Abilities Tests (CATs)*   These provide information on a child's verbal ability (verbal reasoning – VR) and quantitative ability (quantitative reasoning – QR). They require the pupils to have a basic store of verbal and quantitative concepts and are more closely linked to what they already know. Finally, they assess a pupil's non-verbal reasoning (NVR). This battery of tests assess ability that is not bound by what pupils have learnt in school. The tests are best described as measuring potential.

- *Attendance*   It is important to look at trends in attendance and if it is poor to intervene quickly to find out why.

- *Behaviour*   Negative behaviour is recorded and in some cases pupils will have education plans. These are plans specifically relating to behaviour and indicate how all teachers who have contact with a particular pupil should manage them.

- *Health plans*   Some pupils have health problems that are above what is normally expected. In serious cases schools must put in place a health strategy explaining how they will manage this pupil's health problems during the school day.

Why do we use data?

If children are to move from one year or Key Stage to another or move from one school to another then the information we have on them should accompany them. In addition, we should make an effort to induct pupils into the next stage of

their learning and to explain fully what is expected of them. In the case of a move from one school to another this is more problematic. Some secondary schools have an intake that is made up of pupils from many different partner schools and transferring and collating this amount of data is a logistical problem in itself. However, moving from one school to another is a big psychological jump for many children and this is why so much time and effort is now put into managing this transition. (A transition case study from Bishop Gore School is available on the book's website, at www.pearsoned.co.uk/essentialguides.)

There are two main reasons why so much is now done on effective transfer and transition:

● *To build a pastoral bridge*   A child who moves from one school to another and feels confident about the move because they have visited the school or knows what to expect in the next Key Stage of learning is often a happy and motivated child. If this occurs then the pastoral team have worked well and the pastoral bridge is firmly in place.

● *To build a curriculum bridge*   Teachers need to know what level a child has reached in their study. The time has gone when a teacher relies solely on the work a child did in the classroom. Now the data tell a teacher where a child should be and enables them to challenge the child on entry to their classroom. This prevents pupils having to repeat work or complete work that is too simple. Presenting pupils with a challenge means that they will not become bored and disaffected and allows them to move on to new work swiftly. In school we often refer to this as presenting our pupils with a 'challenge on entry'.

Data which are transferred can include:

● attendance statistics
● reading and spelling ages
● SAT levels
● behaviour data
● special educational needs information
● information about the support that parents are likely to give
● child protection information where applicable
● medical information that may be relevant to an individual
● sporting/academic/musical achievements.

This data provides a way of allowing children to move from one school to another efficiently and effectively. However, whether a child is moving from one class to another, or from school to school, the information should be *used*. It is important that we are data-rich and knowledge-rich not data-rich and knowledge-poor!

How can I use data in my classroom?

Whether you teach in a primary or secondary school you will be provided with data about the pupils in your classroom. Some of it *you* will provide through your own assessment and knowledge of the pupil. CAT results and reading test scores may form part of the data. If you are teaching in the early years you may have been given a summary profile similar to that found earlier in this chapter.

You need to do the following:

- File the data so that it can be easily referred to. It is a working document and should be readily available.

- Identify information that will impact on your subject teaching. If you are teaching in a primary school the reading score result will affect the pupil's likely performance in a range of subjects. However, it is important to remember that because a child cannot read the information, it does not mean they cannot understand the concepts underlying the content. The reverse of this is also true – a high reading age does not necessarily mean that the pupil can understand what they have read.

- Make sure that you are aware of any pupils who have ILPs or EBPs that have been provided by the SENCO as these will need to be reviewed by you and the review returned to the SENCO. Your lesson plans and the way you work with these pupils should be influenced by the advice in such documents.

- Make sure you are aware of the general ability of the class.

- Mark work using an agreed school policy or department policy giving the pupil good formative feedback.

- Use the data to plan your lessons, differentiating the work according to the needs of the pupil.

- Think about how you may group the class for work based on their CAT scores, reading scores, etc. Sometimes you may wish to extend the most able by putting them in a group and giving them a different task (differentiation by task). Sometimes you may wish to have mixed ability groups where the able child will develop the others in the group (differentiation by outcome).

Remember that differentiation does not mean giving more of the same to the able student. It does not mean doing less work on a topic for the less able. It means planning work that enables a pupil to achieve at their own pace and level but sets them clear targets for how to progress.

A quick guide to CATs and what the scores mean

Pupil	VSAS	QSAS	NVSAS
A	88	94	110
B	101	110	78
C	112	96	99
D	82	105	107
E	94	107	108
F	112	96	103

VSAS = verbal standardised age score
QSAS = quantitative standardised age score
NVSAS = non-verbal standardised age score

Looking at the scores shown in the table above, note the following:

● Two-thirds of pupils score between 85 and 115 (pupils with a triple score of 100 should access five A*–C grades).

● 12 points or more difference between VSAS, QSAS and NVSAS is significant; for two-thirds of pupils there is no significant difference.

What do the scores tell us about the pupils?

● Pupils like A with low VSAS and QSAS but high NVSAS take off rapidly with early intervention to improve their literacy and numeracy skills. The NVSAS tells us that they have good innate ability. Pupils like A prefer pictorial representation and might be visual learners (see Chapter 7 for information on learning styles).

● Pupils like B with low NVSAS but high VSAS and QSAS have poorly developed non-verbal skills. They need support in the higher-order skills (e.g. problem solving, algebra). Perhaps girls are more likely to suffer here.

● Pupils like C with very high VSAS but lower QSAS and NVSAS may need support in maths, science and technology. Schools need to play to their verbal strengths here.

● Pupils like D may have specific language difficulties (e.g. dyslexia or have English as an additional language). These pupils would benefit from language support/reading programmes, etc.

● Pupils like E would benefit from language support.

● Pupils like F would benefit from numeracy support.

CAT scores can predict the following (Birchgrove School, 2000):

- The outcomes in Key Stage 3 tests in the core subjects of English, maths and science.
- GCSE grades for English, maths, science, history, geography and French.
- A score of 100 usually leads to five or more A*–C grades.

How can subject team leaders use data to improve pupils' learning?

Many new teachers find themselves in charge of a subject area. This is especially true of primary teachers. Here we consider how subject leaders use data to improve pupils' learning.

The role of the head of department is crucial as they have an overview of progress within a subject and within the school. They will be able to compare progress in English, for instance, with that in science or maths.

Heads of department or subject team leaders should do the following:

- Keep data in a specific file.
- Distribute a second copy of all data they hold to those in their department or team.
- Use data on a regular basis to show how the subject area is performing in relation to other subjects or how pupils are achieving in the subject.
- Compare the performance of the same pupil in different subjects.
- Give guidance on how to use data and what data are relevant.
- Use data to highlight those pupils who need enriching (the provision of special educational support to very able pupils – see Chapter 16) and those who need supporting. It will also help to show those who are not working to their potential (i.e. are underachieving), and strategies can be put in place to remedy this. Those pupils' progress will need to be monitored and they will need mentoring.
- Use data to decide where to place pupils in groups if setting is applicable.
- Use data to decide what courses are appropriate for pupils. Sometimes subject leaders will change examination boards based on what the data tells them about the cohort and how it is performing.
- Set realistic targets for the subject in national examinations/tests.
- Agree targets (with the subject teacher) for the class, set or group and then check progress against the targets.
- Compare the results achieved in the subject with national statistics or benchmarking data.

Most schools use data to improve their teaching and compare themselves with other schools. This chapter highlights some of the information that might be available to help you better understand the type of pupils you teach. Your school could well be using other assessment tests to determine how well pupils are doing and to predict their likely final success.

Why not try this?

Consider the following:

- Think about what data you have already come across in your school.
  - Where is the information kept and how is it used?
  - Is there someone who is seen as the assessment manager or expert?
- Think about the type of data that you would have to use as a statutory obligation. Behaviour plans and individual learning programmes must be followed and a review completed.
  - What data would be most helpful in your classroom?
  - How would you use these data to plan your lessons more effectively?
  - Would you use the data to group pupils in your class so that more learning takes place?
- In interviews, teachers are asked about what data they might use to inform their teaching. You may also be asked why it is important to track a pupil's progress and ensure effective movement from one stage of learning to another. What would your answers be?

Going further

The Association for Achievement and Improvement Through Assessment, 'Baseline assessment', available at http://atschool.eduweb.co.uk/aaia/index.html.

Birchgrove School (2000) 'Making performance data work', Birchgrove Comprehensive School, Swansea.

Birmingham Profile, Birmingham Local Education Authority.

www.nfer.ac.uk

How schools use data to improve achievement

What this chapter will explore:

- How to use data to inform intervention strategies
- How to use data to improve attendance and behaviour
- How to use data to identify pupils who need mentoring and support
- How to use data to identify pupils who need enrichment and support
- Using data to determine the success of the school at all levels
- Looking at value added in detail

Schools are now data-rich and this should mean that they are knowledge-rich about the pupils who form the cohort of the school. Data is power; proactive schools can use this information to put the best strategies in

place for their pupils. This chapter leads on from Chapter 15 to show you how schools can use the data they collect to inform best practice. It sets out to show how specific information on individual pupils can be used to bring about school improvement.

How to use data to inform intervention strategies

Reference was made in Chapter 15 to the types of data that schools gather on pupils. Schools use this information to inform them about progress, and where this is not as it should be to put in place remedial strategies. For instance, the reading ages and spelling ages of a pupil can be ascertained using standardised tests and pupils should have a reading age that is the same as their chronological age. In primary and secondary schools this data can identify pupils who are falling behind. These pupils, once identified, can be given support and this can be provided by teaching assistants. It is usual with spelling and reading support to work for a short time each day with pupils as this has proven to be the most successful. In some cases schools work with parents and pupils, showing parents how they can help their children with their work. In cases where parents are semi-literate the school may help the parents to overcome their problems as a way of indirectly supporting the child. This involves a trained team of specialist staff who are able to work sensitively with families who fall into this category.

Many schools also use interactive learning packages that can be loaded on to a computer. These programs are sensitive to the needs of individual pupils and will

identify what level a pupil should be working at. The program is set by a trained member of staff but it will drop the pupil down a level if they get a set number of responses wrong; similarly if they get a string of answers right the program will move up a level. Teachers who are trained in using the packages will also be able to print out reports on individual pupil progress. These packages can be used to improve reading and understanding, spelling and numeracy, and the reports provide further data for teachers. The programs show how often a pupil has logged on to the computer and for how long they have worked.

Case study

Using reading/spelling and cognitive ability tests to improve attainment

In one school the Head of English and the SENCO work together to improve the literacy levels of all pupils. Each year the English department, supported by the special educational support department, tests the reading and spelling ages of all pupils from Years 7 to 11 using nationally recognised standardised tests. This is important as it means that results for individuals and cohorts can be compared. Individual pupil's results are compared year on year to ensure that reading and spelling ages are progressing in line with expectations. Where this is not happening individual pupils are targeted for extra reading support if staffing for this is available. (Normally in Years 7 and 8 for mainstream pupils.) Other pupils who are identified as needing help with spelling attend spelling workshops that are run every morning by a trained team of support teachers and teaching assistants. Intervention strategies for reading and spelling achieve the best results when they are provided daily for short amounts of time.

Proactive forward planning

The information on year groups provides important data on the ability profile of one year in relation to another. The Year 7 pupils are also given CATs (cognitive abilities tests) and this provides additional information about the year group. This means that in this school it is possible to build an abilities profile for each year group and compare that profile with cohorts that have gone before. CATs are powerful tools when used wisely. The tests provide schools with an indication of how the whole year group is likely to achieve in their GCSE examinations five years hence. This means that schools can use this information to support both strong and weak year groups and to ensure that outcomes are better than predictions. In schools where year groups are identified as being weaker than normal it may mean that option subjects that pupils take in Years 10 and 11 are not suitable. Additional places on

→

vocational courses may be needed and a reduction in the number of groups in academic subjects made. Data of this kind should be used to proactively plan the most suitable range of courses to suit the pupils and to ensure that they all attain their potential.

Building expertise

Where schools are using data as carefully as this school, considerable expertise is being built up. Over time it is possible to see how accurate the CAT predictions were for a specific cohort and whether the year groups, where intervention strategies were used, were able to outperform their GCSE predictions. It was found that this did occur and that in most year groups it was possible to add significant value through the literacy strategies and others that the school put in place. Adding value simply means a year group predicted to get 50% of the cohort five A*–C grades at GCSE was able to outperform the prediction and get more than 50% A*–C grades: in this way the school has *added value* to the cohort that year. This type of data analysis is possible at both primary and secondary level, as is the ability to put in place intervention strategies such as extra reading and spelling groups.

Health warning

Some pupils will outperform their CAT prediction and others will underperform. At the end of the day performance is dependent on attitude and commitment as well as aptitude. This is why it is not always a good thing to explain exactly what CAT result an individual pupil has to the pupil themselves, their parents and sometimes to certain teachers who feel that a CAT result is carved in stone.

Intervention strategy examples

In Chapter 15 the Birmingham Profile was referred to. In the same way as the school in the case study above was able to build up information on pupils year on year, the information gathered by a school using a model like the Birmingham one would do the same. It would be possible to see how pupils developed and progressed having entered the school with a certain level of competencies and skills. Over time a comparison could then be made with those who came in with greater or lesser skills and competencies. This would allow a school to compare cohorts over time making judgements about their strengths and weaknesses. This type of data builds up over time and allows schools to be able to make very accurate predictions about the likely potential and outcomes for a group of pupils. It also allows schools to make valid judgements about the effectiveness of strategies that have been used and what may be needed in the future.

In Scotland over 150 schools are developing better integrated services to raise attainment and promote social inclusion. One essential characteristic will be the targeting of individuals and the developing of personal learning plans. At the earliest possible stage these schools aim to address the needs of vulnerable pupils, including those looked after by the local authority (LACs), children in need and those at risk of offending or of serious substance misuse. Strategies like these all rely on the effective keeping and sharing of data on pupils and the use of data-rich systems to track progress effectively. The aim of one such strategy is as follows:

> *'An assessment is to be made of individuals soon after they enter education and a programme including targets for attainment will be agreed and regularly reviewed.'*

(New Community Schools @ the informal education homepage, www.infed.org/schooling)

How to use data to improve attendance and behaviour

Schools are expected to ensure that pupils attend for at least 90% of the time. In addition, it is expected that any absences are authorised. This means that the reason for absence is identified and a parent/guardian has supported the reason for the non-attendance. Absences for medical reasons, for school trips, extra-curricular activities and family holidays may constitute some of the reasons why pupils are absent from school. Where a pupil's attendance falls below 90% (some schools set the limit at 92% or 94%), strategies are put in place to monitor the individual attendance and follow up the reasons for non-attendance.

Identifying absence patterns

Many secondary schools use an electronic means of registration. In some ways this makes data analysis and tracking of individual pupil attendance easier to manage. Where pupils are failing to attend it is important to identify any patterns that exist in absences. Sometimes pupils fail to attend on the same day each week. This can be due to the lessons that they have on that day. It may be that they feel disliked by a member of staff or have to participate in a subject that they feel they are weak in. In cases like this it is relatively easy to solve the problem using counselling and supporting strategies. In cases where there is no obvious pattern or reason it is more difficult to break the habit that pupils have fallen into. In these circumstances it is important to involve parents, support staff and the EWO, who plays a key part in monitoring school attendance and that of

individual pupils who are seen to be at risk. A clear signal is given to the parents and pupil that if there is no medical reason for absence then the pupil must be in school and that their attendance will be monitored. In certain cases, charges will be brought against parents for failing to get their children to attend school on a regular basis. In some schools electronic registration is used for every lesson and this shows immediately when pupils are truanting internally. (See Chapter 21 for how schools tackle attendance issues.)

Storing data electronically

Good behaviour is vital to the success of any school. Many schools use information technology to store data electronically. These systems enable a school to store a variety of information on individual pupils and this can include negative behaviours and the sanctions that have been used in response to them. These data are important, enabling schools to track behaviour generally and identify the most common forms of negative behaviour. Schools can also track the success of various strategies that might have been put in place and can then review their effectiveness. Schools can identify particular year groups that may cause problems and track the behaviour patterns of individual pupils. Where pupils are involved in repeated negative behaviours schools will use data to support their use of external agencies to intervene and support pupils. These might include any behaviour support units that exist within the local education authority, EPs and those trained in behaviour management techniques. Extreme sanctions include: internal exclusions where pupils are kept in school but apart from their fellow pupils; excluding pupils for a set number of days; or, in extreme cases, permanently excluding pupils.

When a school is trying to improve behaviour, comparing the records of these types of exclusion prior to strategies being put in place and post-strategy are vital. This is one powerful way that data can be used to track the success of intervention strategies being used for behaviour management within a school. If they are succeeding then the amount of negative behaviour and the figures for exclusions of all kinds should be reducing. Similarly at an individual level, data on a pupil who is having help with behaviour should show that the number of negative behaviours is lessening and the intervention is working.

How to use data to identify pupils who need mentoring and support

In many schools a variety of staff use data to track and measure the progress of pupils against their potential. Where a pupil is seen to be underachieving and

thus failing to reach their potential, intervention strategies such as monitoring and mentoring are used. (Mentoring is a term that refers to the way certain pupils are identified and targeted for extra help with organisation of work, etc. Mentoring can be useful with pupils who are not achieving what the data suggest they are capable of.) Teachers normally identify two or three pupils who need support and keep records on their progress. Sometimes it is enough for a pupil to know that they have someone they can talk to about their work and who is prepared to give them some individual time. In some cases this monitoring/mentoring will only go on for a short time (e.g. half a term), but in certain circumstances this may need to be extended. Data are stored on the monitoring files and copies of the records will be passed on to a member of staff who may have responsibility for pupil monitoring/mentoring in the school.

This type of intervention can make a huge difference when it is undertaken as part of a whole school strategy to improve achievement. It ensures that a large number of pupils have some form of strategic support put in place for them and over time most children at risk of underachieving will have some form of support. For instance, if every subject teacher identifies three pupils that they teach in each class and closely monitors them, and this model is replicated throughout the school, then a large number of pupils are being supported.

Improving borderline cases

In some schools the monitoring and mentoring is even more strategically defined. In a school where they are trying to improve the number of pupils who get five A*–C grades at GCSE it might be used to identify those who are on the C/D borderline. Their subject teachers will have identified these pupils by indicating they had the potential to get a C+ grade but were currently working at a D grade or even below. These pupils can be supported in a number of ways:

- They may be sent on intense revision courses that are organised within schools or in neighbouring Further Education (FE) colleges.

- They may be mentored and supported by pastoral teams who help identify individual problems and put in place strategies to help pupils organise themselves, complete outstanding coursework and provide them with revision strategies and techniques to ensure they attain their potential. In serious cases it may be necessary to reduce their GCSE entry by allowing the pupil to withdraw from a subject that they are not going to achieve a positive outcome in and use that gained time to catch up on the others. This is usually a strategy of last resort.

- Parents and pupils will be invited to meet with the pastoral teams to discuss individual progress and ensure that every party involved realises what needs to be done to ensure a successful outcome with the pupil attaining at or above their potential.

This type of mentoring is now more common in primary schools where under-achievement has been recognised in pupils as young as 7 years of age.

Another use of data is to identify those pupils who schools want to achieve level 3 in science, maths and English at the end of Key Stage 1, or level 4 at the end of Key Stage 2, or level 5 at the end of Key Stage 3. When pupils achieve these levels across the three subjects the pupil is said to have achieved the core subject indicator (CSI).

The CSI is an important indicator of how well a school is doing in preparing pupils in the three important subjects of maths, science and English. It is the figure arrived at when the number of pupils gaining a level 3 at Key Stage 1 (English/maths/science), a level 4 at Key Stage 2 or a level 5 at Key Stage 3 is calculated as a percentage of the total cohort.

In some schools a lot of work is done to identify pupils who should get the CSI but who may need extra help in one of the subject areas. Where this occurs schools put in place subject-specific support to try to get pupils to attain this target. This is a good example of a very specific use of data to track progress and a customised intervention targeted at an individual for a clearly defined and measurable reason.

How to use data to identify pupils who need enrichment and support

Data is now routinely used to determine those pupils who are succeeding well above expectations and who would benefit from support and enrichment. Some pupils will succeed significantly above the norm in all subjects and for such pupils it may be necessary to move them up a year group from their chronological age. In other cases it is possible to enrich them in curriculum areas that they excel in. Some pupils may be encouraged to develop their skills in certain subjects early. A primary school pupil taking a GCSE in IT would be one example. Likewise, talented pupils being encouraged to begin AS course modules pre-entry to sixth form. The problem is that to be truly successful there has to be some form of progression built in for that pupil.

More schools realise that they need to be flexible and cater for the individual needs of certain pupils. This does mean a willingness on the part of the school to adapt the curriculum and put in place teaching resources to enable this to occur. Schools have teachers who manage the education of the gifted and talented and very often this is the remit of the SENCO. Identified able pupils are set projects and work that develops their skills and fulfils their individual needs. More secondary schools are building in strategies to identify the gifted and talented and then to support them. This talent may be sporting or musical and again schools are

ensuring that pupils talented in these areas are allowed time and resources, where possible, to develop these skills. In some cases pupils have good 'people skills' and these can be developed through involvement in buddy schemes and through the work of the school council and charity committees.

Finally, bear in mind that where pupils may not be as advanced and where early entry is not right for them it is still possible to enrich their subject education.

Using data to determine the success of the school at all levels

It is possible to use information on the results of a school to determine how well that school is doing. At a simple level the league tables enable the public to judge one school against another using raw statistics such as the percentage of pupils who gained five A*–C grades at GCSE, or the numbers of pupils who gained level 5 in maths, English and science in SATs. This raw data is meaningless unless you know the quality of the pupil intake that the school is working with. For instance, consider the two schools in the case study below.

Case study

Data comparison of two schools – a lesson in not jumping to conclusions

School A

This school is sited in an impoverished inner-city area. There is high social deprivation and unemployment. Pupils come from a high proportion of single-parent families and the numbers of pupils on free school meals is above the UK average at 40%. Parents are mainly employed in the manual sector and few have had further education. This school achieved 48% of five A*–C grades in the GCSE examinations of 2005. There is a high number of pupils with statements of educational need and 25% of the pupils have English as a second language.

School B

This school is sited in a suburban area only a few miles from school A. There is high employment and many parents are employed in the two universities in the city centre and in the two hospitals located within a five-mile radius.

→

249

Over 70% of parents have had experience of further education and most of them work in white-collar occupations. The school has only about 10% of pupils on free school meals. This school achieved 55% of five A*–C grades at GCSE in the 2005 examinations. The number of pupils with statements of educational need is well below the UK average and only 5% of the pupils have English as a second language.

The bald statistics

Bald statistics suggest that school B is outperforming school A, which it is. However, the question should be: Are they adding significant value to their intake? With an intake like that of school B it is likely that these pupils have the potential, due to their background and supportive parents, to achieve at a much higher level than they are currently. In this case school B is significantly *underperforming*. In comparison, school A is overperforming as it has added considerable value to its intake in order to get the percentage of passes at GCSE.

When inspection teams visit schools they look at the raw statistics as a starting point only. However, inspection teams (and in fact schools) are able to get more information than this in the form of benchmarking data. It is benchmarking data that really provide information about a school's progress. They not only tell a school how it is doing in relation to the school next door, which is often a meaningless comparison (take schools A and B in the case study for instance), but also allow it to compare progress with schools all over the country that are similar in size, ethnic mix, numbers on free school meals and so on. This benchmarking allows schools to compare how they are doing in very specific ways.

Data comparisons at secondary level

At secondary level you can compare:

- the numbers of pupils who enter examinations at age 16
- the numbers who gain five A*–C grades
- the numbers who gain one A*–G grade
- the numbers who gain the CSI
- the average number of points each pupil gains
- the average number of GCSE subjects pupils take
- attendance levels
- the percentage of pupils with statements of special educational need

- authorised and unauthorised absence figures
- the attainment gaps that may occur between boys and girls in all subjects.

It is likely in the case of school B in the case study that if benchmarking data were to be used then this school would in fact fare badly. It would probably be in the bottom quartiles for many of the comparisons cited above.

Other comparisons

Benchmarking data can be used further to compare the efficiency of one school against another in terms of resource management. For example, data can compare:

- the staffing levels in equivalent schools
- the amount of money spent on capitation
- the number of pupils who continue into the sixth form
- the amount of non-contact time staff have.

Schools can also measure their success against other schools within their local education authority as well as the targets that they have set. Schools will determine targets for their pupils at the end of each Key Stage. Where schools are under LA control, the authority will also be tracking the progress of the school against agreed targets. Where these targets are not met then valid reasons have to be put forward to explain why there has been a failure to achieve them. In addition, schools can measure their performance at a national level. This is only really possible with examinations that occur at age 16 and after because of differences between the nations regarding SATs, etc. With examinations that occur at ages 16, 17 and 18 national data are available that suggest how the full cohort for a subject has achieved and it is possible to see how pupils have achieved comparatively across the four nations.

Schools like to see subject areas attaining above both the LA average and the UK average. Where this occurs schools are probably adding value to their pupils. Schools can also determine whether they are getting enough pupils achieving A* grades and passing extension papers at A2 and therefore enriching the most able in their entry cohort. It is also possible to identify how each subject teacher has performed with their class in relation to others in a department.

Looking at value added in detail

The table overleaf shows five teachers in a department, the numbers of pupils in their Year 11 class and the numbers of those pupils who got various grades. The

Data set for five teachers

Teacher	Student numbers	A*	B	C	D	E	F	G	U	Average	All average	Residual
1	27	4	15	4	4	0	0	0	0	50.22	47.45	+2.77
2	27	0	0	7	18	2	0	0	0	41.11	38.79	+2.32
3	27	1	1	14	10	0	0	0	0	42.74	42.99	−0.25
4	27	0	0	5	5	16	1	0	0	37.11	35.62	+1.49
5	18	0	0	0	4	10	2	2	0	33.33	29.53	+3.80

Data by subject

Subject	Entries	A*	A	B	C	D	E	F	G	U	X	A*–C	A*–G
Art and design	53	1.9	15.1	20.8	41.5	17.0	3.8	0.0	0.0	0.0	0.0	79.3	100.0
Business studies	58	7.4	22.2	55.6	7.4	3.7	3.7	0.0	0.0	0.0	0.0	92.6	100.0
English language	223	2.2	7.2	17.0	34.5	22.0	10.3	3.6	0.4	2.7	0.0	60.9	97.3
Maths	198	0.5	7.1	18.2	15.7	23.7	12.1	0.5	3.5	0.5	0.0	43.9	99.5
Biology	16	18.8	31.3	18.8	31.3	0.0	0.0	0.0	0.0	0.0	0.0	100.0	100.0
Single science	29	0.0	0.0	13.8	24.1	20.7	13.8	20.7	3.4	3.4	0.0	37.9	96.6
Drama	33	6.1	27.3	42.4	24.2	0.0	0.0	0.0	0.0	0.0	0.0	100.0	100.0

average column indicates the numbers of points gained by the combined named pupils in that class. This is compared to the points that the same pupils gained in all their other subjects together when those data have been averaged (shown in the all average column). If they have done better in this subject a positive residual is shown. So teacher 1 has added value to her class by gaining 2.77 points on average more than they achieved in other subjects. This is a significant improvement and is the equivalent of more than one level. The department uses setting to group pupils and you can see this from the difference in the average for each class, with set 1 (taught by teacher 1) gaining the highest average compared to the lowest set, which gained an average of 33.33.

The data show which teachers have added value and the one teacher who has not in this case, although −0.25 is statistically insignificant and only +/−0.50 is usually regarded as having statistical significance. This type of information is important and curriculum managers in schools are now expected to be able to interpret such data. In many cases such data is produced by the LA for schools. Schools are also expected to be able to gather information of this kind themselves and interpret it in order to monitor, evaluate and review their progress.

It is also possible to compare how subjects have done in relation to one another. The second table (opposite) shows the type of data that any UK secondary school can be given. It tables the achievement by pupils in one school in a few of the subjects offered at GCSE. Such data is compiled by education authorities in the four nations and refers to the respective examinations taken within their nation.

How do we judge which department is doing the best for its pupils? Do you judge the department against the LA and national outcomes for all pupils in the subject? For instance, the national figure for the percentage of pupils who gained an A*–C grade in single science was only 20%. Therefore, should we assume that this science department did well to get 37.9% of its pupils an A*–C grade? There are two departments that achieved 100% A*–C grades. How then can you compare these departments with others? The numbers of pupils taught? The numbers of A* grades achieved?

Here are the value added figures for the various subjects:

- Art and design +.81
- Business studies +0.94
- English +1.32
- Mathematics −0.88
- Biology +2.83
- Single award science −6.69
- Drama +7.78

Remember that value added is achieved by analysing the individual results for named pupils who took your subject and comparing this result with the average grade achieved in all their other subjects.

Value added figures really provide a school with the best indicator of success. Although on the face of it the single science result looks good compared to the national figure, the value added tells a different story.

Why not try this?

Think about what data has been referred to in this chapter and then find out what data is used on a regular basis in your own school.

● What data is available to the ordinary class teacher?

● Who manages the data in the school and who analyses it?

● Is the school data-rich and knowledge-rich or has it got access to a lot of data which is not being analysed?

● How are ordinary teachers expected to use data and add to it?

● Does the school receive statistical data from the LA?

● Has LA data been analysed for the school for a specific purpose? If so, what purpose?

Going further

www.infed.org/schooling – New Community Schools @ the informal education homepage

Reporting to parents – best practice

What this chapter will explore:

- Reporting on progress
- What makes a good report?
- Meeting parents face to face
- Making contact with home
- Reporting difficulties
- Review days – what are they?

Good teachers know their pupils well and are able to report at length on an individual's potential and progress in their subject area. This chapter is about how teachers gather the information on a pupil, store it for reference and then use it to report either orally or in a written format to a parent or guardian. It is intended to provide you with good diagnostic reports from the primary and secondary sectors in a variety of subject areas that will provide a benchmark for your own good practice.

Teachers and schools by law must provide parents with a full written report on an annual basis. At the end of each Key Stage the school also has to provide information about the levels that the pupil has achieved in all their subjects. Where SATs still exist pupils will be awarded a test level and a teacher-assessed level. Where these are different the teacher is expected to give some explanation as to the reason for the discrepancy. Both test and teacher assessment have equal status and are complementary to one another. The school is also expected to report on the numbers of pupils within the school awarded each level. Where national information is available this should be provided as well so that parents can see how well the school is doing in comparison to the rest of the country. School prospectuses are also expected to have this information in them.

Reporting on progress

Many schools actually provide more information on progress than expected and provide one full written report, access to teachers for a face-to-face meeting (parents' evening) and a half-yearly progress report.

In some cases schools provide more than one parents' evening. These might occur at key points in a child's learning, such as the following:

- *At the end of Key Stages* – both in primary and secondary school.
- *On application to secondary schools* – parents are offered help and guidance on their applications.
- *In Year 7* – when new pupils and their parents will meet with form teachers to discuss how pupils have settled and to highlight any issues that need addressing.
- *At the end of Key Stage 3* (and prior to options choices being made) – when careers advice will also be available.
- *In the middle of Year 11* – to discuss coursework in particular and progress in the subjects (many schools have two parents' evenings in years where pupils will be externally assessed either at age 16 or 18).
- *To discuss university entrance procedures* – allowing parents to ask questions about finance, etc.

Some agencies such as the Basic Skills Agency insist that if schools are to be awarded the Basic Skills Quality Mark then parents must be given at least three reports on progress throughout any one year. These need not all be written but can include face-to-face discussions.

What makes a good report?

One word can be used to answer this question – knowledge. A teacher delivers a programme of study through a course of lessons. As the lessons are being delivered and the pupils are learning, evidence of this learning is being compiled. This evidence may be transitory – through oral questions and answers, discussions and practical work such as that found in subjects like drama or physical education. It will also be seen in practical outcomes, like the making of a product in some subjects or in the written work of pupils in others. Therefore good teachers should also be good assessors. Delivering good-quality lessons where pupils are thought to be learning is not good enough. The teacher must *ensure* that learning has occurred by assessing the quality of the outcomes from that lesson – no matter what the format. In addition, some recording of this outcome should take place and the data added to on a regular basis. These records should be manageable and should be in line with school and department policy. They may also take account of other teachers' assessments if a class is shared.

A report is a statement that imparts this knowledge of the learning outcomes. It shows that a teacher has looked at the programme of study and has taken from it critical criteria that the pupil has had to meet to succeed in that subject. The teacher reports on this progress over a set period of time and the report refers specifically to this progress. The report encapsulates, for a parent, what the child has done over the course duration and how their learning has measured up to the identified criteria and the skills that need to be mastered at the time.

The report should encapsulate and state:

- what has been taught
- what has been learnt
- how the pupil has done in relation to the expected norm for a child of that age on that course
- what strengths the pupil has shown
- what weaknesses need to be addressed by the pupil
- the pupil's attitude within the subject area towards classwork/homework/independent learning/working with others
- clear targets for improvement that should be subject specific.

In essence, the report allows parents an insight into learning and ensures that they are part of a partnership made up of pupil, parents and the teacher/school.

When a report is good it is possible to identify the subject being described without a subject heading being needed. The description of what has been learnt and the outcomes tells the parent clearly the subject being referred to.

Below are examples of good subject-specific reports from a secondary school. Each of the reports also includes targets and comments by a form tutor and year tutor/pastoral coordinator.

Examples of good-quality reports at secondary level

Physical education

Course details

In physical education pupils have the opportunity to develop knowledge, skills and understanding selected from the areas of experience in physical education, including sport and exercise activities. They are taught to plan, perform, monitor and evaluate a safe and effective health-related exercise programme that meets their personal needs and preferences.

Effort: A

Comments

X is able to produce the skills required in the game of basketball with control, accuracy and confidence. During the basketball lessons he has been able to evaluate and analyse both his performance and that of others in the team. This year he is helping to organise a competition that is running through the year. Through this he has developed good leadership skills and communication skills.

Art and design

Course details

● Pupils should research by recording their observations, experiences and ideas (AO1) 25%.

● They should analyse and evaluate images, objects and artefacts made by other artists, designers and craftworkers (AO2) 25%.

● They should develop and explore ideas using a variety of media in a creative way (AO3) 25%.

● They should make a personal response (artwork) showing the connections with their chosen artists or culture (AO4) 25%.

Target grade C

Currently working at D Paper Tier GCSE

Effort: B

Completion of homework: C

→

Comments

X has been working on completing Unit 2 this term. She is able to use a sketchbook to record information on the chosen theme of man-made objects and architecture. More time needs to be spent improving drawing skills. She could show another still life at the start of her project. She has some good ideas but needs to increase the amount of work she does. She could also use the PC to make Chirico landscapes by scanning her photos and drawings and manipulating them together. Thorough preparation needs to be carried out for the mock examination. Extra effort both at home and in school should ensure the target grade is met.

Targets

Complete more work at home and in school. Experiment with a wider range of media such as collage and pastel or print. Meet all deadlines.

Technology

In this course students display capability of designing and making products, related to their chosen area of design and technology. Throughout the course students will be taught knowledge, skills and understanding through product analysis, techniques and skills related to their chosen speciality, and design and make assignments.

At the end of the course, students can be awarded up to 60% for their coursework project and 40% in the terminal examinations (GCSE) or 80%/20% (entry level).

Target grade 2

Currently working at grade 2 Paper Tier Entry level

Effort: B

Comments

So far this year in technology the group have been developing their drawing skills, producing plan and elevation drawings of the tables they are currently manufacturing in class. They have also been producing some good illustrations of their tables using CAD software on the computers.

X has been working well this year but some absences recently have seriously affected his progress. He must catch up with his design work. He is very capable practically and the standard of his finished work is high.

➜

English

English GCSE and Entry level pupils develop: speaking and listening skills; communication skills; comprehension and extended written responses to literary, media and non-fiction texts; and writing in a variety of style and forms.

GCSE Speaking and listening assessment 20%

Written coursework (4 assignments) 20%; two examinations 60%

Entry level coursework 70%; examinations 30%

GCSE English literature – The study of literary texts from all three genres: poetry, prose and drama. Pupils study a wide range of pre- and post-1914 poetry, drama and prose texts. The study of the texts includes close analysis of plot, characterisation, themes, structure and style, pursuing literary argument, empathetic responses and comparisons between texts.

Written coursework 30%; examinations 70%

Target grade B

Currently working at C Paper Higher

Effort: B

Completion of homework: B

Comments

X has worked well this year and has successfully completed all the coursework required. X writes fluently showing sound basic skills. Work is paragraphed and for the most part punctuated accurately, though she needs to edit finished work carefully to ensure accuracy. X reads fluently showing good understanding of characters and their motives. She responds to literary and non-literary texts showing some understanding of author purpose but her ideas could be more fully supported with further textual evidence. X is able to comment on aspects of style within a text and writes for a variety of audiences. She is a good oral speaker contributing with thought to class discussions on contemporary issues.

Using and recording data for reports

In order to write reports like these teachers need to keep detailed records of pupils' progress against the criteria for the course. (See Chapter 9 for suggestions on how teachers should be storing information about progress and marks attained for homework and classwork.)

Some schools use standard recording sheets that teachers are expected to fill in and copies of these are passed to the line manager for this subject. This ensures that there is consistency across the school and that monitoring strategies are built in. It also allows a central record to be kept of marks, which could be for:

● standard assessment tests that are used in the department to chart the progress of individual pupils, to group pupils for learning and to set targets

● end-of-year examination results – again these can be used in the same way as outlined above

● end-of-term grades for attainment and effort

● coursework marks for individual pupils – this allows for monitoring of the teaching and learning going on in individual classrooms and ensures that the scheme of work is being followed consistently.

Meeting parents face to face

Most schools arrange a parents' evening for a specific year group and these are scheduled throughout the year. The evenings are usually strategically placed so that a parents' evening for Year 9 will occur just before they are due to make decisions about which subjects to specialise in at Key Stage 4. This could take place in March/April. Many secondary schools have two specific evenings for Year 7 parents. The first is scheduled relatively early in the first term and may entail parents meeting with the form tutor to discuss general progress and to ensure that a new pupil has settled into the school. A later parents' evening will be scheduled involving subject teachers and will focus on academic progress, attendance and attitude.

In primary schools two parents' evenings might be held for parents of pupils in Year 6. One might be held early in the year to discuss with parents the transfer to secondary school, focusing more on the transition than the individual progress of their son/daughter. The next might be late in the year at the end of the Key Stage in late June/early July and may be used to explain the *summative levels* attained by their child, the progress they have made and what the future might hold in their next school (summative levels are final end-of-course levels based on a summing up of all attainment). Whenever these occur it is important that teachers are well prepared for them. Parents are discerning and can tell when teachers cannot recognise their child and have little real knowledge of their achievements.

Preparing for a parents' evening

Ensure that all pupils' books are marked up to date for the evening so that parents can see samples of the work that their child has produced within the subject(s) that you are going to discuss. In primary schools, teachers may be responsible for all the subjects delivered; however, in secondary schools this will not be the case. In a secondary school a teacher may teach three classes within a year group and for a short time only each week. If this is the case then it is important that you are able to identify the pupil you are talking about. Some teachers have found it useful to make notes about the physical appearance of a pupil in their markbook. These should be short, concise and obviously non-discriminatory (for example, Hannah, short, blonde curly hair, loves yellow). This technique is especially good for those teachers who find matching names to faces a challenge. However, part of being a good teacher is making the effort to know all the pupils you teach.

Some schools expect teachers to have a standard mark sheet on show and this will indicate the marks achieved by a pupil in various elements of the course. If your subject involves various skills then identifying how a pupil has performed across the range is important. For instance, if a teacher were reporting on progress in music they would need to refer to standards in:

- composition work
- practical skills in playing an instrument or using voice
- basic skills
- attitude and completion of classwork
- aural work
- ability to work alone and as part of a group
- progress in line with norms expected for a pupil of that age and at that level of study.

Most new teachers have had an opportunity to shadow a member of staff at a parents' evening prior to being involved in reporting themselves. Parents are expected to make appointments beforehand or indicate that they will be at the meeting. However, some pupils purposely fail to tell their parents about these evenings and it is often the case that some parents will turn up on the night without prior warning, having heard by chance of the event. Therefore it is advisable to have the work of all the pupils you teach available, with those who are definitely going to turn up arranged in order of the appointments. This is time consuming but the evidence you are compiling for this evening will be useful and can also be used to inform the final year report for that pupil. It is worth remembering that this is one of the statutory duties of a teacher and it is this expertise, among other skills, for which teachers are paid.

TOP TIPS!

When preparing for and attending parents' evenings:

- *Have books and all evidence of a pupil's work to hand marked and with detailed comments and targets identified.*

- *Make notes about each child so that you have a rough idea of what you want to say to a parent. Even some experienced teachers do this. These notes can be useful to send out to a parent who couldn't attend but wants a progress report.*

- *Work out roughly how much time you will have to spend with each parent. Schools organise these events differently. Seek advice and plan accordingly.*

- *Be honest with parents. If their child is not working appropriately, is easily distracted or behaves badly then now is the chance to state it. However, you need to ensure that you have put strategies in place to stop poor behaviour or have moved the pupil from others who may be accused of distracting them. If this has been going on for a long time then in reality other interventions and staff should be involved in trying to engage this pupil in their learning. Parents do not take kindly to being told that their child has been playing up for a whole year without their being informed.*

- *Ensure that the parent cannot complain about your performance. You must follow the scheme of work and be seen to be assessing the progress of the pupils in your class. You must also be seen to be treating all pupils equally and respectfully.*

- *If a parent becomes rude, aggressive or abusive then politely ask them to leave and/or call for support from an experienced teacher nearby or a line manager. (This is very, very rare!) Avoid getting into an argument. You are the lead professional and need to remain calm and in control.*

- *Make a note of any action that you need to take following the evening. You may have promised to pass on information or to get further information for a parent. Make a note of contact numbers and ensure you carry out what you promised to do.*

- *If you are asked a question you are unsure about then be honest and say that you don't know but will find out. Either do so by asking a senior member of staff who may be available to help* →

> *or say that you will investigate and that the information will be passed on either by you or by another member of staff. Take a contact number and add this to your action list.*
>
> ● *Your action list should be in your diary or in your teacher planner. Avoid bits of paper that can be mislaid. Experienced teachers keep diaries/planners as records from one year to the next, filing them securely.*

Making contact with home

Many schools use pupil planners. These are similar to a pupil diary and allow pupils to record homework and other important information. They are also used as a means of communicating between home and school, and vice versa. Teachers can record merits and sanctions in them and the reasons for either. There is usually room for parents to enter any absences with reasons and this helps reduce the pressure on busy parents. Ensure that where possible absences are authorised and that schools are kept informed about illness, medical appointments, etc.

However, it may be necessary or useful for teachers to make direct contact with parents and the only way to do this may be by phone or letter. Schools usually have set policies and procedures in place for this and it may be inappropriate for class teachers or subject teachers to do this without it being discussed first with the line manager. When writing a letter certain formalities might need to be followed. Ensure that a copy is made and that the letter's contents have been agreed with a senior member of staff. If it is appropriate for a new teacher to ring home then make a note of the important and salient points they wish to make. Make a note of the discussion held by logging it in a diary or teacher planner. Some parents have a reputation for being difficult and therefore it is useful to make sure that your intended phone call is not to a parent like this. If it is then make sure that there is a witness to the conversation by your side.

Reporting difficulties

Some children come from families where parents are separated or divorced and in some cases both parents will request a copy of a progress report on a child. Normally it is appropriate to accede to this demand and simply provide two

reports. However, in some cases there can be injunctions in place against one parent or another. It is important that where there is a legal restriction the school complies with the wishes of the court. In some cases pupils may be in foster care but it may be appropriate for the real parent to be given a copy of any reports provided on the progress of the pupil. Pupils can be in care for a number of reasons, including the illness of a single parent. It may be the case that the parent is still very involved in the life of their child but physically unable to look after them. This is why it is normal for a school to have someone in charge of the reporting procedures for the school. They will be aware of any specific arrangements involving individual pupils that need to be dealt with. In large secondary schools the pastoral team will have information of this kind and the team will arrange for the extra duplication of reports. These will be passed on to the form tutor for distribution. Dealing with issues like these needs sensitivity. Form tutors and pastoral teams encourage pupils to get parents to write in if they want an extra report.

In some cases the parents may not speak English. Though it is not possible to translate a whole report, it may be possible for a summary of the report to be passed on verbally through ethnic minority language staff or community workers.

Review days – what are they?

Some schools now have something called review days. This is a day when a form tutor or class teacher will spend time with their own pupils discussing their overall progress in all subjects and negotiating SMART targets with them. The word SMART stands for specific, measurable, achievable, realistic and time-related. How individual schools prepare and organise these varies, but the usual practice is as follows:

● The school calendars a review week for a certain year group. During this week all subject teachers discuss with each pupil the progress they are making.

● In order to do this schools may have a ladder to learning placed in a pupil's book. This shows in pupil-friendly terms what learning goals/level they have achieved in this subject and how and what they need to do to achieve the next learning goal.

● Schools often share the 'big picture' to learning with pupils and this may be placed at the front of their exercise books. In this way, the pupils are able to see what work they will complete over the course of a month, half-term or term, and how this work will add to their learning ladder.

- Once a pupil has completed their review week, they will have a list of targets that are subject specific. These are recorded and shared with the form tutor, who is in a position to see how the pupil is doing across all subjects.

- Pupils who are at risk of underachieving are referred to the head of year/ progress manager; they may then be mentored by a member of the year team or the senior leadership group in a school.

- These targets, which may have been recorded in a consistent manner in a pupil target diary, are then used in a parents' evening so that pupils, parents and teachers can share the knowledge about future learning targets and needs.

There is no set format for organising and running pupil review days. In some schools the timetable is collapsed, whilst in others this is not seen to be necessary. In some schools reporting to parents is still undertaken by subject teachers, whilst in others form tutors now meet with parents to discuss the overall progress of a pupil basing their knowledge on the subject-specific data they now have. In all cases the advice given earlier in the chapter for preparing to meet parents is still relevant and vital.

The two case studies which follow show other ways of setting targets and managing pupil progress.

Case study

Pupil review days without impact on attendance

Selly Park Technology College for Girls, Birmingham

The school sees the value in ensuring that pupils have an opportunity to review individual progress and have clarity with regard to individual targets. However, the headteacher does not think it is appropriate for the school to be closed to pupils for those activities to take place.

The school ensures that individual pupils have review through the following:

1. Weekly timetabled tutor review for all pupils.

2. An assistant head leads on pupil review work at Key Stage 4.

3. A Key Stage 4 surgery is offered to pupils who may not be on track to meet their targets.

4. Every half-term the school holds super learning days for Years 10 and 11. The timetable is collapsed and pupils have access to computer rooms to look at their individual targets. Super learning days are staffed by the head and senior staff.

➡

5. All pupil targets are screened every half-term.

6. Currently the school is planning to appoint a member of staff with specific responsibility for assisting Key Stage 3 pupils to ensure that they understand and are enabled to meet their targets.

7. The school offers a traditional parents' evening run on an appointments system.

Ofsted report

The teachers go out of their way to encourage, support and assist the students to improve their examination results in Years 10 and 11, and students respond to this very well. There is now a stronger emphasis on making use of assessment to focus teaching and learning, and this has helped the students to know what they need to do to improve further. The school sets itself challenging targets and exceeded them in 2005.

Case study

Structure of the school day and use of tutor time

Wanstead High School

Rationale for the change:

1. Tutor time is not used effectively as a time to carry out academic tutoring due to the difficulties of managing a whole group while talking to individuals.

2. As part of the Ofsted post-inspection action plan need to improve student guidance and support in terms of learning.

3. To reinforce the school's commitment to raising achievement by focusing students as individual learners.

4. To reinforce the target-setting progress so that it is ongoing and action taken when student underachieve.

At present the school runs a fairly typical school day as follows:

8.40	School starts
8.40–8.45	Registration
8.45–9.45	Lesson 1
9.45–10.45	Lesson 2
10.45–11.05	Break
11.05–12.05	Lesson 3

→

12.05–1.05	Lesson 4
1.05–2.05	Lunchbreak
2.05–2.25	Tutor group period
2.25–3.25	Lesson 5

Proposed new structure:

8.40	School starts
8.40–8.50	Registration/tutor group time
8.50–9.50	Lesson 1
9.50–10.50	Lesson 2
10.50–11.10	Break
11.10–12.10	Lesson 3
12.10–1.10	Lesson 4
1.10–2.05	Lunchbreak
2.05–3.05	Lesson 5
3.05–3.25	Tutor interviews

The main changes:

- Tutor time to be transferred to the end of the school day.
- One 20-minute end-of-school session to be used for assemblies.
- In the other four end-of-school sessions tutors would meet for one-to-one interviews with students to discuss academic progress, achievement and related issues – probably two students per session, eight a week on a rolling programme.
- Those students not interviewed would not be required to stay and could go home.
- In reality many students would stay for after-school activities – those staff not tutoring would supervise what would in effect be a break time.

Schools are able to decide both how to manage the review days and what they want to achieve with them. In some cases it means form tutor and pupil agreeing targets already discussed with subject teachers, whereas in others the parents could be invited into this discussion. Where this occurs the schools have often dispensed with parents' evenings entirely and replaced them with review days.

Key ideas summary

In this chapter you have learnt about reporting and how to report on pupil progress, either through a written report or in a face-to-face meeting. Try to ensure that you know your pupils well and track their progress meticulously. If you do this you will make a significant difference to how well they do in your subject and your classroom.

Why not try this?

Consider the following questions:

- How do the teachers you have worked with store data and record pupil progress?
- How do they determine how well a child is doing both against criteria for each subject and other pupils?
- Are there standard recording sheets used within the school or department?
- Do the reports include information about the strengths and weaknesses of the pupil in the subject?
- Do the reports include targets for improvement?
- How are parents' evenings arranged?
- Do teachers show marked pupils' work to parents?
- Do the teachers prepare some comments beforehand that they will share with parents?
- Who is in charge of reporting arrangements in the school?
- Who arranges for duplicate reports to be made and distributed?

Part
5

The pastoral programme and the curriculum

The role of the form tutor and pastoral team

What this chapter will explore:

- The pastoral system
- What does a good form tutor do?
- What is the role of the pastoral line manager?
- The role of the Key Stage manager
- Teaching and learning responsibility allowances

As well as being employed as a classroom teacher all teachers are involved in looking after the pastoral welfare of the pupils in a school. This chapter is about what that role entails and how staff are generally involved in the pastoral welfare of pupils. Good schools have strong pastoral systems and teams. This chapter sets out how these work and who does what within the pastoral framework.

The formal pastoral curriculum of any school is determined by guidelines that outline what a child should be aware of and achieve by the end of each Key Stage. However, the way schools look after pupils on a day-to-day basis and cater for their individual welfare and well-being is referred to as the *pastoral system* of a school. Schools that achieve well and are successful usually have a very strong pastoral system that supports other systems at work in the school and cares for the well-being of all pupils.

The pastoral system

The pastoral system has a structure that varies between primary and secondary school but in both the class teacher or the form tutor is the most important person in the system. This is because they are the equivalent of front-line personnel and will know the individual children in their class well. These class teachers/form tutors will have first-hand knowledge of the home circumstances of the pupil and will be aware of any changes that occur that can affect a pupil and their ability to work in school. In addition, they are able to monitor subtle changes in behaviour, presentation (here referring to the way a child is dressed and comes prepared for school) and attitude that could indicate causes for concern. The role that a form tutor/class teacher holds is a crucial one and enables them to build up a close and trusting relationship with many pupils. For this reason they may be the person to whom a pupil will divulge serious or confidential information that may need to be passed on to the child protection officer of the school (see Chapter 21 for more on the role of child protection officers).

In a primary school the class teacher will have the benefit of teaching the pupil for all or most subjects. This has advantages as the academic performance of the child is known at first hand. In a primary school the next person involved in the pastoral system may be a Key Stage manager (KSM), who is in overall charge of Key Stage 1 or 2. However, in smaller primary schools the deputy headteacher or another member of staff with considerable middle-management responsibility performs this role.

In a secondary school this is not always the case and a form tutor who may be with a pupil for the first five years may never actually get to teach them in a formal context. At this level the system may be more complex with a pastoral coordinator/head of year in charge of a year group. It is often the case that year teams will move up the school with their year group so a pupil in Year 7 may have the same form tutor and pastoral coordinator for five years. However, this is not the only model and in some schools a Year 7 team may stay in Year 7, building up links with partner primary schools and working as the expert team on primary–secondary transition. Some schools do the same with a Year 9 team where they are the experts on delivering options and

careers information to this age group. In a school where this occurs the Year 7 and 8 teams will rotate but Year 9 will stay in place. When this happens information about pupils will need to be carefully passed on to new form tutors and pastoral coordinators.

There are advantages and disadvantages to both systems. One advantage is the way that a team can build up expertise and build on that year on year when they stay in a particular place in the school. The delivery of the formal PSHE (personal, social and health education) programme may also be better (see Chapter 19). However, the disadvantage is that knowledge of pupils that takes time to build up can be lost if proper transition arrangements for the passing on of data are not secure.

In most schools data transfer is being formalised through the use of advanced IT packages. Baseline information gathered at the beginning of a pupil's life in school is passed on to relevant teachers along with Key Stage levels. In addition, other information about pupil attainment and potential as well as attendance, attitude and home circumstances is forwarded.

The form or class tutor plays a vital role in monitoring the progress of pupils in their class as they have an overview of how the pupil is doing in all subjects. However, the academic progress of a pupil is just one aspect that is monitored. The form or class tutor also gets to know the pupil on a personal level, learning about their family background as they collect contact information. They will know who lives with two parents, one parent or a legal guardian and will be the first to know if there are problems at home that the school needs to be aware of. In a primary school where the class teacher is also the subject teacher this information may not need to be passed on, but in a secondary school ensuring that subject teachers are aware of issues that can affect a child's progress is vital. For instance, pupils can react badly when any of the following occur:

- divorce or separation
- serious family illness of a close relative or friend
- bereavement of a parent, sibling or close family member
- criminal incidents involving the family as victims or perpetrators
- loss of a family home (e.g. through fire or bankruptcy)
- prosecution of a parent for child abuse
- being taken into care or being on the 'at risk' register.

All these are real situations that can and do arise and it is important to support a child through times like these by making allowances for them and ensuring that all subject teachers are aware of the issues. This is where a strong pastoral system is useful. It enables a school to support a child when they most need it. It also places a responsibility on the school in that it has to work closely with

other agencies involved, such as social services, health professionals and the police.

The role of the form tutor is changing and the workforce remodelling that is ongoing has taken the majority of administrative tasks away from teachers. In many schools this has meant that teachers will not give out letters for parents, collect money for trips and so on, but this administrative aspect is a minor part of what makes a good tutor. For more on workforce remodelling see the book's website, at www.pearsoned.co.uk/essentialguides.

What does a good form tutor do?

A good form tutor does most of the following:

- Ensures that pupils are attending on a regular basis and that they arrive in school on time.
- Plays a large part in promoting the values of the school and a positive ethos. Each school is unique and has an individual identity determined by the way it operates and interacts with pupils, one determined by the vision propounded by the senior team and the staff. The form tutor is a key part of that framework.
- Ensures that parents come to parents' evenings where possible and remain informed about their child's school and any relevant activities.
- Monitors the well-being of pupils, noticing differences in their health and happiness or a change in their circumstances. There is a reason pupils come to school hungry or upset or in a dishevelled state with clothes that are not clean.
- Counsels pupils about behaviour and if necessary uses the school's systems of sanctions and rewards to keep them on track.
- Knows about the hobbies and interests of the pupils in their form as well as any successes they have had outside school in sports or extra-curricular activities. Recognising and celebrating achievement, however small, is a good way of promoting inclusion and mutual respect in any school.
- Ensures that pupils in their class are keeping up to date with homework in all classes if they are in a secondary school.
- Is a good listener and mentors individual pupils who need help and support with organisation and motivation.
- Works closely, where necessary, with the head of year/pastoral coordinator or the next person in line within the pastoral system to support pupils whose behaviour or schoolwork gives cause for concern.

- Keeps the class informed about what is happening in school.
- Is a problem solver for some pupils who will go to them for support.
- Encourages children and develops their confidence and self-esteem.
- Monitors the social development of pupils, seeing how they interact and communicate with their peers. Where there are issues with this they will be able to get support for pupils who may need external help with anger or behaviour management, or support from the educational psychology service through an EP referral.
- Is a team builder to bring a disparate group of pupils together to form a cohesive group, ensuring that all pupils are valued and protected.
- Understands the school data held on pupils in their form and monitors their academic progress, thus ensuring that each child is performing to their full potential.
- Checks that pupils are being awarded merits or are receiving sanctions.
- Provides parents with an overview of how their child is developing academically and personally throughout the current academic year and through the formal reporting system.

UsefulWebsite

See the websites listed at the end of Chapter 3 in order to find out exactly what is expected of pupils in your nation and in the Key Stage that you are responsible for.

The form tutor will have a line manager who is responsible for the delivery of the pastoral curriculum in that area of the school. In a secondary school this could be the head of year/pastoral coordinator. Whoever the person is will determine what the pastoral curriculum should be for that area of the school based on National Curriculum guidelines. Like curriculum coordinators or heads of department, the pastoral team has the same responsibility to write a scheme of work that interprets the statutory guidelines.

The role of the form tutor as mentor

In many secondary schools the form tutor is expected to monitor the work of pupils on a regular basis and act as a mentor. Form tutors identify pupils within the class who may need extra support and will, over a period of time, monitor their books/files/projects/coursework. Their role is not to comment on the work

set by other subject teachers but to look at the work of the pupil and ensure that they are keeping up. Where the tutor is a mentor they will monitor the whole form at some point in the year but may give more time to some pupils than others depending on the degree of need. An example of a monitoring sheet that you may be expected to fill in is reproduced on the following page. Where this system occurs in a school, tutors will have monitoring files with data on their pupils. This will include Key Stage results, CAT data, etc. This tells a form tutor what a pupil is capable of achieving and their likely potential. (For an account of the personal experiences of a form tutor go to the book's website, at www.pearsoned.co.uk/ essentialguides.)

Tutors will be expected to monitor a number of pupils each half-term. In order to find time to do this they may not be expected to attend school assemblies and will use this time to meet pupils and discuss their progress. The role of monitoring cannot be underestimated and provides tutors with an insight into the progress of their tutor group. As the workforce remodelling takes place it may be that this role will be lost to teachers and will be undertaken by LSAs or other non-teaching staff who form part of a school's 'counselling' team. In fact in some schools this has already occurred. In future, in order for the form tutor to remain in contact with their form's progress they may have to liaise more with LSAs who also work with the class. Monitoring sheets like those shown on the next page will be even more important as they will provide a way of sharing information on pupils with the team responsible for their progress.

Name of pupil	Form	Date	Subjects monitored	Homework completed	Classwork completed	Literacy/ numeracy	Comments/ action
Lisa Rowe	7Y	March 06	History Science English Technology	In Hi/En etc not in science	✓	Lisa finds science and maths work difficult	See science teacher for support
Shafi Begum	7Y	March 06	All books seen	No	No	Basic skills are good and EAL support in place	Shafi needs more support to complete all his work in class and at home. Passed on to PC meeting arranged with parents
Steven Morris	7Y	March 06	All books seen	✓	✓	Excellent	On target

Example of a monitoring sheet

What is the role of the pastoral line manager?

The pastoral line manager plays a vital role in interpreting the curriculum guidelines for pastoral work in the school. They will write the pastoral programme, put together the materials and the scheme of work and ensure that it is taught effectively and appropriately. They will also monitor delivery and ensure consistency of standards and practice. Finally, they will review the process and evaluate its success as part of a school's self-evaluation process.

All schools are now expected to complete a self-evaluation report for an inspection team before it comes into the school. However, many schools have done this for a long time to enable them to have an overview of what is and is not successful. All middle managers review their area of responsibility and contribute to the whole school report on an annual basis. See Chapter 22 for more details.

In most schools the role of the pastoral line manager is now treated equally with that of the subject or curriculum manager. They are both middle managers with a curriculum responsibility – one academic, the other pastoral. The pastoral manager is in charge of a number of staff and will meet with them to determine progress and a vision for the future, taking account of any changes in syllabus determined by changes in national curriculum guidelines for PSHE. The effectiveness of the pastoral system is judged by inspection teams who visit the school, as is coverage

of the pastoral programme. Inspection teams will also judge the impact that the system is having on standards. The effectiveness of the pastoral programme, the system, teams and managers can be judged equally alongside the effectiveness of subject team delivery.

The pastoral line manager has the following responsibilities:

- Ensures that the pastoral team works well to deliver the programme of study that it has written and, like a curriculum manager/head of department, ensures that this is done consistently.
- Ensures, along with form tutors, that the school's vision and ethos is disseminated.
- Promotes high levels of good attendance, behaviour and achievement.
- Ensures that their year group or area of the school is achieving in line with data that they have and uses data to monitor progress and set numerical targets.
- Writes pastoral development plans for their area of the school, sharing the role of visioning for the future with the senior team.
- Contributes to the school vision for developing the effectiveness of the pastoral system within the school.
- Monitors individually targeted pupils' work in the same way a form tutor does and acts as a mentor.
- Liaises with outside agencies involved with any pupils with special educational needs within their area. This does not only mean less able or more able pupils but also those involved with the police or social services, or looked-after children (i.e. those who are not living with their parents but are in foster placements, etc.).
- Meets with parents to discuss the progress of individual pupils who may need support.
- Puts in place behaviour support plans for pupils at risk of permanent exclusion.
- Sets targets for attendance, exclusion figures, achievement for their year/area, in negotiation with subject leaders and senior staff.
- Becomes involved in performance management of staff within the pastoral system.
- Contributes to the reporting system of the school and writes individual reports, providing an overview of the academic and personal development of pupils.

How do we judge whether a pastoral system is effective?

For a system to be effective the staff involved will ensure that attendance figures are high or improving and this will apply to authorised and unauthorised absence figures. (Authorised absences are those that a pupil, parents and the school have

accounted for – e.g. illness, family holidays, hospital visits, school visits, field trips, extra-curricular activities. Unauthorised absences are those for which no reason is given.)

In any school the attendance figures should be over 90% and unauthorised absence figures should be as low as possible. The pastoral system should also contribute to a reduction in fixed-term and permanent exclusions and issues resulting from poor behaviour. The pastoral team will ensure that all pupils are adequately supported and that subject teachers are aware of and take account of any issues relating to individual pupils. The pastoral team ensures that pupils integrate into school life and where transfers occur between Key Stages or from one school to another that these are successful. When pupils who transfer feel safe and assured about what the next step is going to be for them, the pastoral system can be said to have succeeded. It is also successful when pupil information that has been gathered is passed on and used as part of the normal practice of the school. In addition, the system is successful when pupils within the year group or area perform in external assessment and achieve their potential. This will result from careful pupil tracking and pupils who are not on target being focused accordingly.

The pastoral system of a school contributes significantly to how the school feels as you walk through the door. Schools that are orderly environments – where pupils feel safe, secure and confident, where staff and pupils work together in a spirit of mutual respect and where the main focus is on teaching and learning – usually have an effective pastoral system in place.

The role of the Key Stage manager

The KSM is a role common in secondary schools and is increasingly being found in large primary schools. The KSM is responsible for pupils across a range of year groups and for the staff involved in the pastoral system within those years. In some schools this involves as many as 30–40 staff. The KSM provides an overview of a significant area of the school and very often is responsible for transition from one Key Stage to another. The actual process of transition between primary and secondary schools and within secondary schools will be looked at in Chapter 20. The KSM will oversee the process and has a vision for how it can be improved. In addition, they will monitor, evaluate and review the process and its effectiveness. Like all staff involved in the pastoral system they will be looking across subject boundaries at general trends in achievement, attitude, attendance and behaviour, and a significant responsibility for school performance lies with them and their teams.

The KSM will work with many agencies outside the school such as youth offending teams, educational psychologists, social services and family group conferencing

groups. They will also be responsible for many of the referrals that occur in schools in order to support vulnerable groups of pupils. In some circumstances their specific knowledge of the academic ability of a year group might suggest that in the future the curriculum plans for the school will need to be adapted to take account of specific needs. For instance, if a KSM working with primary partners identifies that a future secondary school intake will be weaker than usual they may suggest that more English and maths classes will be needed with smaller numbers to cater for more pupils with specific learning difficulties. This could also work the other way – a potential intake group could be stronger and more enrichment of the cohort will be necessary. In another case they may suggest that a Year 9 group is strong and may not need any special places on college-based courses available to those who do not access GCSE courses in Year 10.

It is impossible for a headteacher to know every pupil. The benefit of a highly developed pastoral system is that it ensures that the pupils are well known by someone within the school. This information, combined with what is known about a pupil's academic performance, gives a rounded picture of the pupil. The academic performance of the pupil is only one area that a school has to be involved in. The personal and social development of the pupil including how they relate to others in the class and those around them is also of vital importance if they are to leave school ready for the world they will become a part of. In large schools the pastoral system allows the school to be broken up into manageably sized units so that this information can be collected and all pupils' needs can be taken account of.

The higher up the pastoral system a member of staff is then the more contact with outside agencies they are likely to have and the more staff they will be working with. In addition, they will deal with the more serious issues to do with behaviour, achievement and attendance. Like pastoral coordinators they will be involved in writing programmes of study for the pastoral curriculum and will have a greater responsibility to ensure its consistent delivery. They will monitor both staff and pupils and will play a key role in performance management of staff. In addition, they will monitor parents' evenings and, with subject coordinators and pastoral coordinators, will ensure that reporting to parents is effectively managed.

Teaching and learning responsibility allowances

Schools have just remodelled their workforces for a number of reasons. With this in mind many schools have taken this opportunity to rethink the staffing structure of their school. In some cases they have appointed new non-teaching members of staff to support positions. One of these posts is that of the pastoral support assistant (PSA). PSAs work closely with the pastoral team of teaching staff to support its work. They may undertake administrative tasks that teachers

no longer do, give out letters, chase up absent pupils and organise meetings with parents. They may also work on a one-to-one basis with pupils in the same way that LSAs do. PSAs may help pupils to organise their work, ensure that they are in class when they should be and know where they should be. They may work with a small group of pupils on behaviour management. The role of the PSA is flexible and determined by the school. There is no doubt that over the next few years there will be more non-teaching staff in supportive roles like this who may act as mentors, counsellors and learning coaches to pupils (for more on the role of non-teaching staff see the book's website, at www.pearsoned.co.uk/ essentialguides). The advantages of such staff is that they are non-teaching and have a more flexible day as they do not have to be in a classroom to deliver a lesson to 30-plus waiting pupils at a specific time. They may also have been recruited because they have experience as counsellors, support workers, project workers, etc., and therefore bring to the school a wider range of expertise.

Why not try this?

Consider the following:

- Have a look at the pastoral system working in your own school.
  - Who writes the pastoral programme and how is it delivered?
  - Who has responsibility for pupil welfare in your school?
  - Are they regarded as having equal status with those who have academic responsibilities?
- Find out which outside agencies your school deals with on a regular basis.
- Is there a clear hierarchical structure in place for dealing with pastoral issues?
- Find out how it works.

The PSHE curriculum in our schools

What this chapter will explore:

- The PSHE framework
- Social and emotional aspects of learning (SEAL)
- What constitutes good practice in delivering PSHE?
- What is circle time?

Schools play a huge role in developing the whole child. This means not just providing pupils with academic knowledge and subject-based skills but also providing for their social and personal development. Schools endeavour to prepare pupils for the world they are a part of outside school. The teaching of personal, social and health education (PSHE) forms an important element in a balanced and all-round education. A successful programme of PSHE should ensure that pupils will leave school

emotionally mature, articulate and confident, with positive attitudes to society and able to play a greater part in the community and the democratic process.

Although the term is referred to as PSHE and includes the health element, some schools, documentation and websites refer to it simply as PSE.

The PSHE framework

The Education Act of 1996 (in section 351) states that each pupil should receive a broad and balanced curriculum which:

'Promotes the spiritual, moral, cultural, mental and physical development of pupils at the school and of society and prepares pupils for the opportunities, responsibilities and experiences of adult life.'

(HMSO, 1996)

> **UsefulWebsite**
>
> See the curriculum authorities' websites at the end of this chapter for detailed guidance on PSHE in your school's nation.

The term PSHE relates to everything the school does to promote the personal, social and emotional development of pupils. Though there are differences between the four nations – for example, citizenship is a foundation subject in the secondary schools of England but not in the other three nations – there are also many similarities.

Most schools have a written policy for PSHE and a scheme of work that is delivered by:

● class teachers/form tutors

and/or

● a specialist team of trained PSHE staff who deliver the programme of study
● outside deliverers such as nurses, doctors, the police, business people, etc.
● subject teachers where their expertise can be used to deliver certain aspects of the PSHE programme.

In most schools the PSHE programme is delivered in a number of different ways, all of which make up a cohesive approach to the teaching of the subject, such as:

● themed assemblies

● discrete lessons

● subject lessons that via their SOW cover aspects of the PSHE course (e.g. science lessons that deal with puberty and pregnancy, the effects of the sun, etc.; geography lessons that deal with environmental issues such as global warming; religious education lessons that deal with different cultures, religions, beliefs and raise issues such as tolerance; English lessons where literature stimuli focus on growing up, health issues for young people, bullying, abortion, suicide; and so on)

● PSHE days that are devoted to careers guidance, health education, industrial and economic awareness, etc.

● inclusion arrangements in the school such as class representatives on year and school councils (see Chapter 13 for more on promoting inclusion).

At present the delivery of good PSHE programmes in schools is inconsistent, with some delivering excellent provision and others not delivering any at all (Ofsted, 2005). However, in the best schools there is a detailed working policy with an SOW that clearly states what will be taught, when and how, and identifying resources that staff can use to deliver the SOW. In many cases schools use outside agencies to help them and form effective links with community police and health agencies, social workers, careers guidance staff, members of local businesses and industries. The PSHE programmes in all nations stress similar aspects that schools need to address.

What have the PSHE programmes got in common?

Most programmes have a number of factors in common, and these are described in this section.

Note that when aspects of the PSHE programme are delivered in different ways – i.e. through a subject area and through other methods such as assemblies – the PSHE coordinator will have this recorded in the scheme of work and this delivery needs to be monitored.

Interpersonal relationships

All the PSHE programmes stress the need for pupils to be encouraged to value good interpersonal relationships: the importance of family, friendship and the need to respect similarities and differences that people might have. As the pupil grows older the need for recognition of what makes a good parent is also a part of the programme of study.

Part of a community

Pupils are encouraged to see themselves as part of a community that begins with their own community but then moves outwards from the local to the national and global. It is also important that within the PSHE programme pupils are encouraged to see the value of good citizenship and to understand how important it is for citizens to understand the political and legal structure of the nation and country they are a part of.

Healthy lifestyle

PSHE programmes stress the need for a healthy lifestyle and cover aspects like nutrition, physical exercise, hygiene and health and safety. It is important that pupils are encouraged from an early age to take responsibility for their actions and understand the effects these can have on their well-being. Pupils are given knowledge in order to help them do this. From an early age they are given information about road safety, the danger of certain substances in the home, the threat from certain adults, the danger of overexposure to the sun, etc. In the new inspection framework well-being which will encompass these elements found in the PSHE programme will form a part of the judgement made on a school.

Sex education

PSHE programmes help pupils to understand how they develop sexually. Sex education forms a part of the statutory programme of study. Pupils are given information about how they grow and develop, puberty, sex and sexuality, sexually transmitted diseases, contraception and abortion as well as relationships. Pupils are encouraged to think about being morally responsible, about being aware of their own feelings and about how to behave in a relationship. They are also encouraged to keep themselves safe.

Emotional development

Through the PSHE programme pupils are encouraged to consider their own emotional development. They are encouraged to think about how they feel and how they respond in different situations. Programmes stress the need for pupils to be encouraged to build up their self-confidence and self-esteem and to learn coping strategies for dealing with stressful situations. Increasingly, there is further emphasis in this aspect to encourage pupils to cope with conflict, anger and to manage their own behaviour. Pupils are also encouraged to cope with the changes that will occur both at a personal level and in their progression through school. Coping with moving from one school to another, with divorce or bereavement are all likely events for children to have to deal with at an emotional level.

Spiritual development

Schools are expected to play a part in the spiritual development of pupils. Individually, pupils are encouraged to develop an understanding of values and through discussion to come to some sense of where these values come from and how society works to uphold them and why. They are also encouraged to think about their own beliefs, spiritual and otherwise. They should have knowledge of the different religions of the world and schools are expected to promote tolerance and respect among pupils for those whose religions and beliefs are different. Specialist teachers of religious studies provide a focus for this work within the subject scheme of work, but this aspect should be evident across the whole school within the assembly structure and in discussions that may occur in other subject areas. Schools are expected to hold a corporate act of worship every day and this should have a Christian dimension to it.

Moral values

Schools also have a responsibility to instil moral values, and departments in schools are often asked by inspectors how they contribute to the spiritual, cultural, moral and social aspect of the school. Every area of the school should be promoting values such as respect, honesty and integrity. Recently it was suggested that schools in England would be given a sum of money to encourage pupils to get into the habit of giving. This care and concern for others forms part of the moral aspect of the PSHE programme. Pupils are also encouraged to think about the purpose of having school rules and regulations, and the importance of working in a safe and secure environment where these core values are promoted. Pupils are encouraged to develop their own code of conduct and to make decisions based on sound moral judgement.

Study skills

Throughout school, pupils will be given support in study skills. The PSHE programme supports pupils by teaching them how to be effective learners and how to manage their own learning. It encourages them to identify their preferred learning styles and shows them ways to use this knowledge to improve their performance. Improving learning and performance is one of the key skills and as such pupils can also gain accreditation for this. Self-assessment and self-review are also important parts of this aspect and increasingly pupils are expected to set targets for their own improvement. Schools also stress that pupils are going to be learning after they leave school and the emphasis is on seeing school as part of a life-long learning process.

Environmental awareness

Environmental awareness is another aspect of the PSHE programme and is covered in some cases through subject areas like science and geography. However, when pupils get to Key Stage 4 not every child will follow the same courses in science and some may not take geography at all. Therefore, in order to ensure consistency and that every pupil's entitlement to this aspect is met, education about the environment also needs to be delivered as part of the overall PSHE programme. It is important that pupils are taught to respect the environment and understand the part that responsible consumers play in protecting the world and its resources for future generations. This aspect begins in the primary school, where schools might look at a local level at the environment, and develops into pupils having a global perspective on environmental issues. Many schools are also involved in sustainability projects of their own, which provides hands-on knowledge of how important it is to protect the environment and to consider ourselves as temporary custodians of the planet.

World of work

Pupils are encouraged from an early age to think about the world of work – industrial and economic awareness, careers guidance and work-related experience (WRE) are important aspects of any effective PSHE programme. In primary schools this aspect may focus on local businesses and pupils may visit local shops and factories to give them some insight into the world of work. Schools may also encourage outside speakers to talk about their jobs, and national schemes where parents are encouraged to take a child to work support this aspect. As pupils progress through the school the PSHE programme is underpinned by good careers guidance from outside providers as well as detailed transition programmes. Pupils are given detailed information about the changing workplace.

Work experience

At present pupils are expected to undertake some form of work experience organised by the school and much PSHE time is spent on preparing pupils for this WRE. However, as pupils have become more reliant on the money they can earn from Saturday jobs and more than ever are gaining experience of the world of work prior to formal work experience, concerns have been raised about whether schools need to provide this WRE. Increased concern about pupil safety has also led to calls for criminal checks to be put in place for work placements. There are two questions that are now being asked in relation to WRE:

● How much longer will this type of organised school placement be necessary for today's pupil who is often already involved in the world of work?

- How viable is it to organise WRE for large numbers of pupils if police checks become necessary?

Schools try to prepare pupils for the world of work, employment and adulthood by providing advice on how to manage their finances and those of a household. The aim is to ensure that pupils will arrive at the point of employment having made meaningful and correct decisions about their chosen career. They will also be prepared for the changes that occur in employment nowadays and will be able to make sound financial decisions in relation to managing their own affairs.

Social and emotional aspects of learning (SEAL)

In May 2005 the primary national strategy for social and emotional aspects of learning (SEAL) was launched in England. It is a programme of study that provides guidance, a framework and resources for the explicit development of social, emotional and behavioural skills. The study pack was developed over two years with the help of over 500 schools. It is intended to be used by primary schools who have identified that some of their pupils have problems understanding and managing their feelings and emotions. SEAL is intended to help these schools address some of the issues that prevent pupils from engaging with learning. However, it has been recognised that much of what is dealt with in the SEAL packs is also relevant to secondary schools. The materials are intended to promote positive behaviour and to encourage pupils to learn effectively. The pack focuses on five social and emotional aspects of learning: self-awareness; managing feelings; motivation; empathy; and social skills.

The materials include:

- a guidance booklet
- a getting started poster
- a whole school resource with photocards.

The whole aim of the packs is to build on the already effective work that goes on in schools by encouraging pupils to work cooperatively as part of a group, to keep trying despite suffering setbacks and to cope with conflict and emotional stress. The aim is that these materials will support the whole school ethos that many schools have sought to develop through their use of inclusion policies such as school councils, buddy schemes and the increasing use of circle time.

The success of the SEAL initiative in the primary sector was noted and it was not long before secondary senior staff were suggesting that such an initiative would be useful there too. SEAL is used to provide interventions and in the secondary

sector these have been used to improve attitude, attendance and promote greater engagement in the learning process. SEAL encourages schools to take a whole school approach to improving the emotional intelligence of its pupils. It helps to develop emotionally literate climates, ethos and relationships.

What constitutes good practice in delivering PSHE?

In January 2005, Ofsted published one of the most recent reports to date on the quality of PSHE delivery in secondary schools. The report found that personal, social and health education was delivered through discrete lessons as well as through the delivery of the national curriculum, tutorial programmes and assemblies. The report also cited work experience, mini-enterprise schemes and other initiatives that enrich the lives of pupils in school and develop them as individuals as playing a part in delivering the PSHE programme. The report was based on inspections in 60 schools and by referring to over 100 inspection reports.

Ofsted (2005) reported the following concerns:

- The findings suggested that the delivery of PSHE was inconsistent across schools with some schools ignoring its delivery in any form.

- There was a narrow focus in some schools with a failure to deliver information on financial management, coping with stress, maintaining good mental health and good parenting.

- The need to deliver citizenship as a foundation subject had in some cases eaten into time required for other important aspects of the PSHE programme.

- There was undue emphasis on giving pupils knowledge and delivering content, and too little time spent on allowing pupils to explore issues and develop their own ideas, understanding and beliefs.

- There was a tension between the role of the form tutor and the need to deliver the programme; on occasions too much time was spent on monitoring and target setting at the expense of the PSHE programme.

- Few form tutors had any training in delivering PSHE and this adversely affected the quality of the delivery.

- The most significant finding was that pupil achievement and contribution in this area was not being assessed and no account was being taken of what they had learnt and the progress that had been made.

- The quality of lessons in PSHE was not monitored as rigorously as the delivery of subject-based lessons; in many cases they were not monitored at all.

- Few schools consulted pupils about what was provided on the course.

- The majority of staff who are PSHE coordinators provided good guidance and leadership.

Although this report deals with the secondary sector it is likely that some findings would also apply to the primary sector. A further report, entitled 'Time for change' (Ofsted, 2007), highlighted the fact that although pupils' knowledge and understanding of PSHE had improved over the previous five years, there were some important short-comings that schools needed to address. It suggested that schools should make an effort to ask pupils if the curriculum met their needs. It also suggested that the major failing in all schools is the way that schools have failed to assess the impact of the programme on the pupils. Schools are well versed in checking how good the delivery of a programme is but have failed to evaluate how pupils' attitudes have changed, or the extent to which pupils have developed skills during the course of the programme.

What constitutes best practice?

The following points need to be considered when thinking about best practice:

- Like a national curriculum subject, there is a programme of study for PSHE that schools need to take account of when developing the SOW that will be delivered to each year group.
- Schools need to identify what can be covered in assemblies, subject lessons and discrete PSHE lessons.
- Schools need to identify who can deliver what and where the expertise lies in the school. Where parts of the PSHE programme are delivered by subject specialists this must be highlighted in the SOW for PSHE and in the subject SOW. Cross-referencing between the two is essential to ensure consistency.
- A detailed SOW identifying the aims and objectives of the course for each year group needs to be written.
- A coordinator needs to have responsibility for this SOW and a senior member of staff should have an overview of the whole PSHE programme.
- Resources for the delivery of the course and the use of outside links and agencies should be identified and written into the SOW. These should be regularly reviewed and updated as well as measured against any new additions to the PSHE framework.
- Teachers need to be trained to deliver the PSHE programme although best practice suggests that some teachers who have an interest or are specialised in certain aspects of PSHE are better able to deliver high-quality lessons.
- Pupils should be encouraged to evaluate what they have learnt and their views should be taken into account when planning, monitoring and reviewing.

- Monitoring the delivery of PSHE is as important as monitoring the quality of subject delivery.

- Pupils' knowledge and understanding of the issues being discussed and the progress they are making should be assessed somehow.

- Teachers need to have continuing professional development and training to ensure the effective delivery of the PSHE programme.

What is circle time?

Circle time refers to a method of working with children that improves their ability to talk confidently in front of others and to listen with appreciation to others' points of view. It has the benefit of being suitable for all ages and fits very easily in PSHE programmes because, at a fundamental level, it can be used for classes to get to know each other and for bonding purposes. As time progresses and the group becomes cohesive and less self-conscious it can be used to discuss spiritual, moral and cultural issues.

Primary teachers use this method of working as and when the need arises. Although they follow a timetable it is sometimes possible to suspend this routine to deal with a more pressing issue. Circle time can be used to raise issues that are causing concern. In one school, where staff felt behaviour was an issue, it was used to initiate a discussion about feelings. This then led to a discussion about respect and behaviour in later circle time sessions. This flexibility is not as easy to achieve in secondary schools, but circle time is still a valuable way of opening up discussions and allowing all to feel that they can have a valued opinion.

How should circle time be managed?

However old the pupils are it is important to follow a few simple rules. For any class it is important that they are encouraged to get to know each other. Therefore there are stages of circle time that need to be worked through before any teacher can use it effectively to tackle big issues.

The introduction

Like any teaching and learning that goes on in a school, it is vital that circle time is introduced and the learning intention stated. Explain that circle time will give everyone an opportunity to get to know each other, have a say about an issue and allow them to practise the skills of talking and listening. This will need to be restated regularly at the start of circle time until it becomes a type of mantra.

Getting to know each other

Arrange everyone in a circle so that everybody is visible to everybody else. Many teachers who use circle time like to give the speaker an object to hold, like a soft toy. Only the person with the object can speak although others can indicate that they wish to (or can say 'pass'). In early sessions it is useful to get people to move around first, by saying things like 'All those with shoelaces in their shoes move now', 'All those with pierced ears move now', 'All those who have watched the latest Harry Potter film move now'. Other examples include, 'Change places now if you hate …', 'Change places now if you love …', 'Change places if your birthday is …'. This acts as a warming up activity and also encourages pupils to move out of friendship groups and to sit next to a person they may not know very well.

Why not try this?

Circle time needs to be planned and it is useful to write down a list of questions that you can ask. Trying to ad lib this type of activity is not a good idea. This is a lesson and as such needs the same careful planning that is given to one with a subject base. Ten minutes is enough for young children as a start; for older ones 30 minutes is a good cut-off point.

Beginning to speak

The aim of circle time is to develop the speaking and listening skills pupils will need as they grow. Once established it is also a way of getting pupils to articulate a point of view and to get to know how others feel about certain things. Pupils will move to an understanding of what constitutes a 'norm' in our society and circle time should reinforce those values and standards that are important. No matter what the age of the pupils, encouraging them to speak aloud means the teacher being resourceful enough to break down inhibitions and develop the confidence of the group.

In early sessions pupils will be asked to end a sentence, such as the following:

My name is …

I live with …

My best friend is … because …

My favourite book/film is …

My favourite food is …

I hate … because …

I love … because …

Talking from the heart

The real aim of circle time is to get to a point where pupils feel able to talk about issues of real concern to them. When circle time is done well, pupils are not only speaking and listening but are also actively involved in putting forward a reasoned and rational point of view on an issue of importance to them. This skill is highly important and is one that will improve their ability to structure a written argument as well. Circle time also develops self-confidence and respect for others. It ensures that those who can sometimes dominate and take over discussions have to give way to those who are more reluctant to speak.

Establishing rules

The group or class can establish circle time rules but one of the most important rules is to ensure that no one uses circle time to get at another person in the group. There should be zero tolerance of this type of behaviour. It is also useful to use a focus sheet that pupils can fill in at the end of the session. These can be adapted to suit the age and ability of the pupils.

In many secondary schools circle time forms a part of a whole school model for delivering parts of the PSHE programme – especially in lower-school classes. Where this happens it is often possible to see a very visible 'moral values system' operating around the school. These come from the pupils themselves and are generated initially in the classroom (as in the circle time sheet reproduced on the next page) and are then passed up to the school council, where they become embedded in the school ethos.

Circle time sheet

Date . . .

Circle time today was about FEELINGS

These are our ideas about feelings.
We thought about how we feel when good things happen like having presents or going somewhere nice.
We thought about how we feel when bad things happen like having a row with a best friend or doing something wrong.

This week we are working on why it is important to have rules and how people feel if they are broken. We talked about how we feel when it is not good in the lesson because people are bad and then we can't do what the teacher has promised.

These are our ideas.
We should have rules that we all listen to.
If we don't listen then the teacher feels bad and we don't have a good lesson and we feel bad.
In our school council we should talk about rules and put them up around the school and maybe words like respect to remind people.

Sample circle time sheet

Why not try this?

- Access the appropriate website for the nation in which you are currently teaching:

  www.ccea.org.uk – Northern Ireland

  www.qcda.gov.uk – England

  www.scotland.gov.uk – Scotland

  www.wales.gov.uk/dcells – Wales

  Look at the PSHE framework for the age group relevant to your work. What are the attitudes, values and skills listed? Make a note of these.

- Who is in charge of the PHSE curriculum in your school?

- Have you seen the policy and the scheme of work?

→

- Have you seen any lessons of PHSE delivered?
- Is this part of a whole school programme that includes assemblies, tutorials, subject lessons as well as discrete PHSE lessons?
- Does the school have links with outside agencies that help deliver the programme?
- Does the school monitor, evaluate and review the programme of study and its delivery?
- Does the school use circle time?
- Have you seen any teachers using circle time?
- How could you use circle time in your subject to discuss an important issue?

Going further

Bliss, T. and Tetley, J. (1993) *Circle Time: A Resource Book for Infant, Junior and Secondary Schools*, London: Lucky Duck.

HMSO (1996) 'The Education Act 1996', London: HMSO, available at www.opsi.gov.uk.

Ofsted (2005) 'Personal, social and health education in secondary schools', HMI 2311, London: Ofsted.

Ofsted (2007) 'Time for change: Personal, social and health education', April, London: Ofsted.

www.circletime.co.uk – Circletime

www.standards.dfes.gov.uk – Social and Emotional Aspects of Learning (SEAL)

Pupil induction and transition from Key Stage to Key Stage

What this chapter will explore:

- Ensuring a smooth transition
- Induction and transition: good practice guidelines
- Supporting pupils making choices

This chapter shows how schools induct new pupils. All new students will have experienced a period of induction and where possible will be made as familiar as possible with the day-to-day routine and the teachers they are likely to come into contact with. Transition is also discussed in this chapter. Schools now gather a lot of information about pupils, and in order for pupils to move between classes, Key Stages or even schools it

needs to be collated and passed on. **This information provides schools and teachers with valuable data about, for example, a pupil's attendance, aptitude and extra-curricular activities. Many schools have strategies in place to ensure that teachers gather and transfer this data and in most there will be individuals with responsibility for this task. This chapter is also about how pupils are prepared for the next stage of their learning – which may mean making them ready to move from primary to secondary school or from secondary school to tertiary institutions.**

Ensuring a smooth transition

The aim of transition at all stages is to build bridges between pupils, schools and parents. There are three types:

● the pastoral bridge
● the curriculum bridge
● the loyalty bridge.

First, schools want to ensure that pupils transfer feeling safe and secure, confidently knowing where they are going to and who will be there for them, as well as what they will be doing. Second, the transfer is intended to build a bridge between what has gone before and what is going to happen in the future. When learning has already taken place, as in the primary pupil moving to a secondary setting, the aim is to build a curriculum bridge so that learning that has occurred is built upon. Finally, schools want to ensure that there is a built-in loyalty between the parents and their chosen school. Along with this is the need for a secondary school to build up the confidence of a partner primary school so that the primary believes that this secondary school will provide a vital next step for their primary leavers.

Induction and transition: good practice guidelines

Moving from primary to secondary school will affect nearly every child who goes to school in this country. Some find the move traumatic and it often involves some level of anxiety, no matter how well the transition is handled. Remember that there are three bridges that need to be built in any transition and the most important one is to ensure that pupils feel safe, happy and excited about the move to secondary school. This is the pastoral bridge and the transition pastoral team will be working to ensure that pupils do feel safe and secure.

Some secondary schools have recognised partner primary schools and pupils may be expected to progress to that secondary school. However, pressure on certain schools for places and parental choice do not always mean this will happen. Wherever a child is moving to there will be some established form of contact between the two schools. Etiquette is such that secondary schools are encouraged to formalise contacts with primary schools that are designated partner schools. The following strategies, if all in place, present an ideal model of transition encompassing all relevant good practice:

- Primary headteachers, the secondary headteacher and those with responsibility for transition will meet regularly in calendared meetings.

- There will be regular visits between key personnel including SENCOs. A Key Stage 2 manager and Key Stage 3 manager meet on a regular basis to transfer information about pupils and discuss issues as they arise. Information about the level of attainment of the new intake is vital as this can affect the way the curriculum is managed in the secondary school. The secondary deputy headteacher in charge of the curriculum can take account of a weak intake with more support classes, or for a strong intake by moving resources away from support and towards enrichment.

- Noticeboards in the primary partner schools contain information about events in the secondary school and regular newsletters to the primary schools inform them about life in the secondary school.

- Secondary school newsletters contain information on partner primary schools and their activities.

- Primary school pupils from Year 4 upwards have regular contact with the secondary school and will visit to play sport, take part in events put on by the secondary school (e.g. drama productions, carol concerts, etc.). The aim is to make the buildings and its staff familiar to potential new pupils.

- Specialist secondary staff will help deliver parts of the Key Stage 2 programmes of study in science, information technology, technology, music, drama and physical education. This can happen in any subject area but many primary schools identify these curriculum areas as ones that can cause them problems owing to the lack of specialist facilities, such as science laboratories, or the absence of specialist staff. Secondary staff in these subjects will gain information about what has been covered in the primary school and what needs to happen next to present a challenge to excited new pupils eager to learn.

- There will be regular visits to the primary school by secondary pupils involved in the buddy scheme so that new pupils have older pupils to support them. They normally work with the Year 6 pupils to build up friendship groups and reassure them about the myths that surround the move from primary to secondary school. However, buddies may also write and illustrate stories,

taking them to read to nursery and reception classes. They may also work on numeracy with young pupils.

● There will be specialist insets delivered to primary schools by secondary experts and vice versa. Primary schools have smaller budgets than secondary schools and in the summer term, when Years 11–13 are involved in external examinations, primary schools and secondary schools can combine to share valuable resources. This builds up an important loyalty bridge.

● A newly emerging innovation has been the 'blog' set up by the secondary school and intended to encourage partner primary school children to set up a dialogue with pupils in Year 7. These blogs allow nervous Year 6 pupils to ask questions about their new school and have any fears allayed.

Such strategies have many advantages. For example, one primary school wanted to deliver a full-day African drumming inset that would have cost them £400. This information came to light in a scheduled meeting between primary and secondary senior staff. Their partner secondary school had a music teacher who was an African drum specialist and offered to deliver the course for free.

Combining to share resources

Below are examples of the kind of strategies currently used by some schools to ease transition:

● Primary colleagues will deliver inset to secondary teachers on the use of key skills in their everyday classroom teaching and the varied teaching methods used at primary level that could be used at secondary level.

● There will be an open day at the secondary school for all interested pupils from any school.

● There will be induction days for all potential pupils providing taster programmes of study.

● Teachers from the secondary school core subject teaching team will visit partner primary schools to deliver sample lessons to Year 5 and 6 pupils or to team teach. This ensures that potential pupils get to know some of their new teachers before arrival in the new school.

● Teachers from the primary school will visit the secondary school to teach former pupils now in Year 7.

● Primary and secondary schools will share schemes of work, ensuring that pupils are not repeating work already done but that the new school is presenting the pupils with a challenge. This is not easy when a school may take pupils from, say, 26 different schools but only six are partner schools. Etiquette is important in relationships between primary and secondary schools and finding out what is taught in a primary school that is not a partner is sometimes difficult.

- There will be information sharing about the pastoral programme and its delivery.

- There will be information sharing about school policies and school councils. If a partner school has spent a lot of time developing pupils in a certain way – for instance building up their self-assessment skills – a secondary school will wish to build on this where possible. If another school has a well-established school council and pupils coming from there could be valuably used in the new secondary school council then this is also worth knowing. Information transfer is not just about the pupil – it is about the school as well.

- The Key Stage 3 manager will produce a booklet for secondary staff that contains detailed information on all pupils. This includes academic achievement, medical history, attendance history, extra-curricular achievements, support needed or in place, etc. This is added to throughout the year as more information is gathered and forms the base-line information for the secondary school and its staff.

Remember that the above is the ideal and not all primary and secondary schools will put in place all of these strategies. However, many of these initiatives will be common in transition arrangements. In addition to the above, all primary schools will use their pastoral programme to discuss issues that arise on transfer such as making new friends, preparing for change and making decisions. Thus the pastoral programme is used to support pupils through this transition. (A transition case study from Bishop Gore School can be found on the book's website, at www.pearsoned.co.uk/essentialguides.) Many secondary schools stagger the start of the new academic year. They may have only Year 7 and Year 12 pupils in school and put on a specific induction day for each group. This enables form groups to get to know each other and for the Year 7 pupils to get to know the school when it is not full.

Case study

Bridging the gap

How do you bridge the curriculum gap when your intake comes from 26 primary schools? In order to ensure that teachers are provided with useful information about new pupils, one school provides all new pupils with a bridging pack. This pack contains work in English, maths, science and history. It also has free coloured pencils, pens, a rubber, ruler and pencil sharpener and a free exercise book that has ruled pages and blank pages. Pupils also receive Basic Skills Agency cards with the times tables on them and information about spelling rules. The Parent–Teachers' Association →

(PTA) in the secondary school pays for the packs that replace some of the curriculum bridging that would normally occur but cannot when so many schools are involved.

All pupils are given these packs to take home on their induction day in July and the work has to be completed over the summer holiday. The work is differentiated and pupils get merits for its completion, its quality, etc. The tasks include the type of work that has been done in the primary school and should ensure that skills are not lost over the six-week break. Pupils are expected to keep a diary of their summer holiday and they are encouraged to include postcards or pictures in their exercise book and to illustrate it in any way they wish. Pupils' work is marked using diagnostic marking sheets. For instance, English teachers use a marksheet similar to the extract shown below. To make things simple they put a name at the top of each marksheet and tick the relevant boxes. A class summary sheet is provided at the end.

☐ *Can this pupil punctuate accurately using full stops, commas and paragraphs?*
☐ *Can they spell simple words?*
☐ *Complex words?*
☐ *Can they structure their writing and sustain it?*
☐ *Have they got a mature vocabulary?*
☐ *Is their handwriting legible?*
☐ *Are there causes for concern?*

This enables the teachers to determine where individual pupils are on a learning continuum and they can then differentiate work for the classes that they are teaching from the outset. This school was inspected within one week of the beginning of the autumn term and inspectors were impressed at how quickly Year 7 pupils were settling and progressing within these subject areas.

Supporting pupils making choices

Transition occurs throughout a pupil's school career and the next large move is from Key Stage 3 to 4. It is at this point that pupils will need to choose the subjects that they will study to GCSE level. Although pupils normally remain in the same school the transition from one Key Stage to another is a very important

one, determining the next stage of learning. Many schools put in place a lot of counselling for pupils around this time and careers advisors and staff, through the pastoral programme, will stress the importance of making sensible choices based on interest, aptitude and present attainment in subjects. In some cases where subjects offered are new, schools will put on taster lessons. The following suggests the type of strategies that may be used to ensure that pupils and parents are informed and that pupils make sensible, well-informed choices:

- Options booklets are given out to all pupils and contain information about the courses on offer both in school and in other establishments. Increasingly schools use outside providers for certain courses, such as construction, hairdressing, catering and electronics.

- Careers teachers and the pastoral team deliver a series of PSHE lessons that focus on making choices and careers advice – 'Which way now?'

- An options fair is held in the school with visitors from outside industries, the army, navy and careers advisors. Parents are also invited.

- Parents are invited to meet teachers to discuss their child's progress in the subjects that they are thinking of opting for.

- Parents attend a meeting with pupils and the senior staff involved in curriculum planning and the options are discussed. Parents are free to ask questions.

- A series of taster lessons is put on for pupils who want to start new courses that were not offered at Key Stage 3. Visits to colleges are arranged for some pupils.

- Pupils' choices are scrutinised to ensure that they have chosen a broad and balanced range of subjects and that they are within their capability. Where staff have concerns, pupils are interviewed to ensure that they are making an informed choice. For instance, a very able child may want to take triple science GCSE but is equally able across the board and has no career in mind as yet. In this case they may be better advised to take double science at GCSE. This enables them to take another subject other than the third science. If in future they decide to take A levels in biology, chemistry and physics this is still possible. This allows the pupil time to make a more definite choice about a future career and enables them to take a broader range of subjects that may open up a wider career choice for the future.

- In an effort to provide better and broader learning opportunities it is likely that in future many pupils at age 14 will be offered opportunities to study some courses at local colleges and other schools. At present it is only the disaffected who may be offered an opportunity to study on an alternative curriculum somewhere other than their home school. In the future it is likely that ALL pupils will be offered alternative courses in alternative locations through a shared option menu common to a number of schools and colleges in one area.

> ## What do we mean by broad and balanced?
>
> Pupils are normally advised to choose a range of subjects. Pupils who choose triple science need to be sure that they are making the right choice, similarly those who choose mainly languages or technology subjects. If in future they find they are unhappy with this choice they may find it harder to remedy than if they had taken a broader range of subjects to start with.

Finalising choices and administration

Pupils are usually given a school deadline of the start of June to finalise choices. Once this is done class lists will be drawn up and resources for the courses will need to be ordered by subject leaders. The take-up for courses can vary dramatically from one year to another and a course that attracts 16 pupils one year may have 30 another, and this has stock and resource implications. In addition, some courses offered may not attract enough pupils and decisions may need to be made to withdraw that subject option. Running courses costs money and these days courses need to be cost effective if they are to run. All this occurs at the end of the summer term and therefore sufficient time between making final choices and the official end of the summer term needs to be allowed for all administration to be completed. Most schools now complete a timetable on computer and class lists and pupil timetables will be generated from the computer system. When pupils start in September they will be given an individual timetable with the subject, teacher and classroom clearly stated for each lesson.

Sixth form transition

Pupils who have studied to GCSE in a school may now stay on and enter the sixth form if the school has one. In some cases pupils will be attending an 11–16 school and will progress on to tertiary education provided by colleges. Whatever the situation, the transition process starts again with pupils being given clear information about the next step for them and the options available. The pastoral team and programme will once again fully support this process.

A sixth form produces its own prospectus that outlines in detail the subjects offered for study. Some may be traditional A and AS courses but others may be alternative qualifications that are unfamiliar to many pupils. Sixth forms often offer a wide range of subjects that may not have been available to pupils before, such as psychology, law, sociology, photography, media studies and business. They will also put on subject fairs with current sixth form students attending to explain what life in the sixth form is like. Many schools have a day set aside in Year 11 for transition where pupils meet a range of advisors, sixth formers and the pastoral team to discuss their options. In the case of an 11–16 school the subject

fair may take place in colleges and pupils will visit the ones that they may attend after GCSEs.

Some schools have now combined to deliver certain subjects that would not be viable if they were to teach them alone. These schools often produce a consortium prospectus. In most cases they offer a core of subjects in their individual schools but will rationalise the delivery of minority subjects (i.e. those that will not attract ten or more pupils). Funding is crucial in sixth forms and is often dependent on a subject being seen to be viable, thus explaining why schools try to rationalise delivery of some subjects. In order for this to work, schools ensure that timetables are consistent and certain afternoons or mornings will be blocked off for this rationalisation to occur. The obvious benefit is that courses are protected, along with small sixth forms, that may not be viable without this provision and would cease to exist. One of the disadvantages is that pupils like to stay in their home school and do not always like to travel to other schools to attend the odd course even when transport is provided free and door-to-door. Another disadvantage is that schools may lose the expertise to deliver an A level in a certain subject if this happens year on year. One way around this problem has been for schools to decide who will deliver subjects on a biannual basis and then the provision is moved to another school. This is a little more difficult to arrange but does allow all teachers the opportunity to deliver A level courses at some point. This can be an incentive for some staff who particularly enjoy the challenge of A level teaching.

Transition to further and higher education

For some pupils there will be another transition that the school also plans for – the move on to further education. The pastoral team of the school will work closely with careers advisors to ensure that pupils are well advised as to what options are available to them. Pupils will be supported in attending open days, filling in application forms, applying for financial support, writing personal statements for Universities and Colleges Admissions Service (UCAS), preparing for interviews, studying for examinations, etc. The school's pastoral programme will also focus very clearly on preparing pupils for independence, living away from home, managing money, health and so on. This is especially true of the move from the sixth form to the world of work or university. In many schools a dedicated team of staff will be on hand the day the A2 results are received. Their role is to ensure that pupil transfers from school to university are assured, and where difficulties arise they will contact universities to support their pupils' entry.

A planned approach

In all these cases the consistent theme is that the transition is planned and pupils are well prepared and therefore able to make informed decisions about their next move. The pastoral team plays a huge part in the transition and transfer processes

that occur throughout the life of a pupil. Senior staff in all schools will have a clear overview of the process and are very much involved at a strategic level in helping to plan the pastoral programme. It is the senior team in a school who will ensure that days are set aside in the academic calendar for transition and transfer issues to be covered with potential new pupils at whatever Key Stage.

The best schools are those whose academic subject and pastoral teams are equally strong and where as much thought goes into the planning of the pastoral scheme of work as it does into the academic scheme of work. It is important that the delivery of the pastoral programme is monitored, evaluated and regularly reviewed. Those in the best position to judge how well it has gone – the pupils – should always be asked to evaluate the effectiveness of the transition.

Why not try this?

Think about the school you are currently working in and answer the following questions:

- What strategies are in place to induct pupils into the school?
- Who is in charge of this?
- Is there a team involved?
- What transfers occur from Key Stage to Key Stage?
- What data is transferred and how is this done?
- Who monitors, evaluates and reviews its effectiveness?
- What booklets, if any, are used to support the transfers?
- What meetings are held and who are they with?

Attendance, child protection and anti-bullying strategies

What this chapter will explore:

- Attendance – a key inspection issue
- How does the Educational Welfare Service work?
- What strategies are in place?
- How schools use project workers
- The role of the child protection officer
- Anti-bullying strategies

This chapter examines the issues that can prevent children learning. In order for pupils to learn they need to be in school: new teachers will be shown the strategies used to improve the attendance of those at risk. This

chapter is also about child protection: at some point in every teacher's career they will come across a child who is at risk for some reason. Schools usually work closely with other organisations and adopt a multi-agency approach to this area. Every school has to have a child protection officer and their role is clarified. Further, the problem of bullying is considered. Every school has to deal with it at some time, both supporting the victim and dealing with the perpetrator and the cause. There has been a lot of success in counteracting bullying and in adopting overt measures to eradicate it as far as possible. Recent bullying events involving the internet and mobile phones will result in schools' anti-bullying policies being amended to include a response to such acts. Furthermore, laws are already in place that will support a school in taking action against pupils who carry out these acts outside school but where there is an impact on school life as well.

In order for pupils to succeed in school they need to attend. Figures are collected for attendance and schools are expected to achieve at least a 90% attendance figure over the course of a year. The reasons for pupil absence should also be recorded and where this occurs it is termed an authorised absence. Where no reason is given this is recorded as unauthorised. Pupils are expected to attend school unless there is a valid reason for non-attendance. Valid reasons include illness, a medical or dental appointment, attendance at a family wedding or funeral, or participating in extra-curricular activities. Although some pupils go on holiday in term time this should be an exception not the rule.

There may be reasons that are not immediately apparent for a pupil's non-attendance in school and this chapter explores some of these, as well as looking at how pupils can be supported by various strategies.

Attendance – a key inspection issue

LA performance for attendance and the recording of authorised and unauthorised figures are audited by respective national governments. LAs are subject to inspections, like schools, and attendance is a key issue for inspection. To have a successful inspection report an LA must provide evidence of the following:

- robust policies and strategies for improving attendance
- a well-established multi-agency approach to tackling truancy and attendance issues
- advice provided to schools for improving the attendance of minority groups like traveller children and of pupils absent due to bullying

- regular sharing of good practice regarding attendance
- systematic use of legal powers available to Education Welfare Service (EWS) (policies for prosecutions in place and truancy sweeps used)
- monitoring and reviewing of effectiveness of attendance strategies
- attendance being a key issue for self-review in every school
- rigorous monitoring of child employment
- improving rates of attendance in line with those of other authorities
- a cost-effective service.

How does the Education Welfare Service work?

In every one of the four nations there is an EWS whose job it is to ensure that pupils attend school regularly and that they get the best out of school. The EWS works on behalf of the LA in ensuring that parents fulfil their responsibilities and get their children to attend school regularly. The EWS may also be involved in monitoring child employment and ensuring that working children are of legal age and that they work no more than the maximum amount of hours permitted. In most counties one of the educational welfare officers (EWOs) will have a responsibility for this aspect of the provision. The EWS will also prosecute parents who fail to ensure that their children attend school. One person, normally the head of the EWS, will be the named person who has the jurisdiction to do this.

> 'The parent of every child of compulsory age shall cause him/her to receive efficient full-time education suitable to his/her age and aptitude, and to any special educational needs he/she may have, either by regular attendance at school or otherwise.'

(Western Education and Library Board NI, the equivalent of an EWS for Northern Ireland, www.welbni.org)

The EWS is made up of EWOs who may be regarded as educational social workers or advisors, but they also work closely with schools to identify pupils whose attendance is giving cause for concern. In some counties they are called education and social welfare officers and they are a part of the social services provision for that county. Some large schools may have a full-time EWO but many will share the services between a cluster of schools. In some areas the ratio is one EWO per 2700 pupils.

The EWO visits homes and works with families and schools to ensure that attendance issues are, where possible, resolved. They investigate the reasons for absence and can advise families about specialist support services. In primary

schools the EWO may work with a deputy headteacher or a teacher with overall responsibility for attendance. In a secondary school where there are pastoral coordinators for all year groups each may alert the EWO about pupils whose attendance has been poor. However, there will be a senior member of staff with overall responsibility for attendance. This could be a Key Stage manager, an assistant head or deputy headteacher. They will take the lead in monitoring, evaluating and reviewing the whole school strategies employed to maintain the high level of attendance or improve it where necessary.

All schools should have an attendance policy and many have strategies in place for monitoring and improving attendance. Though there has been much debate about the level of absenteeism despite interventions, many educationalists feel that the measures have been in part successful and without them the numbers failing to attend would indeed be higher.

What strategies are in place?

Many schools have an attendance policy. The policy will identify how the school ensures that attendance is targeted and how individual pupil attendance is monitored. It will also identify key personnel who are responsible for this task. In some secondary schools registration is electronic and pupil attendance is carefully monitored throughout the day through the use of lesson registrations. Pupils who fail to turn up for school are registered as absent. In some systems a phone call home is generated automatically, alerting parents to the fact that their child has failed to turn up for school. In other systems a person in charge of attendance (called an attendance officer) will ring home to find out the cause for absence.

In all schools parents are encouraged to ring the attendance officer/school before 8.30 a.m. to give a reason for a pupil's absence. This is then recorded on the system with a code being entered for a medical absence or illness. An attendance officer, who is usually a member of the administrative staff, enters the codes centrally. Each subject teacher takes a lesson register throughout the day. It is easy to see when pupils have failed to attend a lesson and this form of 'electronic tagging' of individual attendance has helped to reduce internal truancy figures. In addition, this type of system has been extended in some schools and is linked to an automatic system that generates a phone call home when a pupil who was present suddenly shows up as absent with no coded reason having been entered.

The electronic systems are on the whole successful but are subject to human error and if a teacher forgets to register a class then unnecessary phone calls may be triggered. Fully electronic systems that have a call system built in are also extremely expensive to run and rely on a stable database and working IT equipment.

Teachers with a responsibility for attendance will track individual pupil attendance and focus on those pupils where it falls below the norm. Initially teachers will look to see if there is a pattern to absence. Children may be missing school on particular days or at particular times. This may coincide with times when pupils have a particular subject or teacher. Discussions are held with pupils and parents to discover the reasons for absence and interventions are put in place. Where a school has the services of a good EWO then they can be used to work with the family to support them. Other interventions include amending the school week for some pupils who are bordering on being school refusers. This might mean encouraging pupils to attend for mornings or part of the week only until they build up their confidence and can cope with attending full time. In some cases pupils refuse to attend for other reasons: they may have problems outside school related to drugs or crime. In cases like this the EWS or the school staff may work with outside agencies like the Youth Offending Team and agencies that support pupils with addictions. In other instances, parents, for a number of reasons, collude with pupils and give reasons for absence that are untrue. It may be that they are ill and need support at home and the child provides this level of unpaid help; or it could be because the older child is useful in helping to look after younger siblings. Dealing with absences caused by parental collusion is difficult.

There are also pupils who fail to attend for no significant reason other than that they do not want to come to school and no amount of persuasion or coercion can make them do so. In cases like these parents are still responsible for their children's attendance and are liable to prosecution when their children persist in the non-attendance. Parents are usually given an opportunity to improve the attendance of their child but if an improvement is not seen in a short time then court proceedings can be instigated.

EWOs also take part in truancy sweeps supported by the police who have powers to pick up pupils found truanting but not to arrest them. Pupils are then taken to a central location or back to school.

The Learning House – helping children to attend

In some authorities strategies are provided centrally for pupils who are school phobics or lack the social skills and confidence they need to manage in school. In some LAs Learning Houses have been set up and schools nominate pupils who would benefit from this type of intervention. Pupils will attend the Learning House for a set number of days a week and will spend the rest of the time in their 'home' school. The intervention lasts for a term and at the end of this time pupils return to their school on a full-time basis. These strategies can be successful. However, some children who flourish in the protected environment of the Learning House, where pupil numbers are very small,

→

313

often need very intensive support when they return to school on a full-time basis. The Learning House experience is normally shared between a number of schools and they can be used for primary or secondary pupils depending on the designation of the resource. Teachers and teaching assistants permanently staff the house, not only delivering subject-based learning but also concentrating on improving the social skills and confidence of the pupils they are working with.

The role of project workers

Project workers work on specific projects. Their brief is different from that of EWOs and they take on tasks that an EWO would not normally be able to accommodate in their working week. Project workers are also provided by the LA through funding that is applied for and comes from outside the normal funding streams.

Project workers usually have training in counselling and may have social services training. They will always work with children who are identified as being at risk of non-attending or of being excluded. They may, for instance, work on transition projects with pupils who are moving from primary to secondary school. The pupils they work with may lack confidence and be at risk of non-attendance on transfer. The project worker works with individual pupils, spending time with them to gain an understanding of their concerns and worries. They can take them on visits to the new secondary school and can also offer rewards like taking pupils on a special visit or trip. Project workers are usually shared between a number of schools and work with a number of pupils over time.

The role of the child protection officer

Every school has to appoint a designated child protection officer (CPO). These are usually senior members of staff. In secondary schools it is usually a deputy headteacher who is responsible for pastoral teams within the school. In a primary school it may be the headteacher but this can cause problems if an allegation is made against a member of staff. In such cases another member of staff usually investigates and presents the information to the headteacher who then makes the ultimate decision about how to proceed. It is not usual for the same person both to investigate and to decide.

The CPO will have an overview of pupils in the school that may be 'looked-after children', i.e. those in foster placements or in a children's home. They will also

know who is on the child protection register. All these pupils will be subject to regular reviews involving representatives from a range of services, including the school where the representative may be the CPO or someone delegated by them. The CPO is also the person who takes charge if a child in the school makes a disclosure to another teacher, adult or fellow pupil. (A disclosure is when a child has revealed that something has happened to them that is inappropriate. Disclosures include information about physical or sexual abuse, or risk at home due to negligence for a number of reasons, including abandonment.)

The CPO must work under the direction of the headteacher and therefore must keep the headteacher informed at all times. In extreme cases of disclosure the police and social services need to be involved. All action will be in accordance with local child protection procedures. The CPO will also take the lead if a child is thought to be at risk for some reason.

The CPO has clear guidelines about what procedures need to be followed in a number of scenarios and if unsure can ask for support from the LA, social services or the police. However, if the CPO feels that a criminal offence has been committed then they must alert the police. In addition, if they feel that the child is at serious risk if they go home then they have to call in other agencies to support them. Every CPO has a file provided by the LA with contact numbers, and in all cases if the CPO is not the headteacher then they must keep the headteacher informed about all current child protection issues.

CPOs keep detailed records on the children they deal with and these should be regularly reviewed and updated. All relevant meetings and information must be filed appropriately and when inspections of schools take place the work and effectiveness of the CPO is reviewed.

Anti-bullying strategies

In 1988 the Scottish Office pioneered the first government-sponsored research into bullying in the UK. The project was carried out in ten secondary schools with a sample of 942 pupils who were between 12 and 16 years of age. The research showed that 6% of Scottish pupils had experienced bullying at some time or another and 4% admitted that they had bullied others. The research showed that more boys were involved in bullying than girls. The research also showed that some schools were far more successful at containing bullying than others. Further research suggested that some schools, despite the lack of anti-bullying policies, had for some reason managed to curb bullying to some extent in their schools. The location and social class of pupils or their parents were found to be insignificant. However, what the successful schools did seem to have in common were strategies that had been used in other countries where bullying was being tackled:

- These schools had been honest about bullying and admitted its existence.
- They openly discussed bullying and its causes.
- Teachers, pupils and parents were involved in putting together anti-bullying strategies and policies and were interested in making these work.

Since 1999 LAs have had specific duties to combat bullying. Schools *must* have anti-bullying policies and LAs must ensure that their schools comply with their duties. In December 2003 the Department for Education and Skills published an anti-bullying pack entitled *Bullying: Don't Suffer in Silence* (www.dfes.gov.uk/bullying). This was intended to give schools helpful guidance. Surveys of children and young people suggest that bullying in schools is more common than most adults seem to think.

A report by Ofsted in 2003 suggested that although schools had policies in place which varied in their coverage and depth, they were generally good. Their effectiveness tended to depend on the commitment of the headteacher and staff to keeping the issue high on the agenda and making the policies work in practice on a day-to-day basis. It was generally found that schools with the most successful approaches to bullying took full account of pupils' views and ensured that curriculum and tutorial time was given to discussing relationships and issues like bullying. Other features tended to include checking the school site frequently and ensuring that there were safe play areas. In some primary and secondary schools, for instance, areas are set aside that are strictly for younger pupils or, in secondary schools, for Year 7 pupils new to the school. These are in central areas where teachers are visible and accessible.

Where schools were successful they also had sound procedures for the reporting and investigation of bullying and spent a lot of time investigating when concerns

arose. Communicating with parents was also a part of the process. In many schools the circle of friends, peer counselling, learning mentors and outside agencies were used to support the victims and ensure that their confidence was rebuilt. These groups were also used to modify the behaviour of bullies.

It is important that schools take seriously their responsibilities with regard to pupils. If a pupil feels that they are being bullied and reports this then the school has a duty of care to respond. The perception by a pupil that they are a victim is enough and means that the school has to act to support that pupil and investigate the circumstances carefully. The pastoral team in any school plays a vital part in this and some members may have had training in how to identify and deal with bullying. It is important that all incidents of bullying are logged and that detailed records are kept of the intervention strategies used. Witness statements, where possible, should also be included and most schools keep named files on pupils who have been the victims of bullying.

At the time of the Ofsted report there were no firm national statistics of reported or proven cases of bullying in schools. Childline and other organisations have figures that indicate the numbers of young people who have contacted them about being bullied. Bullying was the biggest single reason for young people to contact Childline and in 2009 35,562 children were helped with issues to do with bullying.

The effects of bullying can be extreme with victims suffering from depression and anxiety. This can also result in their missing prolonged periods from school which is itself counter-productive as they lose their friendship groups and this makes them more vulnerable as individuals to bullying.

TOP TIPS!

What do you do if a pupil alleges that they are being bullied?

All teachers should be familiar with the school policy on bullying, child protection and other important policies and these should be re-read at the start of each academic year.

- *Take as many details about the incident or incidents as you can from the victim. Always date information of this kind. Tell the victim that you will see them later in the day when you have discussed this. If you feel the victim is at risk if they leave you then your duty is to keep them with you for safety. If it is the end of the school day and the victim is going to be at risk when they travel home then you need to ring a parent to come and get them and pass on relevant information to them. You must explain that*

→

you are taking it seriously and will, with advice, investigate the allegations.

- Try to work with a more experienced member of staff and discuss your findings with them. They may suggest you proceed alone but if you do not feel confident ask if you can shadow them and learn for the future.

- If the victim has given you the names of witnesses then you or another member of staff will need to interview them. Follow school procedures ensuring that interviews take place, where possible, in the presence of another member of staff or in an appropriate location. However, in sensitive cases like this witnesses may want to remain unknown to the bully or bullies and discretion will be necessary. You may need to find an office that is available and allows some privacy.

- If there is insufficient evidence and no witnesses then ask the pupil to keep a log of what is going on. This can be a small notebook that they record in so that you build up information against the bullies.

- If you think it is necessary you will need to contact the victim's parents if you haven't done so already and keep them informed about your investigation.

- When you are sure that you have enough evidence you will need to interview the bully. If there is more than one this needs to be done individually. It is good to get them to own up to their crime! Dealing with pupils on a one-to-one basis makes this more likely.

- Look at the school policy and seek advice as to how the bully should be punished. It may be that an exclusion is needed or some form of serious sanction. Warn the bully that you do not want them involved in any form of intimidation again. You will need to warn them that you do not want their friends involved either. Some bullies will pass the baton to a friend to carry on the bullying, others may be stopped at this point.

- In many cases this should put an end to the problems but some bullies are persistent and encourage others to carry on where they left off.

→

- *If the bullying persists it may be that you will need to use other resources. Some schools have trained mediators or counsellors and in serious cases outside agencies like the police will need to be used.*

- *The LA will also have people who can support you.*

- *To be wholly successful and to eradicate as many of the causes of bullying as it can, a school has to state overtly and repeatedly that it is against bullying and that it will not be tolerated.*

Schools that are successful in combating bullying take the issue seriously and investigate cases and causes rigorously. They also record incidents of bullying so that patterns can be analysed and keep records of both bullies and victims. These schools also have a very good buddy system in place and a lot of extra-curricular activities going on. This gives vulnerable children a place to go other than the playground.

'As I quickly learned when I became a head, dealing with bullying is a never-ending process and one that needs to be proactive rather than simply reactive. It's about being vigilant and taking every opportunity to develop a school ethos that rejects stereotypes, values everybody for his or her own unique self, and promotes the ability to empathise. Achieving and maintaining that fundamental shift in attitudes and behaviour is hard work and it has to involve every member of staff all the time.'

(Ofsted, 2003, p 8)

In many of the successful schools another key feature is the willingness to involve pupils in the process. School councils are involved in discussions and many schools undertake repeated surveys as a basis for a discussion about the issue. These surveys provide valuable information about the most vulnerable groups of children, the extent of the bullying and the range of intimidation that went on. Staff training is another important element. It is important that all staff are united and refuse to allow intimidation in their classrooms, ensuring that no put-downs of any kind are allowed. In this way staff present a united front in refusing to allow intimidation and overtly state that the ethos of the school is one that does not allow bullying of any kind.

Why not try this?

Consider the following questions:

- Ask to read the school policies on attendance, child protection and anti-bullying. Are there any strategies used in the school that have been mentioned in this chapter?
- Who is in charge of attendance and has the school got the use of an EWO?
- How many days a week is the EWO available to the school?
- How does the school support pupils who have problems attending?
- Who is the CPO?
- Ask the CPO about some of the issues they have to deal with.
- Has the school got a school council?
- What training have the teaching and non-teaching staff had over the last three years in tackling bullying?
- Is there a safe zone in the school for young or vulnerable pupils?
- How successful is the school at preventing or dealing with bullying as and when it arises?

Going further

Ofsted (2003) 'Bullying: effective action in secondary schools', HMI 465, London: Ofsted.

www.dfes.gov.uk/bullying – *Bullying: Don't Suffer in Silence*, anti-bullying pack; also available at www.thegrid.org.uk/learning/hwb/bullying/guidance

www.everychildmatters.gov.uk – Every Child Matters, 'Change for children'

www.scre.ac.uk – Scottish Action Against Bullying

www.welbni.org – Western Education and Library Board, Services for Parents, Students and Youth

Part
6

School improvement and continuing professional development

School inspections – what makes a good school?

What this chapter will explore:

- What makes a good school?
- The inspection framework in the four nations
- What is the purpose of an inspection?
- Self-evaluation in schools
- How should you prepare for an inspection?

This chapter looks at the elements that make up a good school and discusses how you should prepare for inspection – an event that causes anxiety in many schools.

What makes a good school?

In reality the most important aspect of any school is the quality of teaching and learning that goes on there. When the teaching is of a high quality, is differentiated appropriately to the needs of the pupils and complies with national programmes of study then pupils will engage with the teaching and progress. However, pupils are complex beings and good-quality teaching and learning needs to be supported by a strong discipline structure and a strong pastoral team. Inspectors will look for these aspects among others.

Attendance is another key issue that can affect pupil performance: in order to do well pupils have to attend for at least 90% of the school year or the school is deemed to be failing in this crucial area. Schools have a team of staff to ensure that strategies are in place to maximise pupil attendance and that interventions are put in place to ensure this occurs. This team could comprise project workers, EWOs and attendance officers (see Chapter 21).

Good schools are self-reviewing organisations and this self-review is evident at all levels within the management structure. There are common themes that run through the school development plan and these are also evident in departmental development plans. Monitoring is regular and rigorous and all plans are evaluated for their effectiveness – the school is data-rich *and* knowledge-rich. The school knows if pupils are achieving in line with expectations and results are evaluated. When issues arise strategies are put in place to address them.

Organisations that are successful are also consistent in the application of strategies. To ensure that this happens the school has clear written policies that all teachers are expected to follow and this is monitored by key personnel in the school. They will set numerical targets and will, through departmental development plans, be able to see how the whole staff can work to ensure that targets are met. These schools have clear strategies in place to monitor, evaluate and review their development plans. They also build in success criteria, like that of school A below, to ensure they have something clear to aim for.

Reflecting on practice

Clear aims and targets

School A: teaching and learning is our number one priority

Over the next year we want to:

● Improve the percentage of lessons that gain a grade 1 or 2 instead of a 3, when lessons are observed by senior staff or heads of department, from 50% to 75%.

→

- Ensure that all departments include in their scheme of work lessons that have more innovative methods of teaching and appeal to auditory, visual and kinaesthetic learners.
- See written evidence of this in schemes of work and evidence when monitoring classroom teaching.
- See a bank of innovative lessons develop in the staff library of resources.
- See a reduction of at least 5% in poor behaviour and fixed-term exclusions as a result of this.
- See evidence in all subjects of teachers helping pupils to understand how to learn and teaching them to learn skills.
- Revise the present teaching and learning policy in the light of this work and the evidence. This will be done in consultation with all staff.

In education these are often called SMART targets, meaning that they are:

Specific

Measurable

Attainable

Realistic

Time related.

Good schools are also well managed and the senior team and all managers have a clear, shared vision for the future. Staff and pupils feel valued and the teaching and non-teaching staff have access to good-quality professional development and recognition of their hard work. The school is fully inclusive and all pupils are provided with equal opportunities; the vulnerable are supported and the able developed. The school is well resourced and the budget is managed efficiently. Links with outside agencies are strong and the school has an established relationship with partner schools and organisations, and this is consistently managed.

Results are consistently above the national and LA average and the school is in the upper quartile for benchmarking. The school has many additional awards, such as the Basic Skills Quality Mark, Investors in People, Curriculum Awards and Careers Awards. The school is oversubscribed and staff turnover is low.

The inspection framework in the four nations

Inspections are conducted in primary and secondary schools throughout the UK, but there the similarity ends. The amount of warning schools are given, the time inspectors will be in the school, the time lapse between one inspection and another and the focus of the inspection all vary according to which nation you happen to teach in.

Schools in England get from zero to two days warning of an inspection and will be inspected once every five years if the school has been deemed to be good or better. Schools in this category will be asked to send data to assure Ofsted that they are maintaining rigorous standards. If a school has in the past been judged satisfactory then the inspection will occur every three years. In Wales, under the proposed new inspection framework, schools will have three weeks' notice and will be inspected every five years. Scotland and Northern Ireland are also inspected approximately every five years and get three weeks' notice. A possible reason for the difference in warning times could be because in England self-evaluation is an online process and it is easy for an inspection team to find detailed information about every aspect of the running of the school just by accessing this document. This information is not available in all four nations.

In some countries the inspection teams are made up solely of inspectors who are employed by the department of education in that nation. In England and Wales inspection teams tender for inspections and the team is made up of people who have undergone training to become team inspectors or registered inspectors. However, in Wales this is likely to change with a return to more inspectors who are full-time employees undertaking the inspection. Where inspectors are not full time then it is likely that the rest will be made up of teachers from all forms of educational background.

The reality is that in order to be sure about the inspection framework within your own nation you need to keep up with ongoing developments. It is likely that the lead time for inspections in all nations will be dramatically reduced so that schools have less time to prepare, as this has proved to be successful in England. The advantages are obvious. Teachers and pupils have less time to get stressed about the intrusion into their working space and inspectors feel that they are getting to see the real school rather than one that has had time to prepare artificially.

What is the purpose of an inspection?

The purpose of any inspection is to ensure that standards of teaching and learning in the school are sound. Pupils should be:

- achieving at a level in line with their potential on entry to the school; the school should actually be *adding value* to pupils (see below)
- behaving in an orderly fashion in a school which is a safe environment for them to learn in.

Pupils are assessed on entry to a school. This assessment level determines what pupils should achieve at the end of their stay in primary or secondary school. If a pupil exceeds this prediction the school has added value. If schools do not get pupils to achieve at this level they have taken value away.

The school should be:

- well managed, with resources being used effectively and efficiently; governors should play an active role in its running
- obeying statutory orders and following national curriculum programmes of study
- a self-reviewing establishment where all levels of management regularly monitor, evaluate and review progress – it should be able to identify strengths and weaknesses, and in the case of weaknesses put in place intervention strategies to remove them
- proactive and ensuring that current initiatives are built into its development planning (the development plan should reflect the needs of the whole school and individual departments)
- taking account of and giving consideration to parents' and pupils' points of view – the school should be a fully inclusive organisation and provide equal opportunities for all
- working well with partner schools and the community
- providing an independent evaluation framework
- keeping national government informed about standards
- identifying and promoting good practice, enabling it to be shared with other organisations.

Self-evaluation in schools

Self-evaluation is important in all schools. Many LAs have produced a self-evaluation form/school profile that is completed by schools in their area. The headteacher usually fills in the form online but the information is provided in consultation with other senior managers and the middle management teams. Basically, the completed form provides vital information for the inspection team.

Where a form has not been completed the inspection team will ask the relevant questions once it gets to the school. It is therefore in the best interests of the school and the LA to have completed documentation like this in place.

The form will provide a context for the inspection. It will state the location of the school, size, numbers of staff and pupils, percentage of pupils who are on free school meals, the ethnic mix of the school and the number of pupils who have statements of educational need. It will also indicate the financial income of the school and the expenditure, which will be itemised under cost headings. The curriculum of the school and the amount of time spent on specific subjects will also be specified. In addition, the external results for the school will be included for a three-year period.

Many authorities have a team of statisticians who analyse the results for their schools and the form will be annotated so that trends can be identified. Where a difference in a year is significant this will be highlighted. For instance, 5% differences up or down are seen as statistically significant. If a school gets 65% of its pupils at level 3 in English one year and the following year it is 71% that would count as a significant trend and a green arrow pointing up would indicate this. This information is useful for the LA and the inspection team. However, it is the school that needs to indicate whether this has occurred due to interventions used or whether the improvement is down to a more able cohort. In each category, space on the form is available for more information to be added. This might include details of strategies the school has put in place to address issues or hindrances that have prevented improvement.

Inspection teams have information on the statistical achievement of all schools in the four nations. In particular, they will gather as much statistical evidence about the examination performance of a school over the three-year period prior to its inspection. The use of a three-year period ensures that the inspection team is able to look at trends over time and not rely on one cohort's results. The cohort could be atypical (i.e. weaker or stronger than usual) and this would significantly weaken the accuracy of the team's findings. The team then looks at schools of a similar size and intake and will compare results in a number of categories for all these schools. This is called benchmarking. If a school is doing well they would be in the upper quartiles when compared with other schools.

The local authority will want to know the same information as any inspection team. The most important way of judging how a school is doing is to assess the results that pupils attain. Pupils are assessed on entry to a school and teacher assessment and standard assessment tasks give an idea of the potential of the cohort. The aim is to ensure that pupils attain or exceed their potential. Inspection teams will also have more detailed information on results. They will be able to tell if a school is producing the appropriate percentage of pupils attaining level 3 at age seven or A*/A grades for their cohort at age 16. A school may be achieving good levels or A*–C GCSE grades for their pupils but could still be failing to extend pupils at the top end of the attainment spectrum. Similarly, the school may

achieve good results for the very able and able but below-average children may not be supported sufficiently to achieve their potential.

If a school is fully self-reviewing, they will identify issues like this for the inspection team and will identify the strategies that have been put in place to improve the situation. Similarly, a school could have an issue with a gender gap and they may be trying to improve the performance of boys in English and girls in maths. The self-evaluation form provides a school with an opportunity to show what is in place to remedy problems but it also enables schools to identify strengths that they have. When schools are reviewing performance effectively they will also identify weaknesses and the strategies that have been put in place to remedy these.

In some cases the self-evaluation form mirrors that of the inspection framework. This is because some schools have to self-evaluate taking account of the inspection framework. By the time they are inspected, the school has already prepared a form and has kept it updated so does not need to prepare a large report again. Using the self-evaluation form schools also grade their performance in each area, for instance teaching and learning, managing staff and resources, contribution to the personal, social, emotional and cultural development of pupils according to the inspection framework grading system. The forms are also useful for LA planning and this is why many LAs have introduced them. An LA that is strategically managing a number of schools uses the forms to provide it with powerful information about how its schools are doing, enabling it to use resources strategically. If in one authority a lot of schools are struggling with the same problems, then resources could be effectively and efficiently deployed to support schools as a cluster. The sharing of self-evaluation data with the LA is vital.

Before an inspection team comes into a school it will have carefully scrutinised the performance data and read the self-evaluation report of the school. Then it will devise a list of questions that it wants answered. The aim of the team will be to find the answers through practical observation of teaching and learning, looking at past work in pupils' books or through questioning the staff and pupils, asking for further evidence.

How should you prepare for an inspection?

Ensure that:

- all pupils' books are marked and ready for viewing by an inspector
- lessons are well planned and lesson plans are available.

Most teachers, no matter how experienced, plan lessons. However, for an inspection you should revert to what is common teaching practice and prepare

lessons more fully. A lesson information sheet is shown on p110. This has been used in many schools when they have been inspected. (To read an NQT's experiences of inspections go to the book's website, at www.pearsoned.co.uk/essentialguides.)

Inspectors will want to see evidence of past work that pupils have done and will be interested in classroom displays. It is important that where possible all pupils are up to date with their work and that missed work has been copied up. Inspectors believe that underachievement is initially the responsibility of the class teacher. This means that the class teacher should have supported any pupil who has missed a considerable amount of work or who is having problems in some way. It is important to be able to show the strategies that have been used and, if these have failed, what other strategies or teachers have been involved. If a school is fully inclusive then there will be strategies in place to support pupils who have missed a considerable amount of work due to absence and all teachers will use these strategies.

Inspectors are also keen to know if pupils understand the level they are working at and if they understand how to improve the standard of their work and move on to the next level or grade. A ladder to learning, as described on p92, shows pupils how to progress from one level to another and would show an inspector that assessment for learning techniques are being used to good effect in your classroom. Inspectors will observe lessons and look at books, as well as question pupils about their learning. They will also want to know how class teachers keep records on pupil achievement and what information is used to inform parents, either face to face or in written reports, about progress.

Class teachers are expected to form a part of the self-reviewing process and to understand all data available on their pupils. They will be expected to monitor and evaluate progress and assess whether or not their pupils are on track to achieve their potential.

Inspection teams expect to see copies of all documentation in a school and these should be made available to them. Each school has a school handbook that contains detailed information about the school itself, the day-to-day running routines and policies that a school has to have in place. Most schools put all their policies into this to ensure that all teachers have up-to-date copies of all relevant material.

Where there are large lead-in times to inspection this material will be copied and sent to the inspection team beforehand. In England, under the existing framework, there is not enough time for this to happen so this documentation will need to be ready for the team to view. Inspection teams work a long day and can be in a school at 7.00 a.m. reading through information. They will often leave late in the evening, taking more material away with them.

Most new teachers are responsible only for their own classroom teaching and their form or tutor class. However, it is common in primary schools for teachers to have additional management responsibility. If this is the case the documentation will need to be in evidence for that as well. You are not expected to contribute to the school

handbook unless you are responsible for a policy (literacy, numeracy, etc.) that is used across the school but you may have to produce a departmental handbook.

A school/staff handbook

This could contain:

- staff and governors' names
- day-to-day running information
- job specifications
- roles and responsibilities
- lesson times including breaks and lunch
- important whole school policies and procedures
  - child protection
  - anti-bullying
  - teaching and learning
  - assessment
  - equal opportunities policy
  - routines for organising school visits
  - health and safety guidance
  - attendance
  - behaviour.

All this will be available in your school and is normally in one file or booklet.

All staff must know the contents of this handbook well as inspection teams will want to ensure that the school staff are working as a team and that policies are being delivered consistently. This will not happen if some staff are unaware that the handbook exists and are not familiar with its policies.

A new teacher may be expected to produce a SOW for a subject where they are the only specialist teacher. However, if there is more than one person involved in the delivery of a subject it is now common to produce a handbook to accompany the SOW as this ensures consistency of delivery and standards.

A departmental handbook

This is common in primary and secondary schools where one person has responsibility for a subject and others are involved in delivering that subject. It will contain information about: →

- the departmental development plan
- staffing
- location of resources
- schemes of work for all year groups and levels
- policies on marking and assessment
- cross-curricular dimensions (some schemes of work, for instance science, link into PSHE)
- monitoring and how it is managed
- lesson observation
- monitoring of pupils' books and how pupils' work is moderated to ensure that assessment levels are being correctly awarded
- a resources stock list that is checked annually
- copies of ordered materials.

A departmental development plan shows two distinct things

1. The improvement you wish to make within your own subject area.
2. The improvement you intend to make in your subject area in response to the needs of the whole school.

In order to document what you are going to do to fulfil point 2 above you will need to read the school improvement/development plan (SIP/SDP).

What is the school improvement/development plan?

This is the whole school document produced in consultation with all staff, especially those with responsibility for curriculum, pastoral and whole school management. It may also respond to the governor, parent and pupil voices of the school. The SIP/SDP may identify an issue for improvement, e.g. the performance of boys. Although this goal may be stated in the SIP/SDP, each individual development plan should show how it will be addressed and identify how it will ensure this whole school aim is achieved.

New teachers may be expected to produce SOWs early in their career and can even be plunged straight into an inspection. Some schools adopt a standard format for SOWs and others allow teachers autonomy in this. Storing SOWs electronically makes updating them very easy and time efficient. An SOW template can be found on p31.

This chapter has put forward suggestions for how best to be prepared for an inspection. However, good teachers do not need an inspection to ensure that they prepare good lessons, mark pupils' work using detailed diagnostic comments or

have the administrative materials in place to perform their role effectively. Good teachers do these things as a matter of course. Finally, inspections are nothing to fear. During my career I have been involved in at least five full inspections in three different schools. This does not take account of the many other times when inspectors have visited my departments or have been auditing specific areas of school life for which I had responsibility. In most cases the relationship between the inspector and the teacher is one of mutual respect where a meaningful dialogue can be held about the work that is ongoing in the classroom. Inspections allow a teacher to showcase their work and that of their pupils and most cases are positive and profitable experiences for all concerned.

TOP TIPS!

To move a lesson from good to satisfactory:

- *pupils are challenged from the outset*
- *there is planned progression*
- *pupils understand progression and where they are in the learning journey*
- *aims and objectives are clearly stated*
- *key skills and thinking skills are clearly integrated into learning*
- *good control and discipline and a good pupil-teacher relationship are evident*
- *good classroom management at the beginning and end of lessons is evident*
- *clear differentiation occurs even in set groups – there will be big differences in target levels and grades and this should be planned for*
- *teacher expectation, e.g. presentation of work, is demanding*
- *thorough marking is carried out with comments indicating ways to improve.*

TOP TIPS!

To move a lesson from good to very good:

- *the objectives are clear in both planning and learning*

- *there is variety, pace and challenge and a range of pedagogies are used*

- *pupils are fully engaged at all times in the lesson*

- *there is a clear WOW! factor to the lesson with innovation evident*

- *there is clear evidence in the work or it could be on DVD-ROM or CD-ROM depending on the subject and how evidence of progression is retained*

- *the teacher facilitates and orchestrates but does not dominate the class situation*

- *in many lessons of this kind pupils of all ages are encouraged to be autonomous learners*

- *pupils enjoy the lesson and the teacher shares a passion for the subject and has a good rapport with the pupils.*

For instance, in one lesson of this kind a teacher was feeding back to a class on an assignment the pupils had done. She put the class into groups of four and gave the work back. She had put the comments on each group members' work on to four pieces of paper and then asked the groups to match the comments to the individual work. This is a good example of how AFL is used in an innovative way in a class and where learning objectives are clear to both pupils and inspector!

Why not try this?

- Think about the school you are in at present. Obtain a copy of the school handbook, the area/departmental handbook, the school development plan and the departmental development plan.

  - Look at the development plans and see if there are any issues that are common to both.

  - Look at the results for the school you are in and then compare them with the results for the rest of the area and nationally.

- Get a copy of the last inspection report. Look at any aspects that the inspection team picked out as being weak.

  - How is the school addressing these issues?

  - What strategies have been put in place?

➜

– What strengths have been identified?

● How does your school self-review? Ask your mentor or line manager what monitoring is in place, who is involved and how often it occurs.

● What awards has your school got?

● What professional development has your mentor or line manager been on recently? Why?

● Do you think that the school is an orderly place to work in?

● Are the children well managed and is their behaviour good?

Going further

Inspection reports are in the public domain and are free to download from the following agencies:

for England go to www.ofsted.gov.uk

for Scotland go to www.hmie.gov.uk

for Wales go to www.estyn.gov.uk

for Northern Ireland go to www.deni.gov.uk

Reading through these gives you a good idea of what inspection teams are looking for and what they think makes a good school.

Applying for a job, preparing a lesson and the interview

What this chapter will explore:

- Looking at job adverts
- How to write a CV
- The letter and application form
- Planning a lesson as part of an interview
- How to prepare for the interview

This chapter shows you how to go about getting that all-important first post. You may think you already know how to write a CV and a letter of application; however, even if you feel confident it is better to read this chapter first! And, once you are over the first hurdle and have been

short-listed, how should you arrive at the interview ready to impress? We look carefully at how to plan an impressive lesson and analyse potential interview questions.

Teaching posts are advertised in a number of ways: in the local or national press; within LAs via a regular bulletin; on the school's own intranet; on the internet. The *Times Educational Supplement* is published every week on a Friday and is widely used to advertise teaching vacancies. Most vacancies tend to be advertised in the spring term from January onwards but there is a regular supply of job vacancies advertised throughout the year. Some newly qualified teachers are not fortunate enough to gain a job immediately after finishing their course. If you are one of these another way is to fill a long-term vacancy arising from staff absence. Do not underestimate how powerful this can be in securing you a post in the school you are currently working in or in gaining you a very valuable reference for the future.

Looking at job adverts

The advertisement shown on the opposite page is for a job in the secondary sector.

Having studied the advertisement you will need to contact the school or college for an application pack. This will contain some or all of the following:

- a school prospectus
- details about the area the school is situated in
- details about the department you would be applying to join or the area of the school the job is relevant to
- a job specification
- a person specification
- an interview timescale
- requirements for the application – a letter, CV and completed application forms.

The information in the pack must be used to inform your letter of application along with information about your teaching experience and vision for this teaching post. It is very easy to spot the generic application for a post. Though a generic letter may form the basis of your application, it is essential to tweak it to suit the actual post you are applying for. Doing this will attract the attention of the reader and score more highly on the criteria that are used to rank these letters when choosing a short-list for interview.

The City of Leicester College A specialist Business and Enterprise College **Downing Drive, Evington, Leicester LE5 6LN** Required from August 2006, permanent full-time **•TEACHERS OF MATHEMATICS** (MPS) (2 posts) Our mathematics faculty is looking for well-qualified, enthusiastic and ambitious teachers of mathematics. As a specialist Business and Enterprise College we are actively developing enterprise through all aspects of the curriculum. In the mathematics faculty we have a dedicated set of laptops, interactive whiteboards and all staff have their own laptop. These posts would suit an NQT or an experienced teacher seeking a new challenge. A level teaching is available for suitably qualified candidates. There is an established induction programme and professional development is fully supported. Informal enquiries or visits are welcomed and encouraged. For application pack including more details please call the job line on 0116 *******. For any further enquiries please contact The head of mathematics 0116 ******* or e-mail office@cityleics.sch.uk. Initial closing date for applications is 29 April 2006.	**What does this advertisement tell you?** Two posts are available at a specialist college. Do you know anything about specialist colleges of this kind? If not you need to get researching quickly. The mathematics faculty is well equipped but high-level IT skills would seem to be essential. Do you have them? If unsure take up the offer and speak to the head of mathematics directly. Never waste time applying for a post for which you lack essential skills. NQT applications are welcomed and there is the added bonus of A level teaching if you are able to offer it. New staff are well supported and staff development is a high priority. Visits are welcomed and this suggests that the college is open and has nothing to hide. The head of mathematics is empowered by the college and is approachable. The college shows trust with this task and respect for management skills.

Job advertisement for a secondary school

How to write a CV

A curriculum vitae (CV) is in essence a life history with only relevant details. It should be word processed so that it can be kept up to date. It should be current, with no gaps in the timescale, and it should be true! Any application that is not accurate can be deemed to be fraudulent and you can be liable to instant dismissal. This does happen!

A sample CV template can be found on the book's website, at www.pearsoned. co.uk/essentialguides.

The curriculum vitae

A typical CV should contain the following elements:

- Name, address and date of birth
- Marital status
- Contact numbers (including mobile number and email)
- Schools attended in chronological order
- Qualifications obtained. Dates and grades are useful. (However, as you progress up the career ladder the dates are useful but the grades you obtained in GCSEs 20 years ago become less so! Other later qualifications obtained while teaching will be more relevant – in the case of a senior manager, having the National Professional Qualification for Headship for instance.)
- University attended
- Undergraduate qualifications obtained, level and date (if some are pending state this)
- Postgraduate qualifications obtained or pending (the date and level is important)
- Other relevant qualifications. These could include sporting qualifications for refereeing, first aid certificates, life-saving awards, music exam qualifications, etc.
- Work experience or teaching placements if you are training or are entering the profession from another area of work; post details if you are already in post. These should all be in chronological order. (It is important to avoid time gaps and any present must be explained. If you took a gap year then explain what you did in this time, likewise if you were at home looking after children, etc.)
- Courses attended relevant to the post. This may not apply to new teachers but when you apply for future posts this should cover a three-year period prior to the application. Keeping accurate details is important
- Hobbies and interests
- The names and contact details of two referees.

The CV is an important document so spend time on it. Insert a header with the school and post details and make a cover for it with your name on the front. This may seem excessive but first appearances really do make a big difference. If a school employs you from NQT to retirement age they might, by the time you finish, have invested over £1 million in that post and you in particular. This investment has to be carefully considered. You will need to prove to the team that you are worth every penny.

The letter and application form

The letter is a formal one and should follow that format. It should begin 'Dear Sir/Madam' unless you know the name of the headteacher. You should end with 'Yours sincerely' if a name is used and 'Yours faithfully' if a title is used. All of this may seem rather trite, but having seen hundreds of applications over time, it is not! At least 20% of all applications for posts will fail because too little time and attention has been paid to filling in an application form, presenting a sound CV and writing a detailed and accurate letter.

Remember that all posts are now subject to a police check and a medical.

Ensure that your letter is well planned and free of grammatical and spelling errors. Schools rely on staff to communicate via reports with parents. If you are unable to send in a *perfect* application form they will query your communication skills and your commitment to perfection that is needed in a school organisation. Your letter can be handwritten if this is requested but word-processed letters are now standard practice. The letter should be produced on good-quality paper and contain two addresses, yours and that of the school you are applying to. Letters are normally addressed to the headteacher unless you are otherwise instructed.

Your letter should be at least two-and-a-half sides long. This allows you sufficient space to sell yourself, explaining how your qualifications, experience and vision will benefit the school.

Sample letters can be found on the book's website, at www.pearsoned.co.uk/essentialguides.

Fill in the application form ensuring that all parts are accurate and that spelling is correct.

In the letter you should clearly state:

- the post you are applying for and where you saw the advertisement
- the experience you have had on teaching placements or in a post that you feel is relevant to this job
- the vision you have of education and for this post in particular.

What does the word 'vision' mean? It is used a lot in organisations today. It is a word used to encompass a person's individual philosophy about how pupils should be taught. It should also encompass any ideas a person may have about the specific job/role being applied for. It means that you answer questions that are not asked, such as 'How important is marking/using data/use of praise in a classroom situation/promoting high expectations/target setting/lesson planning?' Your letter should contain words such as 'I believe', 'I think it is important ...', 'I believe my placement at ... has taught me the importance of ...'

You may also want to state your vision for your own future: 'I would like to consolidate my teaching expertise and in the future would like to think I could ...' Being ambitious and having a clear career plan is a good thing.

The letter should also build up a profile of you as a person. If you are committed, hardworking, a team player and have a sense of humour then say this in your letter. All these characteristics help a school to gain a picture of what makes you an individual.

In addition, you need to think of the following:

- Any extra-curricular talents you have that a school may find useful.
- Any additional qualifications such as those gained for special educational needs, dyslexia as a specialism, etc.
- Any experience in the world of work that is relevant and makes you more useful to a school.
- Any other subject expertise that may be useful.

Schools these days require staff to be multi-functional. Staff are an expensive commodity and the more skilled you are the better. Being able to coach sport, begin a new club in an area that you have expertise, produce a school play, offer musical support, run a business enterprise, coach a public-speaking team, produce a school newspaper, run a science club or teach swimming in addition to your subject or class role are all useful skills to flag up to your future employer. Do not be afraid to sell yourself, as no one else can do this for you.

The letter, application form and the CV pave the way to an interview. The references will come later, usually at short-listing stage.

Planning a lesson as part of an interview

Many schools now insist that all prospective teachers 'teach' a lesson. The school will give you clear guidelines about the age and the ability of the class and the length of the lesson. Some schools will actually tell you what they want taught. In a modern foreign language lesson they may ask you to teach the past tense of the verb 'to be', for instance. Lesson duration will be short, 20–40 minutes, to allow time for all short-listed candidates to teach a lesson and be observed. The lesson is observed by the line manager or head of department or a senior member of staff in the school such as the deputy headteacher. In many schools now, pupils are being 'included' and 'empowered'. They may therefore be asked to complete a simple evaluation form such as the one shown on the next page (a printable version is available at www.pearsoned.co.uk/essentialguides). I will not employ any new teaching staff for main-grade teaching posts unless I see them teach a lesson and I always ask pupils to evaluate the performance of the

teachers. Governors are trained in our school and also participate in this important part of the interview process.

PUPIL EVALUATION FORM

Name of pupil .... **Lesson** ....

1   Was the lesson interesting? Why?

2   Were you interested all of the time? If not, why not?

3   What did you learn during the lesson?

4   What part of the lesson did you most enjoy?

5   What part of the lesson did you least enjoy?

6   Was this lesson
    Excellent Very good Good Fair Poor
    (Underline or circle one of these only)

Thank you for helping us to choose your new teacher

Example of a pupil evaluation form for a lesson

TOP TIPS!

For help in planning a lesson consider the following:

- *Re-read Chapters 8 and 9.*

- *Look closely at the age and ability of the class the school wants you to teach.*

- *Look at the programme of study for that age and subject. Decide carefully on a topic (if you have a choice), ensuring that it will enable you to differentiate the lesson and show off your skills.*

- *Think about the lesson aims and objectives carefully, preparing a lesson plan that you will present on the day to the observers. Ensure that copies of resource material are also available for them. You may want to put this together in a pack with your name on it. Ensure that you have enough copies for the class and that it is free of errors.*

- *Plan to use a range of activities to encourage class interaction.*

- Check whether the school uses a consistent format for lesson planning, a four-part lesson or insists on all staff using lesson starters. Ask if they have a teaching and learning policy.

- Make sure that the pupils will have learnt something concrete by the end of the lesson and that there is proof of this through oral, written or practical assessment.

- Close the lesson appropriately by summing up what has been taught and learnt in the form of a plenary-type session. Even though the lesson duration is short the introduction and conclusion of the lesson must be obvious to those monitoring it.

TOP TIPS!

When delivering a lesson:

- Feel confident when you enter the classroom and ensure that you look around and make good eye contact with the pupils.

- Give out name tags if they do not have them on. Take sticky backed labels with you and give them to a pupil to give out. Names give you power. For instance, if a pupil is talking when you are, stop what you are saying and say 'Thank you [name the pupil]', and maintain eye contact for a few seconds. Then carry on with the lesson but every now and then ensure that that pupil sees you are watching them. Do not let them repeat the offence. If they do move them. (Note that you do not really need to say 'stop talking'. They will know what they have done.)

- Introduce the purpose of the lesson clearly and get someone to distribute materials for you. Keep an eye on them while they do this. Do not assume that the pupils present will have books with them, this could well be a group that has been brought together for this purpose alone. Make sure that your worksheets have space for written work.

- Ensure that the activities you have prepared are carried out well and that all pupils are on task. Think about providing activities for the class that will ensure this.

→

- *Look at different teaching activities that are suggested by experts like Paul Ginnis in his Teacher's Toolkit (2002). How could you adapt such activities to suit your lesson?*

- *Watch the time and ensure that you synchronise your watch with the person observing so that you are sure to have enough time to finish your planned activities.*

- *Allow enough time to conclude the lesson efficiently. Sum up the learning outcomes and ensure that pupils understand that they have completed the learning objectives that you clearly outlined at the beginning of the lesson.*

- *Ensure that you have differentiated the materials and that if anyone finishes the work you have something else prepared. Ensure that it is an extension of the work and not just more of the same. Your aim is to enrich the most able and challenge them, not just keep them occupied.*

How to prepare for the interview

The school or college will write to you explaining the format for the day. Make sure that you read this carefully. What you wear is a matter of choice and if you teach a practical subject and are going to teach a lesson this may influence your choice. However, first impressions do count so try to choose wisely.

Below are some questions that may be similar to those asked in an interview. Think about how you might answer them:

- Tell us about your teaching experiences to date.
- Tell us about a successful lesson or series of lessons that you have taught recently.
- What are the challenges facing teachers today?
- What strategies would you use to enhance learning?
- We work as a friendly, close-knit department/school. Do you view yourself as an adaptable team player willing to integrate and contribute?
- How important is classroom organisation in creating a well-disciplined learning environment?
- How would you create a welcoming, learning classroom environment?

- What strategies would you use to cope with a pupil disrupting the lesson by constant calling out or low-level disruption?

- Is assessment target-setting important?

- What data are you familiar with using and how do you use it?

- We have a policy of sharing teaching materials in the curriculum area/ learning area. What skills could you offer for the production of these resources.

- How do you see the role of ICT, whiteboards, PowerPoint in teaching today?

- What do you feel makes you particularly suitable for this job?

- Is there anything else that you would like to add that you haven't had a chance to say?

- Many staff in our school offer extra-curricular activities for our children. What extra-curricular activities could you offer us?

- What range of strategies or activities would you employ to attract and hold the attention and interest of potentially disaffected and less able pupils?

- What would be your vision for the teaching of your subject? How would you promote your subject in the school?

For each of these questions the interviewing panel will have a list of points that it wants to hear as part of your answer. These will be scored and a comparison made between candidates. In some interviews candidates may also be asked to prepare a presentation based on questions that are given to them beforehand.

Why not try this?

- Look at the questions above and think about how they might be adapted to your subject or area of the school.

- How would you answer the questions?

- Look at your CV critically to check that it is detailed enough.

- Try writing an application letter for a job that you have seen advertised. Think about how you would impart your vision for education to the school and how you get across something of your personality in the letter.

Going further

Ginnis, P. (2002) *Teacher's Toolkit*, Carmarthen: Crown House Publishing.

Continuing professional development

What this chapter will explore:

- Career entry and development profiles
- NQT induction
- Continuing professional development

If a teacher were to stay in a school for the duration of their career over the 40 years or so of employment, the school will have spent over £1 million on that individual! A teacher is therefore a valuable resource who needs to be updated at regular intervals on the latest developments in their chosen profession. This is done through a school's inset/training budget. However, it is vitally important that teachers keep detailed records of any training that they receive and that they think carefully about what their own development needs might be. This chapter looks

at how teachers can progress most effectively, developing valuable skills along the way, and how they can do this whilst being supported by their school and in some cases by national teaching councils.

Career entry and development profiles

One of the things that the four nations have in common is the requirement that new entrants to the profession should have a career entry and development profile. (All teachers also have to be registered with the respective General Teaching Councils. If you have a criminal record of any kind note that this could prevent you being registered. If you are not registered you cannot teach in any of the United Kingdom countries.) The aim of this is to ensure that new teachers are encouraged to think about their professional development at key points. It is structured around transition points that occur at:

- the end of initial teacher training
- the beginning and end of the induction process.

The purpose of the profile is to ensure that new teachers make links between the training that has gone before and the reality of working on a day-to-day basis in a school. It is intended that new teachers should reflect on individual achievements and be able to set goals and realistic targets based on this reflection. Each new teacher should be assigned a professional mentor. Part of the mentor's role is to lead this discussion and encourage the reflection so that new entrants can determine what their training needs might be. For instance, questions might include:

- What do you find the most interesting and rewarding aspects of teaching to date?
- What do you consider to be your main strengths?
- What aspects of your teaching do you need to develop further or require further training in?

NQT induction

Newly qualified teachers (NQTs) involved in the induction phase of their career are not involved in the performance management processes. In addition, they are expected to have more non-contact time and in many cases do not have the responsibility of a registration group. The headteacher holds partial responsibility

for ensuring that the induction period is conducted appropriately and in line with statutory guidelines. They do this in partnership with other recognised bodies and these vary according to the type of school you are in:

- For maintained schools and non-maintained special schools the appropriate body is the LA
- For independent schools the appropriate body is the Independent Schools Council Teacher Induction Panel (ISCTIP)
- For independent schools not a member of ISCTIP, academies, city technology colleges, sixth form colleges or further education institutions the appropriate body is any LA that they reach an agreement with.

NQTs also have a designated mentor who will regularly observe them teach and meet with them to discuss progress. In the first year of teaching, specific funding is made available for training purposes and this is ring-fenced for individual training only. Many LAs run their own induction training programmes, which all NQTS will attend. Teachers who fail the induction period or prior to this fail to gain registration are able to undergo an appeals process.

Many schools encourage new teachers to keep a portfolio of evidence. This builds on the professional development record. Keeping a record of evidence is a good habit to get into and it should contain:

- reports on your progress and teaching
- reports on lesson observation
- examples of lesson plans
- records of objectives individually set or set in consultation with a mentor or induction tutor
- individual reviews of progress towards qualified teacher status and evidence of course assignments.

Throughout a career, many teachers have a lot of opportunities to take on specific tasks and roles. Keeping evidence of this involvement is important. It enables a person to track their own career development as well as build up information that can be incorporated into an up-to-date CV.

UsefulWebsites

For information on the induction arrangements that exist in your region, go to the website of the agency in your country and search the site using the phrases listed below.

England – www.dcsf.gov.uk; search for 'teacher induction'

Northern Ireland – www.deni.gov.uk; search for 'the professional development of beginning teachers'

Scotland – www.ltscotland.org.uk/index.asp; search for 'support for new teachers'

Wales – www.wales.gov.uk; search for 'career entry profile, March 2009'

Continuing professional development

All schools have a training budget for the continuing professional development (CPD) of its staff. This was originally used to train only teaching staff, but as the number of teaching assistants employed in schools increases, the training fund is used to provide CPD for all staff who come into contact with pupils.

Staff development in schools is managed by a school development officer (SDO); this might be a deputy headteacher. The inset budget is normally allocated under different headings, which include induction, and the SDO manages the budget, ensuring that all teachers' training needs are met. The way the budget is spent is determined by three criteria:

- the school development plan and the training that is needed to realise it
- the needs of individual departments and areas of the school, and the individual plans that have been written to vision the future in these areas
- the needs of the individual and their performance management targets.

Funding is provided in the case of the NQT. However, the SDO has only a limited budget and has to ensure that the funding is used strategically and fairly throughout the school. Teachers who go on courses are encouraged to evaluate the quality of training and, where possible, to report back to others. The competing needs of the school, specific areas and individuals need to be met. In England and Wales the General Teaching Councils provide additional funding for teachers to undergo specific training. The amount of funding varies and in some cases teachers can form groups to carry out joint training. The provision of funding depends on certain criteria being met and all teachers who are allocated funding by these bodies have to submit a final report on their training. The report outlines how the training has provided CPD for the individual concerned. When teachers attend courses it is important to keep the training materials safe and to file them under recognisable headings where they can be retrieved easily.

This is a useful habit to get into, as are the following:

- Ensure that you have copies of your career entry profile and that you review your progress with your mentor.
- Keep documents that prove your qualification status safe. Schools often photocopy degree certificates, etc. and place these in your staff file.
- Ensure that you regularly self-review your progress. Assess your strengths and weaknesses. Use this to determine your own training needs.
- Keep your CV up to date by keeping a detailed record of all training you have attended. File data from courses carefully.
- When you are subject to performance management arrangements, ensure that you have some idea of what CPD you require.

Key ideas summary

Having read this book you should be much better equipped to face the challenges confronting teachers today. You will have a good understanding of the following:

- How schools are organised for learning.
- How to plan differentiated lessons and manage the behaviour of your pupils.
- How to use data effectively to track the progress of your pupils and set meaningful targets.
- How to mark effectively and manage your time.
- How to manage an area of responsibility in a school.
- How to contribute to the pastoral team of the school.
- How to apply for jobs and manage your own professional development.

Conclusion

This book is intended to be a reference book and therefore should not be set aside like a novel that you may never read again. Instead it should be used as part of your own reviewing strategy. For instance, if you find that a class of boys you are teaching are underperforming in relation to their potential, you may wish to refer back to the material in Chapter 4. The same class may also have behaviour issues that need addressing and so the chapters on behaviour management may be of use. In fact from my own experience I predict that there will be many times when information from this could be a life-line for a new teacher. I firmly believe that this book, with its mix of practical advice based on 30 years in the profession coupled with the theoretical information, will be invaluable. If I had started my own professional career with this knowledge I think the journey would have been a lot smoother and the climb a lot easier. Finally, I love the job I do and for me every teacher should be in the classroom to make a difference. You are entrusted with this: good teachers really do make a difference. The acknowledgements at the front of the book are my own testament to this.

Index

Page numbers in *italics* denotes a figure/ diagram

absence(s) *see* attendance
Accelerated Learning 90
achievement/attainment *see* educational achievement/attainment
adding value 250, 251–4, 327
administrative support 140
advanced skills teachers 5
Aiming High initiative 65–6
anti-bullying *see* bullying
apologies for misbehaviour 185
art
    learning ladder 92–3
assemblies 95
assessment 32
    and achievement prediction 327
    curriculum 27–8
    cycle *210*
    and data profiles 232, 235
    differential 31
    English lesson 212
    policy 211–12
    purpose 208–11
    reading age 79–81
    standardised testing 47, 130, 232
    summative 213
    see also formative assessment; self- assessment

assessment for learning 96, 224–5
    and learning gains 213–14
    see also grouping for learning; learning
assistant headteachers 4
attainment/achievement *see* educational achievement/attainment
attendance
    absence patterns 313
    authorised absences 280–1
    inspection requirements 310–11
    intervention strategies 324
    LAs and 310–11
    parents and 311
    and pastoral system 280–1
    and performance 324
    school policy 312–13
    strategies for ensuring 312–14
    unauthorised absences 280–1
    using data to improve 245–6
attendance officers 324
Attention Deficit Hyperactivity Disorder (ADHD) 186
auditory learners 111
authorised absences 280–1

banding 12–13
Basic Skills Agency 57, 256, 303
Basic Skills Quality Mark 256
behaviour management
    and apologies for misbehaviour 185

behaviour declarations 181–3, *182*
body language 163
and CAs 148
class control 164
classroom 187–8
data profiles and 235
exclusion 157
eye contact 163
importance 154
mentors and 186
on-call system 156
parents and 158
policies 155–7, 159, 188–9
in practice 161–2
preventing poor 158–9
recording misbehaviour 183
rules for pupils 162
time-out system 156–7
using data to improve 245–6
voice 163
see also discipline structure; 'hard'
   classes; rewards and merits;
   sanctions
behaviour support assistants (BSAs) 141
benchmarking 230, 251
'best evidence synthesis' 14
'big picture' 91, 92, 266
Birmingham Profile 240, 244
Black, P. *et al.*
   Assessment for Learning: Putting it into
      Practice (2003) 224–5
body language 163
borderline cases 247–8
boys
   characteristics of average 40–1
   gender effect and education 40, 43–4
   performance 43–4
   and single-sex classes 48–9
   strategies to narrow attainment gap
      between girls and 46–50
brain gym 115–16, 171 *see also* lesson
   starters
British Cohort Survey (BCS) 60
British Household Panel Survey (BHPS) 60
buddy schemes 199
budgets
   and staffing 5
bullying
   effective handling 193–4
   policy 193

responding to allegations of 317–19
sanctions 194
strategies for containing 315–20
of teachers 186
Bullying: Don't Suffer in Silence (2006) 316

career entry and development profile 348
caretakers 9
charity committees 198–9
child protection officers (CPOs) 9, 274
   role 314–15
Children's Commissioners 201
circle time 294–7
   sample sheet *296*
Clarke, Shirley
   Unlocking Formative Assessment (2000)
      216
classroom
   control 164
   learning ethos and environment 94–5
   management 168–71, 175–7
   rules 168–71
   use of data profiles 237–40
   see also behaviour management
classroom assistants (CAs) 140
   best practice 147–8
   ground rules 149
   job description 144–6
   liaising about work and behaviour
      147–8
   role 143–7
   working successfully with 146–9
Cognitive Abilities Tests (CATs) 46–7, 130,
   235
   classroom use of data 237–9
   guide to scores 238
community, developing sense of 288
continuing professional development (CPD)
   350–1
core subject indicators (CSIs) 248
cover assistants (CAs) 142
cover support managers (CSMs) 142–3
cross-curricular links 32–3
curriculum
   adapting 248–9
   authorities 28–30
   bridge 236, 300, 303–4
   four capacities 28–9
   hidden 36
   planning 35

curriculum coordinators (CCs) *see* subject
    leaders
curriculum support assistants (CSAs) 142
CV/curriculum vitae 339–40

data
    determining success of schools 96,
        249–54
    identifying pupils needs 246–9
    improving attainment 243–4
    and intervention strategies 242–9
    recording and storing 130–7, 246, 261
data profiles
    behaviours 235
    classroom use 237–40
    developmental milestones 230–2, 233–4
    tests and assessments 232, 235
    uses 235–40
    young children *233–4*
de Bono, Edward
    six thinking hats 100–101
Department for Children, Education,
    Lifelong Learning and Skills (DCELLS)
    28
Department for Education and Skills (DfES)
    45
departmental handbooks 33–4, 331–2
deputy headteachers 4, 10
differentiation 94, 95, 123, 125, 237
discipline structure 324 *see also* behaviour
    management; 'hard' classes; rewards
    and merits; sanctions
disclosures 315
disrespect
    and sanctions 194
dyslexia 140

Education Act (1996) 286
Education Welfare Officers (EWOs) 144,
    311, 324
Education Welfare Service (EWS) 311–12
educational achievement/attainment
    differences among LAs 67–8
    and ethnicity 65–7
    factors influencing 40
    and gender 39–44
    improving 243–4
    income and 58–9
    narrowing the gap 46–50, 68–70
    poverty and 54–7, *55–6*, 65–7

predictions 327
    and socio-economic classification 45
educational behaviour plans (EBPs) 8,
    158–9, 237
Educational Maintenance Allowance (EMA)
    58, 68
educational psychologists (EPs) 158–9, 246
Educational Reform Act (1988) 15
emotional development 288
England
    Children's Commissioner 201
    curriculum authority 28
English
    assessment 212
    engaging pupils 120
    interactive whiteboard 121–2
    lesson starters 114
English as an Additional Language (EAL)
    68
enrichment programmes 101, 195–6,
    248–9
environmental awareness 248–9
equal opportunities policy (EOP) 192
Ethnic Minorities Achievement Grant
    (EMAG) 67
Ethnic Minority Language Advisory Service
    (EMLAS) 8, 131
ethnicity
    and educational performance 65–7
    and income distribution *63*
    and poverty 62–5
'Excellence in Schools' (1997) 15
exclusion 157
    and pastoral system 281
eye contact 163

fighting
    and sanctions 179
finance managers/bursars 9
Flesch-Kincaid Formula 80
foreign languages
    engaging pupils 117
formative assessment 216–17, *220*
    classroom use 223–5
    departmental use 226
    improving 213–16
    and learning 213–15
    in practice 225–7
    preparation for summative testing
        224–5

role of questioning 219–20
school use 226
success factors 215
see also assessment; self-assessment
Further Education (FE) 247

games 117–21
GCSE(s) 12–13, 65, 101, 212
choosing 304–7
gender
and educational achievement 39–44
equality of educational opportunity 44–5
geography
engaging pupils 120
organising lesson topics 136
thinking hats 100
girls
characteristics of average 41
gender effect and education 40, 44
performance 43–4
and single-sex classes 48–9
grouping for learning
banding 12–13
mixed ability 13, 14–19
setting 13, 16–21
single-sex classes/lessons 45, 48–9
streaming 13, 16–19
see also assessment for learning;
learning
Gunning FOG Readability Test 79–80

handbooks 330–1
departmental 33–4, 331–2
staff 33, 34, 331
Hannan, Geoff 51
'hard' classes
coping strategies 180–3
see also behaviour management;
discipline structure; rewards and
merits; sanctions
hard skills 32
heads of department (HOD) *see* subject
leaders
heads of faculty *see* subject leaders
headteachers 4, 10
health and safety officers 9
hidden curriculum 36
history
engaging pupils 120
HODs *see* subject leaders

home/school agreement 160
homework not done
and sanctions 173–4

inclusion
activities 197–9
Children's Commissioners and 201
enrichment programmes 195–6
evidence of 195
full 201–2
individual support 199–200
policies 192–5
staff 195
Individual Learning/Education Plans (ILPs/
IEPs) 8, 131, 237
inductions
good practice 300–3
NQTs 348–9
innovation
and personalised learning 96–8
inspections
frameworks in UK 326
preparation for 329–34
purpose 326–7
teams 279–80
interpersonal relationships 287
interventions 242–9
attendance 324
IQ scores 98

job descriptions 34
classroom assistants 144–6
job-hunting
advertisements 338–9
application packs 338
CV/curriculum vitae 339–40
letter and application form 341–2
preparing for interview 345–6
sample lesson for interview 342–5
see also newly qualified teachers (NQTs)

key skills 32
key stage managers (KSMs) 141, 143, 274
and pastoral system 281–2
kinaesthetic learners 111

ladder to learning 92–3, 266
language, uses 57–8
lateness
and sanctions 172

learning
    consolidation 161
    determinants of effective 20
    engagement 116–21
    intention 115, 121, 161, 216–17
    nine areas 35
    obstacles to 309–12
    personalised 89–104
    skills-based 44
    styles 90, 93, 111–13
    transitions between tasks 177
    see also assessment for learning;
        grouping for learning
learning coaches (LCs) 101, 143
learning ethos/environment
    within the classroom 94–5
    within the school 95
Learning Houses 313–14
learning intention 115, 161
    introducing 121
    sharing 216–17
learning support assistants (LSAs) 8, 94,
        278, 283
    group 141
    pupil 141
lesson starters 113–15, 171 see also brain
        gym
Learning to Learn strategy 99–100
lessons
    checklist 125–6
    delivering 343–4
    differentiation 123, 125
    elements of good 108–9, 109
    four-part 123–5, 124
    importance of first 171
    information sheet 110
    for job interview 342–6
    lesson starters 113–15, 171 see also
        brain gym
    organising topics 136–7
    and personalised learning 91–4
    planning 108–10
    pupil evaluation form 343
    standard formats 123–5
    storing 135–7
lifestyle, need for healthy 288
Local Authorities (LAs)
    and bullying 316
    data requirements 232
    differences in educational attainment 67–8
    and exclusions 157
    Learning Houses 313–14
    and school attendance 310–11
looked-after children (LACs) 9, 94
loyalty bridge 300

mark books 130–1, 132–4, 131, 132
marking
    computers and 133–4
    policies 32, 130
    purposes 208–10, 212
    recording/storing marks 208
    shorthand 133
    what to assess 210–11, 221–3
    workload management 220–3
maths
    engaging pupils 118, 119
mediators 200
mentors/mentoring (for pupils) 8, 246–8
    and behaviour management 185–6
    borderline cases 247–8
    peer 200
    teacher's role 277–8
middle managers 7
mini whiteboard 116–17 see also
    whiteboards
Minority Ethnic Achievement Programme
    (MEAP) 66
mixed ability grouping 13, 14–19
    problems 18–19
mobile phones/MP3 players
    and sanctions 177–8
modern foreign languages
    lesson starters 113–14
monitoring 4, 247
    record-keeping 279
monitoring, evaluating and reviewing
    (MER) 4
moral values 289

National Child Development Study (NCDS)
    60
National Curriculum 27–8 see also
    curriculum
National Foundation for Educational
    Research 80
National Literacy and Numeracy Strategy
    (NLNS) 81, 140
New Deals 57, 68
New Opportunities Fund 57

newly qualified teachers (NQTs)
  career entry and development profile 348
  expectations of 7–8
  importance of first lesson 171
  induction 348–9
  mentors 7–10, 149, 170, 186, 349
  support for 7–8
  see also job-hunting; teachers
nine areas of learning 35
non-verbal reasoning (NVR) 235
Northern Ireland Council for the
  Curriculum, Examinations and
  Assessment (CCEA) 28
Northern Ireland
  curriculum authority 28

on report 174
on-call system 156
Oxford Reading Tree scheme 81

Parent Teacher's Association (PTA) 303–4
parents
  and behaviour management 158
  contacting 264–5
  home/school agreement 160
  loyalty to school 300
  meeting face-to-face 261–3
  providing reports to 255–6
  and school attendance 311
  see also progress reports
parents' evenings 261–4
passing notes
  and sanctions 172–3
pastoral support assistants (PSAs) 8, 141–
  2, 143, 283
pastoral system 274–6
  care team 279–80, 324
  judging effectiveness 280–1
  line manager 279–80
  pastoral bridge 236, 300, 303–4, 307
  programme 280
  role of KSM 281–2
peer mentors 200
personal, social and health education
  (PSHE/PSE) 32–3, 275
  best practice 293
  framework 286–91
  Ofsted report 292–3
  programme content 287–90
personalised learning 89–104

  pedagogy of 91
Philosophy of Children (P4C) 90, 98
PMI lesson plan 101–3
poverty
  causes 64–5
  and educational achievement 54–7,
    55–6, 65–7
  and ethnicity 62–5
Powers-Sumner-Kearl Formula 80
Primary National Strategy for Social and
  Emotional Aspects of Learning (2005)
  291
primary schools
  additional teacher responsibilities 330
  banding 15
  budgets 5
  circle time 294–7
  classroom management 168
  data profiles 230–4
  departmental handbook 331-2
  inductions 300–2
  profiles 233–4
  secondary school partners 301
  transition/transfer 236–7, 281
  use of TASC 97
progress reports
  characteristics of good 257–61
  difficulties 264–5
  providing to parents 255–6
  timing 256
progress review sessions see review days
project workers 314, 324
promoting positive learning (PPL) 159–60
psychological harassment 187
punctuality 169
pupil planners 160
pupils
  data on 130–7
  differential assessment 31
  engaging all 116–22
  evaluation form 343
  grouping for learning 12–21, 81–3
  review days 92, 265–9
  self-assessment 216–19
  see also behaviour management; data
    profiles

Qualifications and Curriculum Authority
  (QCA) 28
quantitative reasoning (QR) 235

readability 74–9
reading
    appropriate resource material 75–9
    developing comprehension 76–8
reading age, assessing 79–83
reading levels
    and grouping pupils for learning 81–3
refusal to obey
    and sanctions 174–5, 184–5
reports see progress reports
resource materials
    choosing appropriate 75–9
    storing 135–7
responsibility allowances 282–3
review days 92, 265–9
rewards and merits 133, 148, 159–60 see
        also behaviour management;
    discipline structure; sanctions

sanctions 148, 155–60, 170
    bullying 194
    disrespect 194
    fighting 179
    homework not done 173–4
    keeping pupils back 181, 184–5
    for lateness 172
    mobile phones/MP3 players 178
    passing notes 172–3
    refusal to obey 175, 184
    truancy 179
    whole class 181, 183
    see also behaviour management;
        discipline structure; rewards and
        merits
schemes of work (SOWs) 4, 30–3, 331, 332
    content 31–2
    and marking 221–2
    PSHE elements 287
School Action 141
school councils 196–8
school improvement/development plans
        (SIPs/SDPs) 230, 350
School Liaison Groups (SLGs) 197
school readiness 57–8
schools
    aims and targets 324–5
    characteristics of good 324–5
    comparisons between 249–51
    learning ethos and environment within 95
    self-evaluation process 279, 327–9

success indicators 254
    see also inspections
science
    engaging pupils 120
    lesson starters 114
    organising lesson topics 136
Scotland
    curriculum authority 28
Scottish Executive Education Department
        (SEED) 28
secondary schools
    move to 199
    organisation 4–7
    primary school partners 301
    staffing 4–5, 7
    structure 4–5, 6
    transition/transfer 236, 281, 300–2
self-assessment (by pupils) 92
    developing strategies 216–17
    encouraging 217–19
    sample sheet 218
    see also assessment
senior leadership group (SLG) 6, 7
senior management team (SMT) 6, 7
serotonin 42
setting 13, 16–21
sex education 288
single-sex classes/lessons 45, 48–9
skills
    advanced 5
    hard 32
    key 32
    soft 32
    study 289
SMART targets 265, 325
social and emotional aspects of learning
        (SEAL) 291
Social Services 9
soft skills 32
Special Educational Needs Coordinator
        (SENCO) 143, 145, 149, 237, 248
special educational needs (SEN) 101, 192–3
special needs 140
spiritual development 289
staff development 350–1
staff development officer (SDOs) 350
staff handbook 33, 34, 331
'stage not age' learning 95
Standard Assessment Tests (SATs) 47, 130,
        232

streaming 13, 16–19
student counsellors 200
study skills 289
subject leaders 4, 9–10
summative assessment 213
support programmes 246–8
support staff 140–3
    administrators 140
    attendance officers 324
    caretakers 9
    cover assistants (CAs) 142
    curriculum support assistants (CSAs) 142
    finance managers/bursars 9
    health and safety officers 9
    learning support assistants 8, 94, 141,
        278, 283
    mediators 200
support teachers (STs) 140
SureStart 57, 68

teachers
    of advanced skills 5
    assistant headteachers 4
    bullying 186
    deputy headteachers 4, 10
    engaging all learners 116–22
    headteachers 4, 10
    mentors 7–10, 145, 170, 186, 349
    pastoral role 275–8
    psychological harassment 187
    and PTA 303–4
    responsibility allowances 282–3
    support teachers (STs) 140
    see also job-hunting; newly qualified
        teachers (NQTs)
teaching
    effective 20–1
    measuring effectiveness 251–2
    personalised learning methods 94
teaching assistants see classroom assistants
team leaders 6
text types 83–4
Thinking Actively in the Social Context
    (TASC) 90, 96–8, 98

thinking hats 100–101
three-strike system 155
time-out system 156–7
Times Educational Supplement 338
tracking for success 96
transitions 236
    ensuring smooth 300
    to FE and HE 307
    good practice 300–2
    key stage 3 to 4 304–6
    to sixth form 306–7
    strategies to ease 302–4
truancy
    and sanctions 180
tutor time 267–8

unauthorised absences 280–1
Universities and Colleges Admissions
    Service (UCAS) 307

VAK learning methods 111
verbal reasoning (VR) 235
videos 122–3
visual learners 111
voice 163

Wales
    Children's Commissioner 201
    curriculum authority 28, 29
washing lines 119
websites
    and pupils' data 134
whiteboards
    interactive 121–2
    see also mini whiteboards
work experience 290–1
workforce remodelling 276, 282
work-related experience (WRE) 290
writing frames 47, 85–7
    examples 86
    using 85
writing, types of 83–4

Young Offenders Team (YOT) 9

The Essential Guides Series

Practical skills for teachers

The Essential Guides series offers a wealth of practical support, inspiration and guidance for NQTs and more experienced teachers ready to implement into their classroom. The books provide practical advice and tips on the core aspects of teaching and everyday classroom issues, such as planning, assessment, behaviour and ICT. The Essential Guides are invaluable resources that will help teachers to successfully navigate the challenges of the profession.

The Essential Guide to
Successful School Trips
John Trant

© 2010 paperback
ISBN 978-1-4082-0447-4

The Essential Guide to
Using ICT Creatively in the Primary Classroom
Steve Woods

© 2010 paperback
ISBN 978-1-4082-2497-7

The Essential Guide to
Taking Care of Behaviour
(second edition)
Paul Dix

© 2010 paperback
ISBN 978-1-4082-2554-7

The Essential Guide to
Classroom Assessment
Paul Dix

© 2010 paperback
ISBN 978-1-4082-3025-1

The Essential Guide to
Understanding Special Educational Needs
Jenny Thompson

© 2010 paperback
ISBN 978-1-4082-2500-4

The Essential Guide to
Shaping Children's Behaviour in the Early Years
Lynn Cousins

© 2010 paperback
ISBN 978-1-4082-2502-8

The Essential Guide to
Teaching 14-19 Diplomas
Lynn Senior

© 2010 paperback
ISBN 978-1-4082-2549-3

Longman is an imprint of

PEARSON

Practical skills for teachers